THE ENCYCLOPEDIA OF GHOSTS AND SPIRITS

Volume II

THE ENCYCLOPEDIA OF GHOSTS AND SPIRITS
Volume II

John and Anne Spencer

HEADLINE

First published in 2001
by HEADLINE BOOK PUBLISHING

10 9 8 7 6 5 4 3 2 1

British Library Cataloguing in Publication Data

Spencer, John, 1954 -
   Encyclopedia of ghosts and spirits
   Vol. 2 John and Anne Spencer
   1.Ghosts - Encyclopedias
   2.Spirits - Encyclopedias
   I. Title II.Spencer, Anne
   133.1'03

ISBN 0 7472 7169 0

Typeset by Letterpart Ltd
Reigate, Surrey

Printed and bound in Great Britain by
Mackays of Chatham plc, Chatham, Kent

HEADLINE BOOK PUBLISHING
A division of Hodder Headline
338 Euston Road
London NW1 3BH

www.headline.co.uk
www.hodderheadline.com

CONTENTS

ACKNOWLEDGEMENTS

We are grateful to all the people who have contributed to this volume in one way or another. Without wishing to diminish the contributions of others, we would especially like to thank: ASSAP's Maxine Glancy, Terry Hewitt and Stephen Hall for permission to reproduce material from their investigations; Nicholas Chance, Private Secretary to HRH Prince Michael of Kent, for information on Nether Lippiat; Ghost Quest's Peter Crawley and Colin Veacock for leads on ghosts in Lancashire; Cynthia Hind, one of Africa's leading researchers of the paranormal, for information on ghost and spirit belief in African cultures; Michael Hudson for leads on ghosts in Kent; The Kingston House Development Committee Inc. for information on the history and hauntings of Kingston House in South Australia; Malcolm Robinson of Strange Phenomena Investigations for assistance and contributions; Derick Shelton for supplying cuttings from local newspapers and for assistance with research into cases in Hull; Robert Titherley, Brooklands Society Director, for his recollections of hauntings reported at the old Brooklands racing circuit; Howard Winters for sharing with us 45 years of research into the Brown Mountain Lights; Michael Walker for giving information and 'leads' on ghost accounts in Lancashire; Anthony Woods for background information on Portchester Castle and alleged hauntings there.

Many thanks also to Margaret Baker, Sylvia Curtis and Catherine and Jennifer for typing and administration.

None of those who have offered reports, assistance or advice can be held responsible for any opinions expressed in this book. Unless clearly stated otherwise, the views expressed are those of the authors.

In many cases the accounts are given in the true name of the witnesses but where anonymity has been requested we have substituted a pseudonym. In all of our cases the real names are known to us.

INTRODUCTION

When we wrote the first volume of this compilation we made the point in the Acknowledgements that 'if we had had 10 volumes to complete there would still have been difficulties of selection' so vast is the available data on this fascinating subject. This has been true again for this compilation.

As before, we could have filled the book just from cases we have investigated or have been reported to us, but we feel that an encyclopedia should by its very nature reflect more than the work of one pair of researchers; so we have again trawled the work of many around the world. We have tried to find many new sources for this compilation to provide as rich as possible a variety over the two volumes.

One major change since we undertook the original compilation published in 1992 has been the explosion of the Internet, the World Wide Web. It has revolutionised the reach of our enquiries and speeded up immeasurably the communication we have with people all over the world. People in America, Africa, and Australia in particular were able to communicate with us several times a day as we checked and re-checked details of reports. And we were able to locate people who would have been very difficult to track down were it not for websites and e-mail. Reflecting this, we have not only attached a bibliography and reading list to the back of the book but a list of useful websites worth accessing.

We have kept the same format for this volume as for its predecessor – the same sections with a variety of cases from different parts of the world, and from different researchers and research organisations.

For those readers not familiar with the territory of this book, or who have not read the earlier volume, it is worth summarising the variety of ghosts to be encountered in this book, classified according to 'type':

'Recordings and replays' type ghosts

There is a belief that one category of ghosts are actually recordings of events that are naturally embedded into the environment, in much the same way as a video records an image and then can replay it at a later date. No-one is certain what the factors are that create the recordings; is it atmospherics? Geology? The state of mind of someone involved? A combination of all of those? Something else? Often such ghosts are reported around the time of structural alterations in a building: why? And what causes the replay; what is the 'playback button'? It is said that these types of ghosts 'fade away' over time; is the effect something like a battery running down, getting weaker as time passes since the recording was 'laid down'? Clearly the combination that creates and replays the phenomenon must be rare otherwise ghosts would be more frequent than they are. The basic characteristic of the 'recordings and replays' ghost is that it is non-interactive; the ghost does not react to the witnesses, it does not address them, nor do the actions of witnesses affect the actions of the ghost. Given that the same description of the ghost, movement and so on, is reported by several different people, the assumption is that anyone who happened to be in the right place at the right time would see the same thing. But would they? Are some people more prone to such sightings than others? And if so, why?

Anniversary ghosts

A sub-set of 'recordings and replays' ghosts for the most part, these ghosts are said to appear on particular days of the year. That day is usually the anniversary of the assumed ghost's death or the day that an event happened; for example, the day a train crashes might be the day of the replay thereafter. The fact is that ghosts are not that reliable otherwise many of their mysteries would by now have been solved. What is more likely is that certain types of ghosts might appear in certain atmospheric conditions that would recur at particular months or seasons of the year.

Presences

Although the traditional concept of a ghost is a sighting of a visual image, many ghosts are not seen at all. They are perceived as a 'sense' of presence, of 'being watched'. Some are detected by smells or sounds. They might be thought of as malign – an oppressive, frightening presence; or they might be thought of as benign, the ghost of a loved one sensed in the house as a comforting feeling, perhaps. Do witnesses imagine these feelings? Or are they genuinely external to the witness? The answer would seem to be a combination of the two. There is evidence that there is an external element in cases where a psychic is brought to a location who has no knowledge of what is being reported there but who nonetheless detects the same thing. There are times when 'non-psychic' friends and relatives feel the same uneasiness as the 'witnesses'. On the other hand there are many such reports which seem to depend on the state of mind of the witness; perhaps some ghost manifestations do need some mental element before they can come into being.

Poltergeists

A very frequently reported type of haunting, and probably the most 'popular' – if that is the word! – type of ghost to the general reader and the media. There is a strong belief, and a considerable weight of evidence, that poltergeists may be for the most part a 'construct' of the witness. The witness may be projecting some inner turmoil in a physical way. If so, then a study of this branch of hauntings may also be a study of the complex processes of the human psyche and the human condition. Poltergeists have been called haunted people, rather than haunted places. Manifestations are generally unexplained sounds, the spontaneous movement of objects, and a variety of 'special effects' such as spontaneous arrivals of objects (apports), spontaneous water pools, sudden fires and so on.

Interactive ghosts

The opposite end of the scale to 'recordings and replays', interactive ghosts seem to have a purpose and are able to speak to, or otherwise communicate with, the living. They are often known to the witness; the classic example would be the ghost who appears to a relative to tell them they are happy in their 'afterlife', or on more dramatic occasions to give information such as details of an undiscovered will. The difference between the 'recordings and replays' ghost and the interactive ghost would seem to be one of consciousness; the recording appears to be just an accidental re-enactment, the 'real' spirit of the ghost seen not actually being present, whereas the interactive ghost appears to have intelligence at work during the encounter between the ghost and the living. As C.D. Broad, Professor of Philosophy at Cambridge, said: 'There is a very small number of cases where it is hard to resist the conviction that the mind of a certain person has survived the death of his body and is continuing to think, plan and carry out intentions.'

Timeslips

Timeslips have come into ghost phenomena because of the uncertainty of what a witness has experienced. They are thought to be windows, or even doorways, between time periods. A person in the year 2001 might find themselves seeing a scene from the Middle Ages, for example, or they might even feel themselves to be there in that former time. Psychometry may play a part in timeslips; perhaps the emotional and other impressions of a time can be so impressed into an object such as a watch, or a place such as a church, that the witness's mind is overtaken by them when they touch the object or enter the location, so that they feel themselves living at that earlier time in every bit as real a sense as in their normal lives. In effect timeslips would then be not much different from the reports of many psychics who 'sense' an atmosphere or a former happening. Timeslips are generally visual images, and the main characteristic which distinguishes them from, say, apparitions (interactive or non-interactive) is that the whole scene changes – some witnesses believe they have been transported into a 'different' time in history.

Ghosts of the living: doubles, doppelgangers, vardogers, and bi-locations

There are many apparitions seen of people who are in fact alive at the time. They are included among the phenomena of ghosts because they are often indistinguishable from such reports, and indeed it may be the same mechanism at play that creates apparitions of the dead. The suggestion that ghosts are 'of the dead' is in any case only one theory, and there are many theories which accept the reality of ghosts without accepting their connection to death or an afterlife.

Ghosts around the time of death

These are often known as crisis apparitions and we have in this compilation extended the 'formal' definition to take in a longer time-span. The original definition, given by Henry Sidgwick, an early pioneer of the research, was of an apparition seen within a period of 12 hours before or after the person seen as a ghost had suffered a crisis. Most commonly the crisis was death, and it was thought that such spirits might not have yet worked out they were dead, or would have unfinished business to attend to, and would 'return' for those reasons. Alternatively, there is the belief that people at a moment of crisis expel psychic energy causing loved ones to 'see them'.

But there are other possibilities. Perhaps the witness telepathically 'knows' of the crisis and constructs the vision as a means of comprehending the impressions gained. The evidence for this is that in many ghost reports, but not all cases, the apparition is as the witness remembers the person, or the vision appears as they last saw them. That said, there are still cases where the apparition seen is not what would be expected, so the position is far from clear-cut. Since there usually seems to be an emotional bond, or strong purpose, at work we have extended the 'time frame' in some cases to account for the fact that emotion, rather than time, may be the significant factor.

Haunted objects

There are many times when people have reported objects apparently carrying 'hauntings' with them. Mirrors seem particularly prone to this; people buying mirrors and seeing images in them of times past, or reflections of deceased people, and so on. Even when these items are taken elsewhere, the hauntings continue around these objects. Some psychics claim to be able to pick up images from the past by holding or touching an object (psychometry) so ghostly images attached to an object should perhaps not be too surprising.

Phantom hitchhikers

These are ghosts seen on roads, generally, who either frighten witnesses or warn people of dangers on the road ahead. As such they can be non-interactive or interactive. Perhaps some have a purpose, to prevent accidents such as the one they themselves were killed in, while others are emotional recordings of an accident and a death at a particular spot. The reason for singling them out in this round-up is that they have many elements of folklore and urban legend about them and may be related more to the 'cult of the car' – that powerful emotional bond peculiar to the modern age that we seem to have invested in our automobiles.

While we have sought to use the framework of the earlier volume in designing this second volume, we have also listened to our readers. Since the original volume was published we have had hundreds of letters, e-mails and faxes from people inspired by the book. They have put forward the accounts they feel to be most significant, and we have tried to re-balance this volume with more emphasis on the ghost reports people most seem moved by. We have also – and this was much requested – inserted more first-hand accounts by witnesses into this volume, so that readers can 'feel' the responses of those who have actually experienced ghosts and spirits.

The labels we put on ghost experiences are less important than the mysteries behind them. 'The thing that's wrong with science and with all our experiences is that you've got to have everything in little pigeon holes, with little labels on,' said Eric Laithwaite, Professor of Heavy Electrical Engineering at Imperial College, London. 'Some things don't fit. That doesn't mean they are not real.' The purpose of research into ghosts and spirits is one of exploration and under-standing: to know what it is that millions of people around the world believe in and have had personal experience of, and thereby to understand something more of the world around us. Perhaps it will lead to a new understanding of what happens after we die; perhaps to the discovery of new, natural laws of physics waiting to be found. Perhaps to an understanding of human psychology, about why we believe what we believe and how we make our beliefs come into being. It is an exciting search and undeniably a worthwhile one.

ENCYCLOPEDIA OF
GHOST REPORTS

Ghosts And Visions Associated With Particular Places

There is no limit to the particular places that ghosts will haunt. Churches, castles, and old theatres all seem to have their stories of ghosts and spirits, but ghosts have also appeared in modern offices, on open roads, on river banks, in private houses – some of them very modern – and even on ships. In this section there are accounts from around the world, some, like the Whaley House, now famous for their ghost sightings, and some revealed here for the first time.

Name: Alcatraz
Location: San Francisco Bay, California, USA
Date: 1963 onwards
Source: Various

The most notorious prison in the United States must be that on the island of Alcatraz. It was a Federal Penitentiary from 1934 until 1963, but was then closed and is now a tourist attraction. It housed many famous criminals including 'Machine Gun' Kelly, Robert Stroud (known as The Birdman) and Al Capone.

The regime on Alcatraz was brutal and based purely on punishment. Rehabilitation was not considered appropriate for the hardened criminals there. Prisoners were generally forbidden to talk except for a few minutes a day during recreation and for two hours at weekends. Capone was imprisoned there for five years until he went insane, partly, it is thought, due to the conditions of his incarceration and partly to advanced syphilis. During his time on Alcatraz he spent three spells in solitary, in cells known as 'The Hole'. His one pastime was playing the banjo in his cell or in the shower block; at one time he was part of a four-man band in the prison.

No visual apparitions have been reported on Alcatraz and fittingly it is the sounds that have been haunting the now isolated and decaying cell blocks atop the island. Guards and tour guides have reported the clanging sounds of doors, voices, whistling, screams and the sound of feet running along the alleys between the cell blocks. Banjo music has been heard coming from the shower room, thought to be an echo of Capone's time there. Cell 14B, one of the solitary 'Holes' was used to confine murderer Rufe McCain for more than three years. Screams have been heard from that cell in the years since the prison was closed.

Name: Backford Hall
Location: Backford, nr Chester, Cheshire, north-west England
Date: 1997-99
Source: Researcher Mike McManus

Most accounts of ghosts come from relatives of a perceived spirit, or from people living in or visiting sites seeing phenomena unexpectedly. But there are other reports which came from researchers like ourselves who have investigated haunted sites. The following account is from a researcher who, with a team, during vigils at Backford Hall, experienced several haunting phenomena.

Mike McManus told us: 'During my many years as a ghost-hunter, I have investigated many properties, but none has fired me up as much as Backford Hall. It is a building that has a long history of anomalous happenings. So I and fellow ghost-hunter David Williams set out with a team to investigate this historic building.

'The hauntings at the Hall came to my attention via an article in the Liverpool *Daily Post* newspaper in July 1996. We obtained permission from Mr Steve Brown, the administration manager at the Hall, to hold all-night vigils. During the course of four vigils we collected a lot of information, the most important of which is set out here.

'It was noted on a couple of occasions that the door to the original cellars was seen and heard to slam shut a number of times. This door, being heavy and solid, could not have shut of its own accord.

'On a number of occasions the sound of a dog was heard padding down corridors, as well as barking and panting in different parts of the Hall. The sound of children playing, laughing and chanting was heard, as was the sound of a woman laughing. Footsteps were heard as if someone was coming up the main staircase even though there was nobody on the stairs. I heard the sound of footsteps coming down the old stairs at the top of the building where the servants' quarters and attic rooms are situated. This was followed by a loud rasping sound close to my ear, which I did not like at all.

'One of our team members had a good sighting of a female in a long pink dress with a cream, laced, striped bodice and what looked like ballet shoes. Her hair was in ringlets and she had a very pale complexion. A male escorted her up the main staircase. This lady was seen on another occasion, but without her companion.

'While setting up a camcorder in the corridor I had a sighting of a grey misty shape. I heard a female voice saying the name "Dave" very clearly. I reported this to the other members, who were elsewhere having a tea break at the time, and no one had been out of the room. David Williams then left the room, and a few seconds later came back in and asked who had shouted to him; he had heard his name being called twice. Other names were heard on an audiotape recorded during one of the vigils, again "spoken" by a female. Some of the names we knew, some we didn't. The names unknown to us were Ann, Joseph and Lucy. A few weeks later I paid a visit to Backford church, which is situated in the grounds, and found three graves next to each other bearing these three names. One of them was a child of five years.

'During a walkabout on one of the tea breaks, David Williams and I were on the balcony and we both heard a very loud "sigh" followed by the slamming of a door. We ran down the stairs to see if any members had been out the room; none had. These events were picked up on audio equipment, as were "sighs" which lasted for over half an hour, and witnessed by every member of the team. Again on the balcony, a dark shadow was spotted "walking" along, followed by the sound of a long heavy "sigh". There were many poltergeist-like events: I heard two raps which came from an office door and they seemed to be responding to me; my camera failed to operate halfway through a film; batteries were drained and camcorders stopped working. A heavy triangular-shaped paperclip appeared from nowhere and nearly hit a member of the team in the face. A large table, which was situated in the room where we had our monitoring equipment set up, began to visibly shake and then jump up and down while four members were seated around one end of it. I witnessed this event and could find no explanation for it. Two objects that were on the table did not even move while it was going up and down. About 10 minutes after this happened, some of us heard the sound of childish laughter.

'On the last occasion I was at the Hall, I was sitting on the back stairs that lead up to the servants' quarters when I heard the sound of a dress rustling along the landing, followed by the sound of a woman laughing. I went up the stairs and could still hear this rustling sound and the laughter. I then came across two male members of the team who had also heard some laughing and the sound of breathing at the same time as I had. A white misty shape was then witnessed by David Williams, other members and myself. This white mist was seen going through a closed door in the reception area and then coming back through it and up to the balcony where we were standing. This was caught on camera.

'To conclude our findings, and to confirm some of them were based on real events, I received two letters from a lady who lived at the Hall between 1951 and 1954 when her father was a caretaker there. She told me that it was indeed a "Lady in Grey" that haunted the building. She had been seen on a number of occasions walking the long corridors and grounds by the lake. My correspondent also informed me that she used to play hide-and-seek with the children, even though she was an only child and no children from the village used to come to the Hall. Her father had a collie dog, which was very much a one-man dog and hated anybody else. When the time came for the family to leave the Hall and go back to the city, he could not take the dog, so he had it put down. Could this be the dog that we heard padding around the corridors and barking for its master? I also recently found out through research that a maid had died falling down the back stairs. Was she pushed or did she fall?'

Name: By The Bookcase
Location: Ashton under Lyne, Lancashire, north-west England
Date: 1990s
Source: Sandra Maddox (witness) / authors' own files

Sandra told us of an apparition in her house. What was more surprising was that the identity of the ghost was discovered, and then confirmed by the ghost's daughter, who was also able to confirm certain aspects of the apparition's behaviour.

Sandra explained: 'We moved to this house in July 1990 and within weeks noticed things moved from where we had left them. We would come home to find the central heating turned off when we knew we had left it on. And more than once we found the TV on when we knew it was off when we had left for work.

'I became very frightened by these experiences and had the house blessed by our local vicar, but the spirit did not leave us. In fact the activity increased; we were then subject to crashes and bangs in various rooms of the house, and occasionally the smell of baking bread would be very strong in the kitchen – this we didn't mind!

'The noises continued and we finally got used to our "lodger". Then my husband saw "him" in our bedroom in the early hours of the morning and managed to take in the man's appearance and clothing.

'By now I felt that I should make some discreet enquiries as to who had lived in our house. It soon came to light that a man called Robert Thomsett, fitting the description of our spirit, had lived at our house 30-odd years earlier. He had died in his late thirties and had often been seen wandering around the house and patio in his dressing-gown during the late stages of his illness.

'One day we had a visit from Robert Thomsett's daughter, Lorraine. She had come to visit our elderly neighbours, in whom we had confided about seeing Robert. Thankfully, Lorraine believes in the spirit world. She confirmed that she still has her father's dressing-gown, and also confirmed that my husband's description was that of her father.

'After Lorraine came to the house our visits from Robert were less frequent; we only seem to have a lot of visits when we alter the house! On one occasion we altered a bookcase and we saw his apparition standing there looking at it. Lorraine told us that he had made a particular fuss in life about that bookcase when he had done alterations there. Our house is very welcoming and although we know that Robert has not left his house, we are comfortable with him being here.

Name: A Child's Grave
Location: West Norwood Cemetery, south London, England
Date: Summer 1997
Source: Ms P. Lee (witness) / authors' own files

Ms Lee visited the 'Victorian' cemetery in West Norwood in the late summer of 1997. Having found the architecture of some of the graves in the cemetery 'quite beautiful', she decided to wander around, enjoying the tranquillity and atmosphere of the place.

Suddenly, she came 'face to face with a little child in Victorian clothes, with a flower in her hand, as if she was putting it on her own grave'. Ms Lee went on, in her account to us: 'Tears streamed down my face for a moment and then she was gone.'

Ms Lee took the photograph shown in the plate section for us, of the approximate location where she had seen the girl.

Name: The Conference House
Location: Staten Island, New York, USA
Date: 1600s onwards
Source: Various

The Conference House is a museum open to the public on New York's Staten Island. It was the scene of an abortive peace conference designed to keep the Colonies under British rule. Benjamin Franklin, Edward Rutledge and John Adams met with the British commander Lord Howe there on 11 September 1776, though the intended treaty was never signed. Howe had hardly started out by impressing the American guests. He posted soldiers all around the house and Adams observed that they looked 'as fierce as 10 furies, and making all the grimaces and gestures and motions of their muskets, with bayonets fixed, which, I suppose, military etiquette requires, but which we neither understood nor regarded'. The Declaration of Independence had already been signed anyway; Howe was too late. He is said to be one of the ghosts still in residence, perhaps regretful that he could not get the treaty signed and blaming himself for losing the Colonies. Other British ghosts are said to haunt the museum; these are thought to be soldiers buried there during the War of Independence.

Before any building was on the site, Staten Island was a scene of fighting between white settlers and the native population; the restless spirits of those conflicts are said to haunt the locale even today.

But the Conference House was once Bentley Mansion, a stately home built by the British seafaring Captain Christopher Billopp. His fiancée, spurned by him just before their wedding, died in the house and it is said that her crying can still be heard there. Many people have reported hearing her moaning and whimpering, including, according to the Staten Island newspaper The Transcript, the workmen who restored the building for use as a museum.

One psychic, Mrs Ethel Meyers, who had been taken to the House by Hans Holzer to assist in his research, detected the presence of a woman murdered in the House. This seemed at odds with what was known; Billopp's fiancée had died naturally. But the custodian of the museum knew of a murder, by a descendant of Billopp, also named Christopher, who had killed a female slave in a rage on the staircase where the medium had received the impressions.

Another medium, Ingrid Beckman, confirmed the impression of the murder, and also detected with great apprehension a feeling connecting an abduction with a tunnel that led from the house to the shore. The records show that Captain Billopp was twice abducted from his own home, possibly through the tunnel.

Name: A Face In A Window

Location: Portchester Castle, Portsmouth Harbour, Hampshire, southern England
Date: August 1990
Source: Anthony and Samantha Woods (witnesses) / authors' own files

Portchester Castle is a Norman castle within the walls of an old Roman fortress on the north shore of Portsmouth Harbour. It is the only specimen in northern Europe whose enclosure remains inviolate and at full height.

In 1133 an Augustinian priory was built in the grounds of the fort, the chapel of which remains today. King Henry II claimed the castle for his own, and it has remained in Royal hands ever since. It was prominent in wars with the French as a defending fortress, as a prison for French prisoners of war and as a starting point for English troops leaving to fight in that country.

One local story of a ghost at Portchester Castle describes it only as 'tall and white'. Two Portchester women, one later herself the custodian of the castle, both separately reported the figure of a monk walking from a iron-grill-covered gateway and disappearing by the main gatehouse. The wife of another former custodian also saw a monk-like figure.

The actor Sebastian Shaw is said to have had his most direct contact with the paranormal while visiting Portchester Castle with his wife. When touring one of the rooms of the castle Mrs Shaw ran out, white and trembling. Her husband asked what had happened and she said she felt as if she had been hit in the face with a wet flannel. Their guide told them it was the room that had been occupied by Queen Isabella of France, wife of King Edward II of England, who had murdered her husband. (Her son, Edward III, had her imprisoned in the castle at Castle Rising in Norfolk for the murder. She died insane in that castle where her ghostly shriekings and cacklings have been reported by many visitors. Her ghost has also been seen wandering in the ruins of the Castle Rising Castle church.)

In 1980 an assistant custodian of Portchester Castle saw a figure kneeling by a grave in the churchyard in the castle grounds; the figure dissolved before her eyes.

Anthony Woods was visiting Portchester Castle in the summer of 1990 with his girlfriend Samantha, now his wife. He described to us: 'We were sitting in my car in this deserted car park just outside the castle gates. I started to eat a roll, and my girlfriend took a photo of me. We had just come back from holiday in the West Country and she wanted to use up the film so that she could get the holiday photos developed. When we developed the photo it showed me eating the roll, but also, just to the left of my face, you can see a face looking in at us. I can assure you there was nobody else in that car park when the picture was taken.'

We asked if he was aware of any strange 'feelings' or atmosphere at the time, but Anthony replied that neither he nor Samantha were aware of anything like that.

'There was not a soul in that car park at the time, and we discussed all the possibilities at length after we first saw the photo, which was about three days after the picture was taken. The car park we were in wasn't the main car park for visitors to the castle; we were in a small town square car park nearby. There was no place in the car park for anybody to hide; we were in the car park for at least a couple of hours before Samantha took the photo. There were a couple of cars there earlier on, but they left long before the photo was taken.

The picture shows a face apparently looking in the window of the car, behind Anthony's head. 'The sky was clear and there was no wind, it was a lovely, warm and clear August night,' Anthony told us. Samantha confirmed that she had held the camera up to her eyes when taking the picture; so the image could not have been a reflection of her, distorted in the window. We had the photograph and negatives analysed by Simon Earwicker of the Association for the Scientific Study of Anomalous Phenomena (ASSAP) who could see no evidence of deliberate fraud. Digital enhancement produced no evidence of tampering. Simon pointed out that the face seemed to exhibit 'proportions . . . different from that of a human face'.

Name: The Figure In The Tail-coat
Location: Hertford, Hertfordshire, southern England
Date: 1989
Source: Sue Laurence (witness) / authors' own files

Sue is a down-to-earth, direct and easy-going woman who has experienced a number of paranormal events in her life. Most of these took place in her younger years, but perhaps the most striking was a ghost experience in her former workplace. She described the event in her own words: 'In Hertfordshire there are country estates that once belonged to the minor aristocracy or landed gentry but which are now in the hands of companies using them as prestigious offices. About ten years ago I worked for one such company, a property company, and when I first joined them they were just moving into a lovely Regency mansion near Hertford. As each part of the house was renovated and restored, so the appropriate department moved in. We in the sales office were the last to move in; we occupied the Morning Room on the ground floor. This room opened out onto a small balcony by way of French doors. Two of the walls were lined with mahogany bookshelves and on the other wall was an architrave which once framed a door, though the door was by now removed and the space filled in and plastered over.

'My colleagues and I were a little puzzled that the bookshelves had not been French-polished as the woodwork in the rest of the house had been. We were told that the French polisher, working late one night on the handrail of the cantilever staircase, felt and saw "someone" walk past him on the staircase and was so shocked that he refused to come back into the building unless it was fully occupied, and only in daylight. When he eventually came to polish our shelves we teased him about the incident. He was a little embarrassed, but he was adamant that he had seen someone. We didn't press him for a description, to save his blushes.

'I shared the office with three other women and there were some very strange incidents in that room. For example, the French windows would fly open in "Hammer Horror" style for no apparent reason. A large, heavy hole-punch crashed to the floor from the bookshelves when there was nobody near it, and I felt the floor flexing once, and felt someone walk behind me when there was nobody there.

'One day a colleague and I returned from a meeting to find our secretary standing outside the door, and looking a little worried. When we asked her what was wrong she said that she felt someone had been in the room with her and the feeling had been so strong she had had to leave.

'The strangest thing that happened to me was when I saw an apparition, and I can see that figure today in my mind's eye as clearly as then. To monitor our sales figures we each had plans of our sites pinned to the walls and the different stages of the sales progress were charted by different coloured pins. It was an unwritten law that no-one touched anyone else's pins unless asked to do so. One of my plans was fixed to the wall over the old, plastered-in doorway. My colleague and I were returning to the office, chatting together, and because she had her arms full she opened the door to the room with her back by pushing against it, therefore backing into the room. She held back the door to let me enter the room first. I saw a man standing with his hands behind his back, apparently looking over my site plan. I thought at first it was my boss and I called out jokingly, "Oi – leave my pins alone!" As the words left my lips he disappeared, right in front of me. I immediately registered that he had been wearing a tail-coat. This all happened very quickly, of course, and my colleague span round to see who I was talking to. Seeing that there was no-one there, she immediately turned back towards me. She told me later that my face said it all. I must have looked like a gaffed fish, mouth and eyes wide open.

'I have no doubt whatsoever that I saw someone. I know for sure that it was not a trick of the light or anything like that. He was as clear and solid as anyone. It's just a pity that my colleague didn't see him as well.'

Sue commented in our interview that while she might think twice about spending the night alone in that building it was not actually a frightening experience.

The description of the figure wearing a tail-coat seems to place it from an earlier era and perhaps to a time when the house was occupied as a home. Was a former owner inspecting the changes to his house? Was he looking at the site plan over the old doorway, or wondering where the door itself had gone? Or was the figure a 'recording type' ghost, a replay of a time when a man stood in the real doorway, perhaps looking through to the room beyond?

Name: Film-maker's Success
Location: Longleat House, Wiltshire, southern England
Date: 1970s
Source: Various

One of the most haunted areas of this magnificent stately home is known as the Green Lady's Walk. It is named after Lady Louisa Carteret whose portrait hangs in the dining room. She is shown there dressed in green, and it is her ghost that is alleged to walk the corridor in grief.

The story goes back to the early 18th century when Lady Louisa married the Second Viscount Weymouth. Their marriage was a disaster, her husband being vicious and unpleasant. Lady Louisa fell in love with another man and they were found together in Longleat House by her husband. A duel was fought which resulted in the death of the lover who, it is said, was buried beneath the cellar flagstones. (Four generations later a body was unearthed there when central heating was being installed.) Lady Louisa died in childbirth on Christmas Day 1736 and allegedly roams the corridors looking for her long-dead lover. Several people, including Longleat's librarian Miss Dorothy Coates, felt unable to walk along the corridor and many people went out of their way to avoid it. Miss Coates once described the feeling she had when walking the corridor: 'Sometimes you daren't look behind you, you just dare not.'

Another spirit occupies the Red Library. Miss Coates believes that there is a presence in the library but 'it's companionable, friendly. I have worked in here a lot and all the time I have been conscious that there was somebody standing, just out of view, watching me. I think of him as the "nice, kind gentleman". I know it's a man, and I know it's friendly. Every time I look around, of course, he isn't there.' Other family members have reported seeing a figure there. It is believed that the ghost is that of Sir John Thynne, the Elizabethan who was responsible for the original building of Longleat.

Other ghosts at Longleat include a malevolent presence thought to be a servant, an unidentified presence that knocks on a door, the ghost of Cardinal Wolseley, and others. Another spirit is that of Bishop Ken, who is commemorated by the Bishop Ken Library. He stayed at the house as a religious refugee for 20 years and his ghost is alleged to have been seen by several staff and security officers.

In the 1970s Frank de Felitta, author of bestsellers such as *Audrey Rose* and *The Entity*, was invited to Longleat to film part of a documentary for American TV network NBC called 'The Stately Ghosts of England'. While he was trying to film in the 'haunted corridor' on the third floor, constant film problems prevented his work; he could get no images on the film at all. The film stock and the cameras were checked and nothing could be found wrong, except that they wouldn't work. His project looked to be in jeopardy. A clairvoyant on the team advised that he should ask permission of the ghosts for the filming, which he did. 'The next day we got perfect film,' he said. 'I cannot explain it.' After that they set up a time-lapse camera in the corridor and filmed striking material. An anomalous light appeared in the corridor and moved between two rooms, passing from one doorway to another. It is a fascinating piece of footage which has been shown in television programmes around the world. Some have called it the most striking evidence in support of ghosts ever filmed.

Name: Foran's Hotel
Location: St John's, Newfoundland, Canada
Date: 1883
Source: Dale Gilbert Jarvis, researcher and folklorist

St John's General Post Office is on the site of a former hotel, thought to have once been the Foran's Hotel. In the hotel one night, after all the guests were asleep, a violent knocking noise was heard coming from a vacant room at the top of the building. So persistent was the noise that soon everyone in the building was woken, but an investigation of the room revealed nothing to account for the clamour. The next night at the exact same time the hotel was permeated with the same violent knocking. Again, no reason was found, and on the third night the knocking was renewed, causing great turmoil among the guests. A party was then organised to stand watch, with a double guard placed at the room door. That night the knocking ceased and was not heard again. The room was closed to the public, memory of the incident faded, and life and business returned to normal.

Several months after the disturbances, a stranger arrived in St John's and made his way to the Foran's Hotel, where he demanded lodging for the evening. At that time the establishment was full, with every room occupied except one. Rather than send the gentleman to a rival hotel, the staff gave the man the room which had been the epicentre of the psychic disturbance months before. The stranger retired to the room, and later that night the entire hotel was aroused by the old knocking, this time in a long and insistent outburst of wrath. Guests and staff rushed to the bedchamber, and upon breaking in found the new lodger lying on the bed fully clothed, and cold in death. A doctor was called, who declared that the man had died from massive internal haemorrhaging, but as the corpse was removed for burial the next day, a distinct rapping noise could be heard throughout the room, which persisted until the body was removed from the premises. The man was never identified and his body was buried quietly in the old Methodist Cemetery at the bottom of Long's Hill in St. John's. The room was boarded up and never used again.

Interestingly enough, stories were in circulation as recently as 1998 that the Canada Post building was haunted. In that year it was reported that strange, unexplained knocking noises were heard by postal workers on one of the upper stories.

Name: The Former Bursar

Location: Peterhouse College, Cambridge, south-east England
Date: 1997
Source: Various

Peterhouse College in Cambridge was founded in 1284 and so is a place of long and varied history. However, in 1997 two butlers working at the college, Matthew Speller and Paul Davies, felt that its history was impinging too closely on their comfort. The story was told by bursar Andrew Murison, who was quoted in the *Daily Mail* newspaper of 19 December 1997 as saying: 'The butlers were clearing up in the Combination Room after dinner and were both at the same time aware of a figure coming out of the panelling and moving diagonally across the room to the William Morris fireplace.

As soon as they began to focus on it, it disappeared into the fireplace. They both looked at each other and knew they had seen exactly the same thing.' The figure they saw was hooded and floating just above the floor.

Murison seems to have been sympathetic to their claims; certainly a few months later he had every reason to be as he himself felt a presence. As he described it: 'It was about 11.45pm and I had gone into the room to get some fruit, a banana and an apple, which I knew was on the table.' Murison noticed that it was unexpectedly cold and then sensed 'something there . . . Then I became aware very much of a presence, and I turned around and in a distant corner of the room was very distinctly a figure – perfectly benign and friendly. But it's not the sort of thing that bursars like to talk about too much because we're supposed to be the sort of chaps who have our feet on the ground, and people might think I'm a complete fruitcake.'

Graham Ward, the Dean of the college and a philosophical theologian, said in a BBC radio interview: 'That something took place in that room is beyond question. I saw the absolute terror on the faces of those two butlers, so I don't doubt something happened. In a college full of unreliable people, they are completely reliable.'

As to who the ghost might be, suspicion falls on Francis Dawes, a former bursar of Peterhouse who hanged himself from a bell-rope in 1789 feeling guilty for having presided over the election of a new Master who turned out to be disastrous for the college. The hooded figure seen by the butlers was said to have disappeared near the spot where Dawes's body was found. Dawes is buried in the churchyard beside the college, which has itself been the scene of two exorcisms.

Another candidate offered was also a former bursar at Peterhouse: the great-uncle of George Washington who worked there in 1695.

Ward called in a priest to try to exorcise the ghost, though that has not yet been done, as the priest has indicated that all 45 fellows of the college would need to be there at the same time which is not an easy thing to organise.

Not everyone was happy with the idea of an exorcism anyway. As reported in the *Sunday Telegraph* of 11 January 1998, one former undergraduate at Peterhouse, James Muckle, commented, 'All right-thinking persons must protest against any suggestions of exorcism. A ghost is a priceless cultural, academic and environmental asset.'

Name: The Former Lakeshore Psychiatric Hospital
Location: Etobicoke, Canada
Date: Recent
Source: Toronto Ghost and Hauntings Research Society /
  Matthew Didier

A contributor to the website of the excellent and energetic TGHRS sent in an account, used here with permission of the society.

He was working as a security officer in the building after a well-known college had taken it over. He had heard all sorts of odd stories. These included the rumour that shortly after three of the old buildings were renovated, a couple of students went to explore the tunnels that connected the buildings. After the students had been poking around in some of the empty rooms, they went back towards the stairs and heard what sounded like someone whistling. The sound came from behind them, but when they turned around it stopped. As they reached the stairs they heard it again, followed by a cold gust of wind.

Another story involved a construction worker who was doing some work in the same tunnels. He was walking through the dim hallway when he rounded a corner and saw a woman walking ahead of him. He thought this was odd since it was late and there should have been nobody else around. The workman then noticed she was wearing a nurse's outfit. He called out to her, but she rounded the corner and disappeared. He followed and now saw her standing with her back to him at the far end of the hallway. There was no way she could have moved that far in the time he had lost sight of her. He approached her cautiously and called out again. Slowly, the woman turned around and faced him. The hapless workman was terrified to see that she had no face and only a flat blank area where one should have been. He ran from the apparition and refused to go back into the tunnels.

TGHRS's contributor took these stories as 'made up to scare people' and had no reservations when he was posted on nightshift at the renovated buildings. The first few nights were uneventful, but he did feel unnerved in some areas. (One of the buildings still has the old morgue in the basement, which didn't add to his comfort.) On the third night, he had locked all the buildings and set the alarm systems when he began to patrol the grounds. While walking by one of the buildings that he had locked, he thought he saw movement behind one of the windows. He shone a flashlight at the window but saw nothing out of the ordinary. He knew that if there was anyone inside, the motion sensors installed in the building would be set off. But he was uneasy and decided to check the building just to make sure.

After turning off the alarm system, he entered the building. Just before switching on the lights he heard a loud noise like a 'whack'. As the lights came on he saw a plastic rubbish bin lid (the kind that flips over) going around and around as if someone had hit it hard. He then contacted another guard who was stationed next door and informed him they had an intruder in one of the buildings. The two guards kept in radio contact while they checked the building. Every room was vacant and the fire exit had not been used. He then checked the rubbish bin, thinking maybe there was a mouse or something, but it was empty, having been given a fresh bag by the cleaners.

He told the other guard that there was no-one there and went to leave the building. As he went to turn off the lights, he heard an audible sigh come from the stairway. He had the distinct impression of someone standing there staring at him, and shut off the lights and left the building in 'one hell of a hurry'. The next day, he was relieved to be transferred back to the dayshift.

Tamara, from TGHRS, visited Lakeshore and commented: 'It gave me some very bad vibes. You kind of absorb a little of the fear and hate and anger and confusion that the old patients left behind. Anyone even slightly sensitive will tell you that, and add that you frequently feel like you're watched, or that any second you will "see" the place as it was. That is one cree-eepy place. There are old hospital beds everywhere, piled into corners of large rooms with high ceilings. The tunnels underground scare me . . . I feel that possibly something still uses them. That place gives you the same feeling as watching *The Shining*, it's just chilling. If there are a few patients still floating around, it's kinda scary that they are possibly insane ghosts instead of "normal" ones.'

Name: Ghostly Eccentricity
Location: The Winchester (Mystery) House, San Jose, California, USA
Date: 1884 onwards
Source: Various

One of the most bizarre episodes of house-building must relate to California's Winchester House. It was built in 1884 by Mrs Sarah Pardee Winchester, who had inherited the Winchester Rifle firm. It was said that she was haunted by the ghosts of those killed by the Winchester firearms and that a medium advised her that the only escape from the ghosts was to buy a house and constantly expand it. This, she was told, would attract a better class of ghost and would protect her from the grubby and vindictive types!

The eight-room farmhouse, as it started out as in 1884, had, just six months later, become a 26-room building, and construction continued for the next 38 years until Sarah died in 1922 at the age of 85. Sarah had designed most of the house herself, but was no trained architect. By that time, the house was a 160-room mansion, sprawling over six acres. It had 47 fireplaces, 2,000 doors and 40 staircases. One obsession that came through in the architecture was the number 13; certain rooms had to have 13 windows or 13 chandeliers, certain staircases had to have 13 steps, and so on. The house has staircases leading nowhere – one stopping at the ceiling – doors opening onto blank walls, windows with no view, and one staircase that switched back seven times but still only raised nine feet.

Rumour has it that some of these architectural eccentricities were designed to confuse and disturb the lesser quality of ghost.

Name: Gingerbread
Location: Belgrave Hall, Leicestershire, central England
Date: Present time
Source: Terry Hewitt, local investigator for ASSAP

Belgrave Hall in Leicester has received many reports of ghostly happenings up to the present time, including many from staff working there. The two main phenomena reported are the apparition of a lady in Victorian-style dress, and phantom smells of cooking, in particular 'gingerbread' smells. The following detail is taken, with permission, from the report being complied by Terry Hewitt for ASSAP which forms part of a detailed and extensive study of the Hall and the surrounding area.

Emma Martin is Belgrave Hall's assistant curator. She gave a 'potted history' of the Hall in an interview in March 1999. 'The house is approximately 300 years old, built in 1709. The Ellis family were probably the most famous family to live here. John Ellis was an MP for Leicester; he bought the house in 1845 and lived there with his wife and 11 children, seven girls and four boys. He was a well-known farmer and respected agriculturist who turned his hand to the railways and industrialisation in general in the 1830s. He died in 1862. Five of his daughters remained at the house: Charlotte, Jane, Margaret, Isabelle and Helen. Margaret was the last to die, in 1923.'

Emma is one of the people to have experienced the 'ghostly smells' at Belgrave Hall. 'The first week I was here, I was wandering around, getting my bearings, and came up onto the main landing – the first floor landing, where the master bedroom is. [There I smelt the] very strong smell of gingerbread cooking. It was only in that very small area, just near the door of the master bedroom as you got to the top of the stairs. If you walked away from that area there was no smell! If you moved back into that area, there was a very strong smell of gingerbread.'

Emma did not consider the smells particularly strange, thinking perhaps they had come from the pub across the road. But later she was talking to Jeannie, who had worked at Belgrave Hall for some time, who confirmed that she too had smelt the 'gingerbread' smells. Emma continued: 'I know other museum assistants who have worked here for quite a few years, who have occasionally smelled cooking! Stewing fruit, meaty smells and things like that.' Jeannie confirmed her own experience with the smells. 'I have worked here now for nearly seven years, and like a few people I have smelled smells. Sometimes it's bread, sometimes it's plums, sometimes it's stew; and the strange thing being, it's nearly always the women who smell it, not the men. There are no cooking facilities, so there is no way anybody could be actually making those things.'

Another of the more famous ghosts of Belgrave Hall is the 'Lady in the Victorian Dress' seen by both the gardener, Mike Snuggs, and later by Jeannie. Mike Snuggs told his story: 'It was around Easter 1998. I was standing in the entrance hall, looking towards the stairs, and just all of a sudden, with no warning or anything, this figure started to come down the stairs. It was a female, I could see the boots and the bottom of her dress, a long dress; and she got to the bottom of the stairs, looked out of the window at the bedding and the flowers, seemed to smile and turned and walked past me through to the kitchen!'

Mike described the figure as 'fifties' in age and quite petite, perhaps 5ft 3in. He thought she was wearing a brown or rust-coloured jacket or bodice, and dark skirt and boots. There has been speculation, loosely based, that it could be the ghost of Charlotte Ellis.

Jeannie also saw the figure. 'I was there for a meeting in the afternoon. And when the meeting finished . . . I went up to fetch my stuff from the women's cloakroom, and I was told to make sure all the doors were locked. And as I was coming back I stopped on the first-floor landing, on the half-landing by the bathroom, and I was looking back thinking, have I locked all three doors or have I only done two? And out of the corner of my eye I saw movement. And I could see the bottom half of a skirt, a long skirt-dress – it was at least Victorian – and shoes or boots at the bottom. It moved across, I could see it through the bannisters, and it moved across as if looking out of the window, as if it was looking out to the garden. [I had] the impression of browns and greys. I turned and looked and it disappeared.'

A CCTV camera at the Hall has recorded an anomalous image which is still the subject of widespread speculation, with theories to explain the strange images on the screen including anything from two ghostly apparitions to moths or leaves close to the lens. Nor is the Hall the only haunted building in the immediate area; the Talbot pub across the road and the church in the same road form part of Terry Hewitt's investigation. In the Talbot, past paranormal phenomena reported have included the figure of a boy seen on at least four occasions, in the cellar and lounge, also poltergeistery in the bar and a very ugly face seen at a window. In nearby St Peter's churchyard, the figure of a lady has been seen to walk through a gravestone, wave and disappear.

The investigation by Terry Hewitt and ASSAP has proved fruitful indeed. During one vigil, ASSAP's then head of investigations, Mike Lewis, came face to face with an apparition in the pub.

Name: Grey Lady
Location: Nether Lypiatt Manor, Gloucestershire, western
   England
Date: 1980s
Source: Various

Purchased by Prince and Princess Michael of Kent in 1981, Nether Lypiatt Manor has a modern history of hauntings. Probably the most authoritative is that of the Grey Lady. A workman who had been working in one of the manor's attics was coming down the stairs and had reached the first floor when he looked over his shoulder to see the grey figure of a woman just behind him. She wore a long shawl over her head and a grey skirt. He hurried down the stairs, obviously realising something was amiss, but on looking back found the figure remained just behind him. When he got out of the building he telephoned the local police station and reported an intruder, though his manner suggested perhaps he realised something was not quite right. The police informed him that this was a local ghost of the property, which seems hardly likely to have cheered him up. The identity of the Grey Lady remains a mystery.

Nether Lypiatt has other claims of ghosts, though those may be more myth than substance. One story is of a blacksmith who failed to complete the manufacture of some iron gates quickly enough and was hanged for his alleged tardiness. The hanging is said to have taken place on a 25 January (year unknown) and an anniversary ghost of the young smith on a large white horse is reported to ride around the courtyard on that date.

There are also reports of a Woman in White, and a frock-coated figure seen at a dinner table. Newspaper reports in 1984 stated that previous owners had had religious ceremonies of exorcism to 'clear out the house'. The reports indicated that something unpleasant had indeed been found and dealt with.

Name: Henrietta
Location: Coalville, Leicestershire, central England
Date: 1990s to the present
Source: June Bowden (witness) / authors' own files

June contacted us after hearing us interviewed about our researches on local radio. She related to some of the stories we had been discussing, particularly since she had been dealing with a ghost in her son's house for almost a decade.

'My son is 35 years old and has been in his present house for the past 10 years. He seems to have a guest who we believe is a young girl between the ages of 7 and 12 years old. I've nicknamed her Henrietta, though I don't know where that name comes to me from. She has manifested through thumping noises and has shown herself to at least two little boys we know of.

'Once, when friends of my son came to visit, their two-year-old son went to the loo. He was laughing and talking while in the toilet and his mother went to him and asked who he was talking to. He replied that he was talking to a little girl and that he had told her that it was rude for her to be there while he was on the loo. His mother asked what she was like and he described her as having red hair. The same young boy saw her again in the bedroom later.

'The next time she showed herself was to another little boy, aged two and half years, who lives next door. The child was out playing in the garden and his mother looked out and saw him waving up to my son's bedroom window. She went out to him, knowing that my son was at work, and knowing the house was empty, and asked him who he was waving to. He said that he could see a little girl at my son's bedroom window. When his mother looked, she could not see anyone, but the child kept insisting that he could see the young girl.

'There have been other incidents. When my son goes to bed he puts his change on the bedside table, and he has woken up and heard his money moving around, a clinking sound as if it is being played with. When watching TV, my son has gone to make coffee or answer the phone, only to find that the TV is off or the remote control missing on his return. He used a tin opener one day, but, shortly afterwards, could not find it again and then later, when decorating his bedroom, found the tin opener under the wardrobe with other lost items. Once, when decorating, he put the paste brush down on the paste board, turned around and it was gone. He went into the middle bedroom and there it was. The middle bedroom is the room my son feels "Henrietta" occupies.

'At one point my son and his partner were so disturbed they had to leave the house. I suggested he return to the house, go into the middle bedroom, sit down or kneel down to her height-level and talk to her. He did, though he told me his hair was standing up on the back of his neck at the time. In the corner of the bedroom was standing one of those artificial Christmas trees with wire branches and fake berries on the ends. While he was talking to "Henrietta" he looked at the tree and one of the branches was moving up and down, as if, while listening to him, "she" was fiddling about with something near at hand, as young children do. I think that Henrietta did not like my son's partner, though my son seems to have taken a liking to Henrietta. In fact, things have been quieter since his partner moved out.

'There have still been things, though, which all seem like a young girl "fiddling". Switches clicking up and down in the kitchen, for example. At one time my son tried to contact the girl. I had suggested that he leave a piece of blank paper outside the bedroom door, with a crayon. When he came back some time later there was a scratching on the paper that could have been an "L" or the start of an "H".

'We have done some investigating, talking to the neighbours.

There seem to be a lot of stories of ghosts in the Coalville area, perhaps because of mining accidents; the area is famous for its mining in former days. The neighbours believe that a young girl died in the house sometime before the war, and we were also told that that child's mother had died in the house by falling down the stairs.

'I think Henrietta should go over to the other side. Perhaps she is sad that she cannot find her own mother. Perhaps she should be told that her mother is waiting for her on the other side and then she will go over and be at peace.'

Name: His Majesty's Theatre
Location: Aberdeen, Scotland
Date: 1942 onwards
Source: Kerry Slaven of Her Majesty's Theatre / authors' own files

Designed by theatre architect Frank Matcham, His Majesty's Theatre opened on 3 December 1906. The managing director of the time, Robert Arthur, was so impressed by the building he commented: 'This theatre will stand as a monument to show what Aberdeen and its workmen can do.' It was an extraordinarily successful theatre for two decades, but went into decline in the 1920s and 1930s, along with many theatres, as a result of the increasing popularity of the cinema. Councillor J.F. Donald purchased the theatre in 1933 and proceeded to renovate it at a cost of £10,000; this included the introduction of Scotland's only revolving stage. This stage enabled the theatre to adapt to the time, as it could 'quick-change' for film, stage or orchestra.

Like so many theatres, His Majesty's is alleged to sport a ghost. Kerry Slaven says: 'John (Jake) Murray was a stagehand in 1942. During the war, the circus was taken indoors in order to conceal any light that might be seen from the sky. The animals were loaded on to the stage by way of a wooden hoist. Only one animal should have been transported at any one time; however, two horses were placed on to the lift and, as a result of the overload, the wooden brake overran and Jake Murray was decapitated.

'It has been said by many that Jake is still present in the theatre. One of his most common treading grounds is an area called the Lambeth Walk. This is a rather dark and dingy stairway, which runs from the top of the balcony ("the Gods") to the very bottom of the building. It is rarely, if ever, used and lends itself perfectly to a ghostly atmosphere. Jake's presence has been felt and heard over the years. Today, the staff look upon Jake as a friendly ghost acting as caretaker; protecting the theatre once the staff have all left for the evening.'

As can be seen from Kerry's account, His Majesty's, like many other theatres, is proud and quite protective of its ghost; and the resident spirit is regarded as protective and benign, rather than malevolent.

Name: In The Crypt
Location: Store room, under Bank Street Chapel, Bolton, north-west England
Date: Approximately 1978-1982
Source: Researcher Maxine Glancy

Our colleague Maxine Glancy is a neighbour and family friend of this witness, Joyce; she has known her all her life. This incident happened sometime between 1978 to 1982; Maxine interviewed her in 1998. The following is largely verbatim from the interview recorded.

Joyce said: 'My boss sold wicker chairs and to store them he rented the crypt at Bank Street Chapel. The chapel is built on quite a steep hill so as you go into the church you are on the ground floor, but to go into the crypt and you go down the hill. When we were unloading chairs there would be two or three of us, but sometimes I'd be sent to price the wicker chairs; then I was on my own. It was a great big expanse of a room – stone floors, brick walls, quite old and often dark, and with electric light bulbs hanging for light. So, because we were always in and out, I tended to leave the door open. I didn't want to be in there when it was shut; no-one did because it was like being underground. I learnt later that there was a boiler room down the steps, so there was another layer beneath – more crypt underneath us – but I didn't [go there], I just saw the steps.

'I was working with my back to the door, busy with my pricing gun, and I had this sense that someone had walked in; this feeling that there was somebody behind me. I knew that there shouldn't have been because I was on my own. I turned round and there was a man stood in the doorway. The sun was shining from behind him so it was shimmering round him, making him look "flimsy", but I didn't think anything about that, I just put it down to the light behind him. I was in the dark, and I jumped. I really felt myself lift off the floor and he said to me, "I'm sorry I didn't mean to make you jump," and I said, "It's OK, it's alright." I turned back thinking, "The silly beggar, making me jump like that. Why didn't he knock? Fancy coming in like that, it's enough to give me a heart attack. I hope he's gone; it gives me the creeps because he is dressed for a funeral."

'He had a long black dress thing on, but what struck me most was he had a hat on, like a top hat, because I don't know what else to call it. An old-fashioned black hat with a brim, but it had a white chiffon bit round it in a big bow and down his back. At the time I didn't think, "Why is he dressed like an old fashioned funeral man?" I just took it that I was in a church, I thought he was the priest and he'd either come back from, or was going to, a funeral.

'I turned round and he was gone. I thought, "Oh, he's gone down the steps to the boiler," because sometimes people do go down there to deal with the boiler to keep the church warm. I'd presumed he'd gone downstairs because there was no other reason for him to be there. I carried on pricing and I forgot about him until a man that I know to be the priest came in. I knew him because he collected the rent off my boss.'

The priest asked Joyce how long she would be as he wanted to lock up. Joyce told him she was finished, but warned him there was 'one of his men' down in the boiler room. The priest told her that there was no-one else at the church that day. She persisted, asking if this man had attended a funeral; but the priest told her there had been no funerals that day. Joyce went cold and felt goosebumps break out.

She continued: 'He went quiet for a minute, then he said, "Would you do me a favour? Would you describe the man?" So I thought, "Oh my, we've got a burglar, should he not be in here?" I described him, "He's got a grey beard, pointy like a rabbi-type pointed beard and he's got his hat on with a chiffon scarf."

'He said, "You are describing to me . . ." – then he said the name of some priest which I can't remember – ". . . who died and was buried in the crypt." ' Joyce thought otherwise, since the man had actually spoken to her.

'The priest then said, "He has been seen before but only in the vestry in the church, he's never spoken to anybody. Would you look through the photographs in the archives and see if you can pick him out?" I said, "Yeah, I'd love to." I still wasn't bothered until after we'd locked up and I was going back to the shop, and I thought, "I'm not going back again on my own." I never did go and look at the photographs. I went back to the crypt, unpacking, but never on my own. I wouldn't go on my own. Not that I'm frightened of him, he was nice. I didn't think at the time, "I've just seen a ghost" or anything. I wasn't frightened until after the priest said, "You are describing a fellow that's dead." '

Having spoken to Maxine, Joyce realised that she had perceived something very unusual. She was sure that the chiffon adornment around his hat was tied in a bow and hung down his back. But how could she know that? He had never turned around and she had never seen his back. Even in the interview, Joyce got goosebumps again thinking it through. She kept saying, 'How can I know that?'

Joyce's description of a ghost is interesting; certainly interactive and not therefore a 'recording' ghost. Not only did he speak, but did so in response to her 'jumping', referring to it and therefore clearly observing her, thinking of what had happened and commenting on it.

Name: Jews' Blood
Location: Clifford's Tower, York, northern England
Date: 1190 onwards
Source: Various

Clifford's Tower stands alone and prominent on a hill in the central part of York. The so-called hauntings associated with it seem more to do with local legend than genuine haunting, and yet there is a twist in the tale.

In 1190 an anti-Jewish riot raged through York, and facets of the riot have resulted in many paranormal claims for the city. The rioters were led by Richard Malebisse, who besieged a large number of Jews in Clifford's Tower. He ordered the tower to be set on fire. Rather than surrender, the Jews remained to face their deaths. The tower was destroyed, but was later rebuilt with stones from Tadcaster. Red stains soon began to appear, and it was held that this was Jews' blood, a supernatural outpouring of the destruction that had taken place during the riots. Scientific analysis, however, has shown that the red markings were in fact iron oxide, present in small quantities in the stones that were used.

The twist in the tale is that no other stone from the Tadcaster quarries contains iron oxide, only – apparently – the stones that were used in the rebuilding of the tower itself.

Name: Lady Blanche de Warren
Location: Rochester Castle, Kent, southern England
Date: 1264 onwards.
Source: Various

The first castle built on this site was Roman, designed to protect the bridge across the River Medway, the Watling Street link from London to Dover. Bishop Gundolf commenced work on the present castle on behalf of William the Conqueror in 1087. King John successfully took the castle after a short siege in 1215, destroying the south-east tower. He burned the props with a fire ignited from the 'fat of 40 pigs', causing the tower to collapse.

On 4 April 1264 the castle was under siege again, this time by Simon de Montfort in his wars against King Henry III. During the battle, Lady Blanche de Warren is said to have been accidentally killed by an arrow fired by her lover, Ralph de Capo. It is said that her apparition has been seen several times, walking the battlements where she died, and some researchers report this as an 'anniversary' ghost appearing each 4 April. The castle has no inner floors to speak of, but the battlements can be scaled and it is there that its most famous ghost resides.

Two visitors from the United States, Karen Stevens and Sue-Ellen Welfonder, told us of their experiences when visiting the castle. Karen commented: 'We found the atmosphere there to be overwhelming. Sue-Ellen's camera, which had worked perfectly for years, jammed after she made a complimentary remark about Simon de Montfort, who had besieged the castle. Perhaps "someone" took exception to her remark. We joked about it being Lady Blanche's revenge.' (Later, a camera repairman said the mechanisms of her camera looked like they had been fused by a lightning bolt.) 'This happened at the very lowest level of the keep. We were standing on the wooden platform overlooking the grass at the bottom and talking about de Montfort and the reputed ghost of Lady Blanche.'

Sue-Ellen added: 'I can only confirm everything Karen's told you [about] the "zapping" of my camera at Rochester Castle after I'd extolled the virtues of Simon de Montfort, a historical hero of mine.'

Name: The Local Tyrant
Location: Wilton Castle, south-east Ireland
Date: From the 19th century
Source: Various

Wilton Castle was the home of the Alcock family from the early 17th century and was largely destroyed by fire in the early 1920s. Only the walls remain. Strange light phenomena seen in the castle are attributed to an actress who died in the fire. Wilton also has an anniversary ghost: the apparition of Harry Alcock, who died in

1840, is seen driving from the castle in his carriage. A local shoemaker is alleged to have spoken to the ghost, and local crowds sometimes gathered in anticipation of the sighting.

One ghost story relates to a neighbour of Wilton Castle, Archibald Jacob, a local magistrate and captain of a local militia company during the time of the anti-British rebellion of 1798. He was a tyrant reputed to have tortured many of the local people. Returning to his home from Wilton Castle in 1836, he fell from his horse and was killed, and for many years his ghost was believed to haunt Wilton Castle and the scene of his death. A Catholic priest was summoned to the castle to conduct an exorcism, and at that time the ghost of Archibald Jacob is alleged to have appeared in the fireplace and then disappeared in a cloud of smoke.

Name: Lord Byron
Location: Newstead Abbey, Nottinghamshire, central England
Date: To the present
Source: Researchers David Cross and Jenny Bright

Newstead Abbey is Lord Byron's ancestral home and several of the many hauntings there are allegedly connected with the poet. Byron himself seems not to have made any documented appearances, but those associated with him have.

The house has an 'omen' ghost, a Black Friar whose cold and dark apparition is said to bode badly for the Byron family. Lord Byron believed the Black Friar appeared during his marriage to Annabella Milbanke, a marriage which Byron regarded as the unhappiest event of his life.

The apparition of a White Lady is said to be Sophia Hyatt, who idolised Byron and lodged on the estate. She was run down by a coach-and-four, but apparently has maintained her wish 'never to leave Newstead'. Boatswain, Byron's beloved dog, has also frequently been seen at the Abbey, recently by a gardener working there.

Researchers David Cross and Jenny Bright, during their time at the Abbey, have heard the sound of ladies laughing and giggling on the stairway leading to Byron's bedroom.

Name: Lucy
Location: Kingston House, Marino, Adelaide, Australia
Date: March 1983
Source: Kingston House Development Committee Inc. / Valerie
   Jones (witness) / authors' own files

Our first knowledge of Kingston House came from a correspondent, Eleanor, who reported to us a timeslip experience in Burra, Australia. While we were discussing this experience (see *The Encyclopedia of the World's Greatest Unsolved Mysteries*) Eleanor also mentioned the reputation for hauntings associated with Kingston House which is near her home. She later gave us some local information and news clippings about the building and shortly afterwards put us in touch with Valerie Jones, who had once lived in the House as its caretaker and who had had personal experience of the ghosts.

In 1836 George Strickland Kingston arrived in southern Australia as deputy surveyor to Colonel William Light. He bought the site and gave permission for an inn to be built there in 1840. The inn was not a great success – a proposed harbour in Marino Bay that should have provided a large client-base was abandoned – and Kingston decided to use the building as a summer home. By 1850 he had enlarged and altered it to its present form. Now the building is looked after by The Kingston House Development Committee, who have the twin goals of systematic restoration and maintenance of the house, and full utilisation of the property as a community asset.

The ghost alleged to be the main resident of Kingston House is Lucy Kingston, wife of George's son Charles, who lived in the house until 1919. Her husband died in 1908 and from then until her own death she acquired a reputation for being a little eccentric. She kept intruders at bay with a shotgun; one elderly resident of the area remembers her taking a 'pot shot' at two men walking on the beach nearby.

In a local *Guardian* article of 26 October 1994, one of the volunteers working there, Mrs Sarah Burgess, told of her own knowledge of the ghosts. Three of her team members had sensed Lucy's presence at some time and many former residents of the house had told Mrs Burgess their stories. 'People who have lived in the house have declared that the lights go on and off and there's been nobody there,' said Mrs Burgess, 'and animals sense it. Dogs and cats have rushed to their owners and scrambled into their laps.' The development committee confirmed to us: 'On occasions, during committee meetings, we have felt that there was someone prowling about the house, but on investigating have found no-one . . .'

Valerie Jones told us of her own experiences of hauntings there.

'My first experience was one night, as we were heading off to bed. David, my husband, had gone down to the bedroom before me; I was in the bathroom. As I walked through the lounge to turn the TV off, I saw a shadow walk past the door. I cannot say for sure if it was male or female. I think it was female. When I saw the figure I wasn't too concerned as I was positive it was someone else that was living in the house. When I got down to the bedroom, David turned on the light. That's when I realised that it wasn't possible for anyone to have passed me in the hall. It turned out that we were the only two in the house, so the shadow I saw was unexplained.

'Another night, when I was staying there by myself, I stayed up until about 1.30am watching telly. I then went to bed with my cat and tried to go to sleep. After quite a few last checks of the room I dozed off, still checking the room; by that I mean I'd be lying in bed and look up every so often because I had the feeling someone was there. Once or twice I thought I had seen a man standing at the bottom of the bed, but by the time I had focused the image had gone, so you could never really say if you had seen anything or not. Anyway, I finally went to sleep and it was about 3am when I woke up. I saw a red light by the bedroom door. Now I'm not sure if this was a car light or what it was, but it was a glowing light that didn't stay long. I heard voices coming from the lounge so I figured it was a friend who was staying with me who had arrived back, so I wasn't at all concerned.

When I got to the lounge and saw that no-one was home, I was a little scared but figured I was this close to the toilet I may as well go while I was up. So I was sitting there in the toilet that was at the end of the hall, my cat was with me, and I heard footsteps. They sounded like men's feet with work boots on – they weren't extra loud or anything but I could hear them walking, turning around, walking again – only about three or four steps at a time. I was waiting for the person to come down the stairs; I was so sure it was an intruder. When no-one had appeared and the steps seemed to have stopped, I grabbed my cat, went into the lounge, got my keys and left.

'I was closing the back door and I hesitated, thinking I was mad and not to be so silly and that I should go back in the house. As I did, I heard this slight grunt noise. That was enough for me, I was out of there. I found out later that others had had similar experiences.'

The identity, and any purpose, of the male ghost Valerie saw and heard is unknown. But the efforts of those who have worked at the house in recent years have been designed to bring the old residence back to its former glory; if Lucy approves, perhaps she will be at rest when the house is again the mansion it once was.

Name: John McLoughlin
Location: McLoughlin House, Oregon City, Oregon, USA
Date: Mid 1970s
Source: Various

Dr John D McLoughlin is known as the Father of Oregon and was the founder of Oregon City. He was a doctor for the British Hudson's Bay Company and in 1821 was sent to the Oregon region, to the company's new headquarters at Fort Vancouver. The company did not have proper title to the land there and as the pioneers' wagon trains moved across America, McLoughlin realised that British claims to the land would fail. He aided the settlers, was generous and helpful and rescued those who became stranded in difficult areas of the Oregon Trail. In 1829 he founded Oregon City, giving away 300 lots to settlers, churches, schools and other groups. In 1845 the land was placed in his own name in exchange for $20,000 paid through the Hudson's Bay Company. The following year he resigned from the company to become Mayor and Councilman of the city.

Despite his generosity and kindness he had few friends in the community, perhaps because he was British, wealthy, a Catholic among Protestants and was married to a Chippewa woman. The American Government disputed his claim to the land and he had no support. He died bitter and disillusioned, and stripped of his ownership.

In 1909 McLoughlin's house was moved to another site where it presently stands. It was restored in the 1930s and opened to the public. In 1970 the bodies of McLoughlin and his wife were moved to the new grounds.

Between his death in 1857 and the 1970s there were no reports of any haunting phenomena; McLoughlin was apparently at peace. Then, in the 1970s, Nancy Wilson became curator of the home and the haunting phenomena began. She herself was tapped on the shoulder when there was no-one else near her, while she and others saw a hulking shadow walking into McLoughlin's bedroom and heard the footsteps of heeled boots in the upstairs hall when no-one was there. Lamps were found swinging when there was no cause, a child's bed would appear as if slept in when staff arrived to open up the house in the morning. Objects would be lost and found in strange places and mysterious voices would sometimes be heard. Phenomena peaked in 1981 when Wilson organised an exhibit of women's clothing, one of which was a wedding dress belonging to the wife of an associate of McLoughlin.

Wilson researched her own family and discovered a link to McLoughlin, which she believed may be why the hauntings were triggered when she arrived. One of her ancestors was helped by McLoughlin but still owed him $43 when McLoughlin died. It is possible that the ghost sought a moderate revenge for the debt, though Wilson believes it more likely that since she has a genuine desire to honour the name of McLoughlin, the ghost is there to give approval to her work. Certainly no-one has suggested that it is in any way malevolent.

Name: The Merritt House
Location: Niagara area, Canada
Date: Present day
Source: Toronto Ghost and Hauntings Research Society/
  Matthew Didier

The House was originally built in the 1820s as the home of William Hamilton Merritt, builder of the Welland Canal. He was born in 1793, served in the war of 1812, and in 1815 married Catherine Rodman Prendergast, the daughter of a New York Senator. William and Catherine moved into the house in 1860 but William died just two years later.

The main house has a series of interesting tunnels which connect it to the carriage house. When slavery was abolished in Upper Canada, the local area became an escape route for fleeing slaves and the Merritt House tunnels were a major part of that route. During the era of Prohibition they found another use: to conceal bootleg spirits. The house has been, in its history, a military convalescent home and an inn, and is presently the headquarters of Canadian radio station CKTB.

Our ghost account starts with a radio interview being conducted there with Kyle Upton, who was discussing the paranormal. As Upton wrote in his book *Niagara's Ghosts at Fort George*: 'I was in the studio with Rob McConnell, the show's host, and we were on the air taking calls from the public . . . Rob had just finished telling a little about the ghosts that haunt the studio building when we heard a voice. I heard two syllables of a man's voice through my earphones. I assumed that something had gone wrong and I was hearing the producer's voice from the other studio. As it turns out, it was not the producer, although he heard a voice in the studio as well. Additionally, the FM broadcaster in a third separate studio also heard a voice. I could only discern that it was a male voice, but Rob is positive that the two words were "Bite me". Strangely, the witnesses in the other studios heard a woman's voice expressing criticism of the show's host.'

Matthew Didier was invited to the location to investigate after other strange occurrences. The producer, Jennifer, had seen part of the figure of a man standing near one of the studio's doors; it vanished while she watched. Next was a long series of mechanical and equipment problems. Anomalous sounds were heard; laughter, heavy breathing and the ringing of a bell. A webcam monitoring the studio picked up an odd mist hovering directly in front of Rob McConnell during a show.

Matthew put together a team with the necessary equipment to investigate the claims. On the initial tour of the premises, Rob took the team upstairs. At the top of the stairs, Matthew was the first to have a problem. He suddenly felt as if he was 'being hit in the chest with a heavy foam bat'. Other members of the team – Tamara, Dave and Toni, as well as a reporter and a technician – felt untoward, too. A psychic, Dorothy, sometime later, complained that she felt as if someone had died there of a heart attack, as she had a tightened chest. She also said that the stairs were being blocked by the spirit of a former lady of the house who felt that the upstairs was 'private' territory and should not be trespassed upon.

The report by Didier and the Society states that in the room at the top of the stairs there had been heard the sound of a baby crying. Tamara, Toni, Dave and one of the psychics were at that room a little later and felt something so powerful that it stopped them from entering. The report says: 'Accompanying us was also a gent named Patrick, invited by Rob to take part. He was playing the part of the sceptic and trying to bring rationality to the night's excitement. While sitting in "Master Control", Patrick noticed a cup trophy balanced on the edge of a large bookshelf. Not thinking about it too much, Patrick (a former military police officer) shoved the trophy to the back of the shelf and forgot about it. After a few moments, he noticed the trophy had moved back to the edge. Again, thinking there must be a logical explanation, he simply moved it back and kept an eye on the cup. After a time, he gave the incident up for "imagination" and let his eyes return to the people in the room. A few seconds later, he glanced up. The trophy was back on the edge of the bookcase. Patrick brought everyone's attention to the trophy and moved it back to the wall side of the bookcase. This time, the room was watching . . . nothing. After what seemed like an eternity looking at this item, everyone started paying attention to the show in progress again. Jennifer noted it first. "It's moved again." Lo and behold, the cup was once again at the edge. The cup was removed to the ground and Matthew balanced a pencil on the end of the bookcase to test for vibrations. The pencil did not move.'

Another poltergeist-like event was finding that a door to the mini-studio was 'barred' twice by 'someone' moving a chair in the room into the path of the opening door, but no-one was in the room to do it. Attempts were made to contact the spirits in the House, and it seems that some members of the Merritt family were contacted; Mrs Merritt complained of her husband's temper, for example. It was also discovered in this seance that a maidservant in the home once fell headfirst down the stairs and died.

One month later, Matthew and a team arrived for a follow-up investigation. Just when Tamara and Matthew commented on how quiet the evening had been, they heard a thud. Looking back, they saw a four-foot piece of wood had landed on the floor behind them. One of the studio engineers confirmed it had happened before.

The next event was experienced by Rick and a couple from Toronto. They were at the bottom of the stairs when they heard a very clear child's voice saying 'Mamma! Mamma!'

As they were leaving, Tamara let out a muffled shriek. She described feeling as if she had touched a 'live electrical wire'. A sudden shock. Interestingly, in January 2000 Matthew and the team discovered that William and Catherine Merritt had, in the last years of their lives, been undergoing what was then a revolutionary kind of treatment for illness; electro-shock therapy.

No doubt this investigation will continue. Its progress, and other investigations by the Society and its affiliates, can be monitored on their website (for the address, see the back of the book).

Name: Molly
Location: Radisson SAS Airth Castle and Hotel, nr Falkirk, Scotland
Date: Present
Source: Revenue Management Assistant at Airth Castle Hotel / authors' own files

The SAS Airth Castle Hotel has received many reports from guests of hauntings in the hotel which they believe relates to 'Molly', a hostess from the 15th or 16th century when the building was a private house. Molly is thought to have been the head hostess, who would ensure that dinner arrangements were correctly made and adhered to.

It is also believed that a fire which destroyed the majority of the building killed Molly and her two children. Since then, Molly has haunted the building, in distress for her lost children. (Some believe she saved herself and is remorseful for deserting her children.) She haunts one bedroom in particular, from where several guests have reported her presence. No-one has thought of her as nasty or malign; indeed, she seems to be a local favourite. The guest book contains several remarks from guests who have reported Molly's presence. Several have commented that they have heard her singing lullabies, presumably to her children.

Her children – the girl is thought to be Alice, the boy's name is unknown – while never seen, have been heard on the staircases and in rooms, laughing and playing. It is thought that they occasionally steal cleaning materials from the cleaners, or chocolates from the rooms, playing mischievous games as children do.

Molly has been seen gazing thoughtfully out of a window. The staff believe she is looking for help to arrive, as she must have done when the building was in flames. One guest arrived downstairs in a state of alarm and wearing only a towel, claiming that a woman had opened his shower curtain: Molly was thought the likeliest suspect.

Name: The Moving Coffins
Location: The Chase Crypt, Barbados
Date: 1812 to 1820
Source: Various

There are several cases around the world of so-called moving coffins, i.e. where crypts are opened to admit a newly-deceased member and coffins formerly known to have been neatly laid out are found strewn at random around the crypt. In some cases it has been possible for this to be explained by the effects of flooding, which might float the coffins and re-distribute them, but in some cases, as in the Chase Crypt in Barbados, no sensible explanation has yet been put forward.

The crypt was created by Colonel Thomas Chase of Christchurch, Barbados, a wealthy Englishman known to have been cruel and short-tempered towards family and slaves on the Island. The first person interred in the crypt was a relative, Mrs Goddard, who died on 31 July 1807. She was interred in a lead coffin that took four strong men to lift it. Just a few months later, Chase's young daughter, Mary-Anna, died of disease and was interred there also. On 6 July 1812 another of his daughters, Dorcas, was interred. During these times the coffins of the previously interred were undisturbed.

Then in August 1812, Chase himself died and the vault was opened for his internment. The three coffins already within the vault were found in disarray. The infant Mary-Anna's tiny coffin appeared to have been thrown across to the corner of the crypt. The coffins were re-laid out in their original positions, side by side, and Chase's coffin placed on top and across them. In case the coffins had been moved by vandals, a fine layer of sand was spread out across the floor of the vault to detect footprints.

It was not until 1816 that the crypt was opened again to receive another baby from the family. When the vault was opened all four coffins were redistributed, though the sand was undisturbed. Just a few weeks later, the body of another family member was interred in the crypt and when it was opened, the coffins were again found in disarray with the sand undisturbed.

The local rumour was that the deceased members of the family were protesting against the unwanted presence of the unloved Thomas Chase, and the rumours created some unrest among the superstitious local population. The Governor of Barbados, Lord Combermere, intervened, being present in July 1819 when the crypt was opened to admit another member of the family. Again the coffins were strewn about and again the sand was undisturbed. The coffins were restored to their original positions. Mrs Combermere noted in her diary, 'In my husband's presence, every part of the floor was sounded to ascertain no subterranean passage or entrance was concealed. It was found to be perfectly sound and solid; no crack was even apparent . . . The floor was sanded in the presence of Lord Combermere and the assembled crowd. The door was slid into its wanted position and, with the utmost care, the new mortar was laid on so as to secure it. When the masons had completed their task, the Governor made several impressions in the mixture with his own seal, and many of those attending added various private marks in the wet mortar . . .'

On 18 April 1820 Combermere ordered the seals broken and the vault opened; there were hundreds of people there to witness it. First, he checked his seal, and found it and the other marks undisturbed. But workmen found it difficult to open the stone slab. When they finally did manage to move it, they found the coffins strewn about once again. One had been on end, resting against the slab door, making it difficult to open. One of the babies' coffins seemed to have been thrown against the stone wall of the crypt so violently that it had left a deep gash there. Another coffin had been thrown down some steps to the bottom of the tomb.

The matter was brought to an end when the coffins were all removed and buried elsewhere and the vault sealed, never to be used again.

Name: Mrs Sellers
Location: Argyle Terrace, Argyle Street, Hull, northern England
Date: 1969
Source: *Hull Daily Mail*, 1969

A husband, wife and six children living in Argyle Terrace, Hull, were reported in the local newspaper as 'living in terror' following sightings of a ghost thought to have been a woman who lived in the house many years previously. The mother, Janet Windley, reported that the ghost had caused sudden drops in room temperature, had pulled the hair of her children, had bruised her baby and had touched herself and her neighbours from behind.

The ghost apparently centred around her then 13-year-old daughter, Vivian. She had first seen the apparition of the woman near a chair. 'Vivian looked as if she had been hypnotised,' reported the newspaper. Bangings and strange noises were heard on other days. A medium came to the house to try to make contact with the ghost, but the hauntings actually got worse after the medium had left. Reverend Tom Willis, Vicar of St John's Church, Hull, blessed the house and although he waited for the ghost to appear, did not see her. Near neighbours Mr and Mrs Sobey of Wycliffe Grove, who had visited the Windleys, found coldness and a sense of presence and indeed were the ones who had called in Reverend Willis to help. Mr Sobey stated, 'On the landing something seemed to be moving me, although I did not want to be moved. I just felt compelled to go.' His daughter, Susan, claimed to have seen the ghost and described her as very old, with a long shawl and long fingernails. Other neighbours had also encountered hauntings in the house.

An anonymous letter was received by the Windleys from a woman who had worked at the house 50 years earlier; she worked for a Mrs Sellers, who she believed to be the person whose ghost was now appearing. She wrote the following as reported in the newspaper: 'Reading about your ghost has brought back memories to me, as I used to work at your house for a very old lady who was over 80 years old. I am well over 60 myself now, and was then a girl of 14. I used to clean up at your address . . . The old lady, Mrs Sellers, wore a shawl and was very tall and slim. She had no family and her husband died just after they were married. She was a very religious person.'

Records do not show a Mrs Sellers living at the address, though local research shows such records were notoriously incomplete. Argyle Terrace no longer exists, having been demolished some years ago, though Argyle Street itself is still there and largely similar to the way it was decades ago. Mrs Sellers, in her present ethereal form, may have had to get used to more modern surroundings.

Name: On Video
**Location: East Ardsley Conservative Club, Yorkshire, northern
   England**
Date: 1993
**Source: Morley Observer (30th September 1993) / Yorkshire Evening
   Post (20 October 1993)**

Security cameras at East Ardsley Conservative Club in Yorkshire picked out a man standing in the doorway of the club. The figure was seen by the club treasurer, Bill Hodgson, who was alone in the club one Thursday afternoon waiting for a friend to join him. Thinking the figure was his friend, he walked to the doorway to greet him – but found no-one there. But when he returned to the monitor screen he saw the figure was still visible, exactly in the spot he had just visited.

The ghostly figure then reappeared some days later at more or less the same time of day, and was again seen by Hodgson. On both occasions the video also recorded the images, which were examined by a number of people. None of them could come up with a rational explanation.

Club members commented that several people had reported 'spooky' feelings in the club, a sense of presence that left some people uneasy. Hodgson commented: 'I do not believe in ghosts, but I can't explain these images. The members are divided over whether it's a ghost or whether it's a load of hogwash. But I'd like to see those who don't believe come in here at midnight on their own and watch the video.'

Name: Party On!
**Location: Pengethley Manor Hotel, nr Ross-on-Wye,
   Herefordshire, central England**
Date: August 1996
**Source: Sue-Ellen Welfonder and Karen Stevens (witnesses) /
   authors' own files**

Pengethley Manor is said to be home to a friendly ghost known as Harriet. It is thought that she had been a maid back in the time when the building was the Manor House, owned by the Symmonds family. In the late 1800s there was a fire in the Manor; some believe Harriet died in that incident. Harriet is especially fond of two bedrooms; there are reports from several people who have detected her presence at the foot of their beds.

In 1996 a group of Americans were staying at the hotel. One of them took some Polaroid pictures in the hotel and these showed some strange lines which she thought were 'paranormal'. We spoke to the general manager, Paul Forster, who stated that he could not find any easy explanation for the images. Paul, in fact, had accounts of his own to tell us. During Christmas 1996 his colleague was closing the bar when a brass doorstopper moved away and the door closed by itself. Paul has himself felt a presence in the reception area, and along an upstairs corridor.

We were fortunate enough to correspond with two of the people who had been in that party of Americans; they gave us their accounts of those nights.

Sue-Ellen's account

'We [Sue-Ellen Welfonder and Karen Stevens], together with our friend Pat Cody, with whom we regularly visit England, were at Pengethley Manor on the nights of 9-10 August 1996. The first night we'd arrived quite late, about 11pm, because we'd been touring and had visited Llancaiach Fawr.'

Although tired after touring, Sue-Ellen could not sleep. She could hear, coming from the next room, a loud party, and later loud heavy footsteps as if a man in boots was pacing back and forwards in the room above. 'That first night, I didn't think anything of it beyond thinking it was quite thoughtless of people to make so much noise in a hotel at that hour. Only at breakfast the next morning did I begin to think there was something odd about what I'd heard. When I joined my companions at the breakfast table, they asked if I'd had a good night. I said no, I hadn't. Loud guests in the room next to mine had bothered my sleep, as well as someone stomping around at 2am in the room above mine. All went silent then. Karen and Pat said it was strange, they hadn't heard anything; the room in question was between mine and theirs and they should have heard party noises, too, if one had been going on. And they queried how I could have heard someone stomping around in "the room above mine" when we were on the top floor. I'd been too exhausted to register that fact when I'd heard the footsteps.'

'But I did think it odd that Karen and Pat hadn't heard the loud partying going on, as it sounded as if it was in the room between us. In any case, I forgot about it and we spent the day touring again. But that second night at Pengethley brought certainty that the noises I'd heard the first night were indeed very strange. For the second night, the same scenario repeated itself! The party noises repeated themselves exactly as they had the night before.

'Like the previous night, the revelry began about 11pm. The noises followed the exact same pattern as I'd heard the night before, too – as if a tape recording was being played in the room next to mine. These noises were so real that, the night before, I'd been tempted to get out of bed and bang on the wall, but I didn't. That's how real they sounded, though.

'Anyway, there it was, 11pm the second night, and it was as if I'd stepped into a time warp and was re-living the previous night. This time I got up and switched TV channels to see if perhaps the party I heard was coming from a TV programme someone in the next room might be watching. There was nothing on that even remotely could be considered as a source for the sounds I heard. I pressed my ear to wall and it was indeed a loud and raucous party going on, in full swing.

'One man's voice was quite distinct: very deep, and there were several women's voices. Like the previous night, I could not make out particular words, just the sound of voices, the man with the deep voice and the women. The women had very high-pitched voices and seemed in quite high spirits. In fact, they repeatedly broke into what I can only describe as hysterical laughter – and, again, this was the *exact* same pattern of noises I'd heard at the *exact* same time the night before.

'There were other sounds, too. Heavy sounds as if large pieces of furniture were being pushed around or dragged across the floor. The first night, I'd assumed someone was messing with heavy suitcases. This was the definite sound of chairs being pushed back, you know: the scraping noise a chair makes when one pushes back from a table, and the sound of footsteps — in short: it sounded like one rip-roaring party going on.

'This time, though, I knew it was "unusual" – no one would have the exact same party two nights in a row, with the exact same pattern of voices, bursts of hysterical female laughter and the sound of heavy objects being pushed or dragged around, chairs scraping the floor and sounds of people milling about.

'Again, I didn't bang on the wall as I'd been tempted to the night before. Instead, I called down to the front desk to complain. The man on duty told me he couldn't imagine a wild party going on in that room – it was occupied by an elderly, lone gentleman. (I found out later that the man from the front desk went upstairs and listened at the door after I'd called him. He heard nothing.)

'When he told me that a lone elderly man was in that room, the hairs on my arms stood up. Immediately, I called my friends Karen and Pat, who were on the other side of the room in question, to ask if they could hear the party. They said no, they couldn't. But Karen suggested Pat go out in the corridor and listen at the door. While Pat did that, Karen stayed on the line with me. Moments later, Pat came back in their room and told Karen she'd pressed her ear to the door of the room and heard nothing. Yet I could *still* hear the party going on full swing even as we spoke. I couldn't believe they didn't hear it. It was *so* loud.

'By then I was scared. I asked Karen to come to my room with Pat, so they'd hear it, too. Now here's the weird part: the very moment she said, "Okay, we'll be right there," the noises stopped. Instantly. As if someone turned off a switch! The noises just ceased.

'They appeared at my room moments later and we sat on my bed, waiting, for about 20 minutes. Nothing happened. When they left to go back to their room, I went with them. Something told me that if I'd stayed, the party would've started up again. I just knew it.'

Sue Ellen later asked: 'Were those rooms at one time perhaps a large parlour? Could the party noises I heard be the replaying of a long-ago gathering? In other words, a 'recording', as you describe in your book *The Encyclopedia of Ghosts and Spirits*? And if so, why me? Why did I hear it and not my friends on the other side of that room?'

Karen Stevens' account

'We arrived at Pengethley late on a rainy evening in mid August 1996, exhausted from a day's touring and more than ready for our beds. We had no idea at the time that the manor was haunted.

'We checked in and were heading wearily up the stairs towards our rooms, when our tour guide, Patty Suchy, felt someone brush past her. No-one was near enough to touch her. We were several feet apart, and could not have touched one another deliberately or accidentally. Believe me, none of us was thinking about ghosts at that point, we only wanted to get to our beds.

'I still had my Polaroid camera with me and immediately took several photos of the stairs and the landing. Two of them had odd "streaks" on the photos. Polaroid has a relatively slow exposure and the light was dim, and perhaps I moved the camera, but I'd been using that Polaroid for years under all sorts of conditions and had only gotten that type of streaking in places reputed to be haunted.

'The next morning I awoke about 7 am and lay in bed awhile, thinking about nothing in particular. I could hear the shower running and my room-mate Pat moving around in the bathroom. A flicker of movement near the windows caught my eye, and I glimpsed a transparent figure of a woman, in some sort of uniform like a maid's, raise her arms as if to open the drapes. I felt no fear; it seemed as though she had a right to be there. I said "Good morning", and the next moment she was gone.

'I wonder if the ghost named Harriet might have been a house-maid whose duty it was to draw curtains in the evening and open them in the morning. That would account for Patty's experience of someone brushing past her on the stairs, and also for my glimpse of an apparent ghost.'

Name: A Presence On The Stairs
Location: Hatfield, Hertfordshire, southern England
Date: Late 1960s to 1974
Source: Jim Ferguson (witness) / authors' own files

Over the few years that Jim lived in a house in Hatfield he often felt a 'presence' which made him, and others, feel quite uncomfortable. Although no-one ever saw the ghost, he felt certain it was there.

Over time the house produced several paranormal experiences for Jim: scratching sounds for which no explanation could be found despite ardent searching by Jim and a friend staying with him; the unexplained appearances of coins in the living room; and electric plugs which had been taken from their sockets, found replaced after, no-one had been in the house. As Jim explained: 'I was very conscious of safety; I would take the electric plugs out of the wall sockets whenever I left the house. But when I came back I would find the plugs back in. Now you know either you're going daft, some-body has a key, or there is something stranger going on. I do not know how an entity could actually put the plugs back in but that is what it seemed like.'

But it was on the stairs where there was a sense of unease: 'I don't think I ever panicked, but I had times when I just felt very scared for no obvious reason; you could just feel it.' At the top of the stairs was a toilet room and the door to this would bang close. Jim found he would come down the stairs sideways, nervously sensing something behind him, but if he took his mind off it, the door upstairs would slam. 'I'm absolutely serious, it would really bang hard.'

A friend of Jim's was also upset in the same place. She was so bothered she had to phone him. 'I got a phone call from my friend saying she had been doing some ironing with her back to the staircase and that she had had this overwhelming feeling of fear that something on the stairway was hovering around,' Jim said. 'She was so scared she could not move.'

Animals, too, would react to that area. Jim's boxer dog put its head under the stairs and immediately shot back, its fur standing on end. The dog was in a panic, yet there was nothing to be seen under the stairs. A cat would suddenly take fright there and run off to hide under a chair. 'The cat, particularly, was very sensitive to what was there,' Jim said. 'You would always see it down on its haunches trying to work things out.'

Although Jim never actually saw anything in the house he said 'You felt it in a very, very strong way. I think there was some kind of entity there which was mildly menacing, and constantly there.'

Name: The Princeton Street Haunting
Location: 4771 N Princeton Street, Portland, Oregon, USA
Date: 1974
Source: H. Michael Ball / Ghosts of North Portland website

Meaghan Ferres related her experiences of a haunting during her years living at 4771 N Princeton Street, which started when she and her family moved in in 1974. The house had been formerly occupied by her aunt and uncle, who told Meaghan and her siblings of how, late at night, they would hear their rocking chair squeaking as if it were being used.

Meaghan made the point that her family had no rocking chair, but they would hear footsteps late at night. She would hear them coming from the master bedroom and walk down the hallway to the upstairs bathroom. More rarely, she heard them returning. This would even happen when the bedroom – her parents' bedroom – was unoccupied, if for instance her parents were out. Of one occasion she related: 'I remember one time in the afternoon, we had caught on to the footstep pattern by now and I had just come home and knew that my dad was upstairs sleeping. I heard the footsteps and wasn't scared because my dad was home. So I ran up the stairs as soon as I heard them, expecting to find my dad making his way to the bathroom. No-one was there! I ran into his room and he was still asleep.'

Meaghan also remembered hearing other sounds: during the day the front door opening and closing, and then someone walking into the house while she was home alone. 'I would think it was my mom coming home from the store,' Meaghan recalled, 'but when I went downstairs no-one was there; or I would yell "Mom?" and get no answer.' She heard the screen door opening and shutting. Meaghan was not the only one to experience this: 'My mom says this also happened to her several times.'

Meaghan continued: 'When I was a teenager, sleeping in the basement bedroom, I would hear a woman's scream just as I was falling asleep. It happened about three times. It was terrifying and I can't prove whether it was a "dream" or not, but I know I haven't heard it before or since. At the time, though, I did hang up a cross from the ceiling over my bed, which remained for the rest of my stay in that room.'

Meaghan's aunt offered a story of a much earlier haunting reputed to come from the house. 'At the turn of the century, a businessman, his wife and young daughter of around five owned the house. The story goes that the wife died while the husband was off on business. Later, the girl would sense her mother's presence and told her father: "Mommy still comes to tuck me in at night." When the father asked her how that could be, she replied that she could see the imprint on the covers of her bed, where her mother used to sit to tuck her in at night.'

During renovation and remodelling work undertaken by Meaghan's father, a small doll was found in one of the basement walls. Meaghan considered: 'About the little girl – could the doll have been hers?'

Researcher H. Michael Ball followed up the reports by questioning a present occupant of the house, who moved in in March 1997. 'He is very friendly and it was a pleasant conversation. He was surprised about the phenomena which occurred in the past . . . he stated that nothing out of the ordinary has happened – so far.'

Name: The River Ghost
Location: River Ise, Northamptonshire, central England
Date: Summer 1998
Source: K. P. Roscoe (witness) / authors' own files

Mr Roscoe owns and runs an electronics and surveillance company and, because of his interest in the paranormal, is now using his expertise in engineering and detection work for ghost research, in an attempt to capture evidence of phenomena. He related this story just a few weeks after the event.

'Around the beginning of July 1998, at three in the afternoon, I was at a remote spot on the River Ise, walking my well-trained collie dog, Pip. Pip had gone off down the river and around a bend; the water at that point was only a few inches deep. I was standing in total silence on a large patch of gravel that is very noisy to walk on, when I turned 180 degrees and had the fright of my life. A young girl of maybe 18 was standing not two yards away looking into the river as though she was ignoring me. She had a very cheeky smile on her face. I was amazed at how, in so quiet a place, she could have got so close without me hearing her on the gravel.

'As I was about to speak to her she walked into the river and picked up a stone. I said, "There are some nice stones here!" And she just smiled and walked to the other side some three yards away and stood by a tree.

'I, by this time, was wondering why Pip would not come when I called him. He was standing some hundred yards away watching the girl very closely, and would not move. I had only turned for a second and when I looked back she had gone. There is nowhere at that spot for anyone to hide. Then the penny dropped: "She must be a ghost." It bothered me for some days afterwards: who the hell was this girl? My daily visits to the river proved fruitless until about ten days later I was at the exact spot again, and not at that time thinking about any ghosts. But Pip was not at ease; so I carried on to what we call the beach, a shingle patch that is flatish, some hundred yards away. I was standing right in the middle of this shingle patch, looking at my mobile phone, when she was there again, just four yards away and looking at the river just as she had before.

'I chirped up: "Christ, girl, do you ever walk anywhere or do you just appear in front of people?" She turned to me and said, "I do that a lot." It was then I got around to thinking about how I was going to handle this. For one thing, she was wearing the most amazing clothing, just as before: a red velvet double-breasted jacket with brass buttons, a real flower in the lapel, and a very old-fashioned dress above her ankles. Her watch looked very old. To get a closer look I pretended that my watch was playing up and asked her what the time was. She said, "Ten minutes past the four-o-clock," a strange phrasing. Anyway, it was really ten minutes past three!

'I tried to engage her in conversation but she said: "The time is late, I must leave." I bid her good afternoon and went to walk up one of the four paths out of that area, but she went right into a patch of nettles up to her neck and almost as I was watching – from only five yards away – she disappeared into thin air. I ran around all over the place looking for her, but she was nowhere to be found. I left the area feeling pretty bothered by all this, but as soon as I got on the path again I looked across a field full of sheep and she was waving at me from at least a quarter of a mile away. She would have needed a Harrier jet to get where she was in the time allowed.

'No more happened for a week or more. On a Sunday I was filming with a S-VHS Panasonic, a semi-pro video camera, at a different spot on the river. I was making a nature film, with the audio switched off as the sound, music and narration would be dubbed on at sound studio, when she turned up again. I was alone, on my knees with my back to the path and in good sunlight. I could see for miles around and I had just "zoomed up" on a tree at the other side of the river when in one of my battery cases I saw a reflection of someone at my side. I jumped up and said: "You've done it again, you scared the life out of me." She just said: "What a beautiful day." I remembered the video camera was still on so I put it quickly under my arm and stood facing her, but she was very disturbed by the thing and asked: "What, pray, is that?" I told her what it was and, thinking that I had got plenty of her on the tape, I went to put it down on the grass. As I did so she was gone. I have not seen her since.'

Not seen her at the river, perhaps, but he has seen her on video; the film Mr Roscoe shot successfully captured the girl's image; rare footage indeed, if the girl is a ghost.

Name: Screamer
Location: Tipperary, Republic of Ireland
Date: 1992
Source: Patrick Flood (witness) / authors' own files

The most famous 'ghost' of Irish origin is probably the banshee; the invisible, terrifying, wailing, screaming spirit on the edge of folklore, held by some to be an omen. Patrick's report to us may not be a banshee, but it was in Ireland, it was a scream, and it was terrifying.

'In 1992, when I was 18, I was living on an estate at the edge of Tipperary. At the back of our house was the open countryside. On the night in question there were five of us sitting on a gate which leads to the fields from the estate. It was about 2am on a clear summer night and very quiet. All of a sudden we all heard screaming coming from the end of the field. We just looked at each other and the scream kept going. It was a woman's scream. Not a girl's; definitely a woman's. At first we thought it could be somebody camping. We went about halfway through the field towards the noise and it stopped. We could see no campfire anywhere, and we could by then hear no voices other than our own. I know we were about halfway down the field because there is an electric pole in the middle of the field.

'We stood around for about a minute, then one of my friends walked on a bit further down the field. He had gone a few steps when it started again. I can only describe it as though the owner of this scream was in great pain. We could see nothing anywhere, yet it came from only about 100 feet, maybe a bit more, in front of us. By now I was scared and decided it was time to go, as did my friends. I can tell you we ran like the wind back up that field. The screaming had stopped by the time we reached the gate. All of us had camped in this field many times before, and have done since, without hearing or seeing anything. And we never heard that screaming again. Now I don't know what it was, but I know that it scared me badly.

'The only thing I know about this area is that there was an Irish soldier shot in the War of Independence and there is a headstone in the ditch where he was shot. But I know that that voice, that scream, was a woman's and I will never forget it.'

Name: The Tudor Lady
Location: Pluckley, Kent, southern England
Date: The past 500 years? Or more?
Source: *Haunted Pluckley* by Dennis Chambers

Several media summaries and many ghost researchers have claimed the village of Pluckley in Kent to be the most haunted village in the county, or even in England. Such a claim would be difficult to prove in a country where stories of hauntings abound in every county, town and village. But the list of ghostly phenomena related to Pluckley certainly makes it worthy of an entry in a collection such as this.

Experienced local researcher Dennis Chambers has summarised the local accounts and believes that there are 12 ghosts that have been reported over time in the village. Many centre around the Dering family, who have left their mark on the area, and the story of the Tudor Lady is perhaps the most fascinating.

Rose Court, a large house standing on the road between Pluckley and Bethersden, is believed to date back over 350 years. Local rumour states that it was built for the mistress of one of the Dering family. It is this woman's ghost that is said to haunt the house and grounds. Her voice is said to be heard around four to five o'clock in the afternoon – the time that she died – calling for her two dogs as she did in life. It is said that she died of an overdose of poison, taking her own life, possibly as the result of a broken or thwarted love affair with a monk living in a neighbouring house. If she is Tudor, as is said, then she lived somewhere between 1485 and 1603. Rose Court may have been standing then, but not the nearby house, Greystones. Her lover could, of course, have occupied a former building on the site.

Chambers investigated the recent claims of hauntings at Rose Court and found that local residents were well aware of the ghost and stories surrounding her, but were not disturbed by her. At the time of his enquiries, the daughter of the present owner confirmed that there was a 'mysterious atmosphere' about the house and gardens, 'eerie but not frightening'. A previous resident had also reported poltergeist-like activity; the movements of objects, strange noises and so on.

Other ghosts of the village include the shade of a Colonel who hung himself in Park Wood (the wood itself has now been given over to agricultural use); a female ghost holding a red rose to her breast seen in the church of St Nicholas; and a sorrowful 'Red Lady' ghost thought to be a member of the Dering family, rumoured to be searching for the body of her baby buried in an unmarked grave.

Name: A Variety Of Hauntings
Location: Dover Castle, Dover, Kent, southern England
Date: At least 1979 onwards
Source: Authors' own files / researcher Robin Laurence and
    ASSAP

Known as the 'Key of England', Dover Castle is one of the most well-preserved fortresses in Britain and overlooks the ancient port. The site is thought to have the longest recorded history of any major fortress in England: it was the site of a Roman lighthouse, and an Anglo-Saxon fortified town. The present castle dates back to the 1180s and the reign of Henry II, though it has been remodelled by both Georgian and Victorian engineers.

There are many reports of hauntings at Dover Castle. A cavalier-like figure dressed in 17th-century costume has been seen on the ground floor of the Keep, resplendent in a black wide-brimmed hat with plume, knee-length boots and a purple cloak. We were told by a cleaner who had been working there that she just looked up from her work, saw the figure by the door, and then it disappeared.

A lady in a flowing red dress has been seen by staff at the West Staircase, also in the Keep. A figure dressed in blue has been seen, again by staff, walking in the Mural Gallery. One strange apparition, also reported by the staff, was of the lower half only of a man's body walking across the doorway of what is known as The King's Bedroom. The member of staff followed the figure into the room, but found no-one there and the room quite empty.

In 1979, in the excavated 'Underground Works', thought to date back to Roman times and believed to include a Roman prison, there was an apparition seen, described as a '17th-century pikeman'. A member of staff, locking up for the night, saw the figure – apparently self-illuminated – in the dark guard room, and watched as it walked through one wall of the room and out through another. Another figure in blue has also been seen in the passageways here.

In 1991 an American couple who had visited the underground works were so impressed by the special effects creating the sounds of screams and moans from another era that they took the trouble to compliment the staff. But there were no such reproductions or special effects anywhere near that area. The staff checked out the location in case anyone had been injured there; they found no-one present.

The authors, working with the Thanet Psychic and Paranormal Research Unit, and particularly local researcher Robin Laurence, have investigated Dover Castle over the past ten years. During one of these investigations, video evidence of something strange was recorded successfully; a doorway known for paranormal occurrences was monitored throughout the night by video and a range of detection equipment. Captured on the video was a protracted period of rhythmic vibration, strangely constant. The possibility of wind and vibration from the road was eliminated, and enquiries were made to the Geophysical Survey to ensure there had been no minor earthquakes at that time (of which there are a number in Britain on an almost imperceptible scale). No explanation could be found.

During other parts of the vigil, unaccountable sounds were heard by team members in pairs throughout the castle. Sudden temperature drops were also noticed, but strangely when areas felt 'teeth-chatteringly' cold this did not register on the thermometers.

On one occasion, our colleagues Philip and Chris Walton (Philip is the current chairman of ASSAP) were walking past the Keep at

2.30am when they were alarmed to hear the sound of a woman's scream coming from the roof. They both pointed their torches to where the sound seemed to be coming from, but there was nothing to be seen. A second and third scream then followed, the sounds apparently suggesting that someone had thrown themselves off the top of the Keep. Chris actually thought that he was underneath a falling body and dived to get out of the way; Philip couldn't move so fast, hampered as he was by a heavy rucksack. A few seconds later the screams were cut off but nothing hit the ground. They could find no explanation for the sounds but were adamant that they had heard a woman's voice screaming.

During a hot 6 May evening a few years later, while we were investigating, but also filming for television, at Dover Castle, a further strange event occurred. One small area of the grounds just outside the Keep became intensely cold and anyone standing in that area could hear whispering sounds as if from people quite close. To 'control' the test, several people were asked to stand in the area (just a few square feet) and not told what to expect. All reported – with surprise – exactly the same thing. While the sounds could have been some sort of strange echo from somewhere (though we could not locate a source), the feeling of temperature drop was stunning. We could see no reason for it, but after about half an hour whatever was happening stopped and the area reverted to being as warm as any other place.

Name: Victorian Lady
Location: Braintree, Essex, southern England
Date: 1995
Source: Rik and Lucy Wade (witnesses) / authors' own files

In the summer of 1995, 87-year-old Lucy Wade was taking photographs of her amaryllis plant. Partially-sighted and not particularly adept with complex machinery, she had asked her son Rik to load the film into the camera, which he did. In all respects she was alert, self-reliant and with good memory and clear thinking, all of which we confirmed when we met them both.

The film was taken to a local processing shop which developed it on the premises. When the film was developed, most of the photographs were normal. There were strange light effects on frames 7 and 8; 9, 10 and 11 were normal, as were those from 13 to the end of the roll, number 24. But frame 12 was anything but normal. The frame contains the very clear image of a woman's face staring straight into the camera.

The woman appears to be in Victorian costume, with a high collar and a bonnet tied with ribbon. As Rik commented: 'The face is benign and seems to be smiling. My mother states categorically that at no time has any person dressed in that type of costume, or any similar costume that could in any way be mistaken for it, visited her in her home.' He also pointed out: 'There are no pictures in the room that could be a source of reflection that may have caused this image.'

When we visited the location and spoke to Lucy and Rik, we confirmed these facts. We examined the full run of negatives, and the prints, and they bore out what Lucy and Rik told us. The only pictures in the room were of landscapes or of vases of flowers. We took 'control' pictures from the same spot, none of which produced any anomalous images or reflections. (Nor, sadly, did the Victorian lady choose to put in an appearance.)

It is possible that if the camera had been faulty, it could have double-exposed some frames. We confirmed with Kevin Langman, technical manager of Fujifilm, that a double-exposure could be the cause of this image. However, Rik pointed out to us when we spoke in 2000 that he had had the camera checked, and also that he had been using the camera since the 'ghost-photo' was taken and it had never malfunctioned even once since.

But however the image was produced, we are still left with the question: Who is the woman? It is a mystery to Rik, as it was to his mother, who has since died but who remained fascinated by her photo for her remaining years. She knew no-one who looked like the face in the film, and she was adamant she had not taken any photos she could not account for.

Name: Wailing Dogs
Location: Sutton House, Hackney, east London, England
Date: 20th century
Source: Various

Sutton House dates back to 1535 and is presently in the care of the National Trust. There are several accounts of ghosts and hauntings associated with the building. At night, those in the building have reported hearing wailing dogs when no such animals are there. They are believed to be dogs that once belonged to John Machell, a wealthy wool merchant who lived in the house from 1550 to 1558. Dogs are emblazoned on his family coat of arms, displayed in the Little Chamber in the house, showing that they must once have been important to him and his family. When visiting dogs have entered Sutton House, many have been known to stop at the foot of the painted staircase, transfixed and unwilling to go further.

Other ghosts have been reported. An official of a union based in Sutton House from 1939 to 1982 saw the gliding figure of a woman in white pass a doorway. The official stepped outside the door to ask if she could be of assistance and found no-one there. Local rumour has it that the White Lady is Francis Machell, John's wife, who died in 1574 in childbirth and is roaming the building looking for the children she never knew in life.

In the early 1990s an architect staying in Sutton House, sleeping in a bedroom that is now the Exhibition Room, woke to see the figure of a Blue Lady hovering above his bed. More recently the Blue Lady was seen by a house steward, who woke to find her violently shaking his bed.

Name: Yankee Jim
Location: The Whaley House, San Diego, California, USA
Date: 1953 onwards
Source: Various

The Whaley House in San Diego, California is now a historic site open to the public. It was built for Thomas and Anna Eloise Whaley, and completed in 1857. The property was built on the site of an execution. 'Yankee Jim' was hanged there but it is said that the gallows were not properly built and the man suffered an agonising death, kicking and struggling while he was strangled by the rope.

The Whaleys' children are said to have heard ghostly footsteps around the house. After the last of the Whaley children died in 1953, the house was renovated. It was soon after it was opened to the public that many people reported apparitions, ghostly noises and some poltergeist-type phenomena.

One visitor saw an apparition, though her companion could not see it. As she described it: 'I see a small figure of a woman who has a swarthy complexion. She is wearing a long full skirt, reaching to the floor . . . she has a kind of cap on her head, dark hair and eyes and she is wearing gold hoops in her pierced ears . . . I get the impression we are sort of invading her privacy.'

Many mediums have claimed that the house contains numerous ghosts; men, women, children and animals. But only two, it seems, have been identified: 'Yankee Jim', still angry at his treatment for a petty crime, and Anna Eloise, whose footsteps are heard as she walks around, still checking her home.

Ghosts Of The Famous

Is it the dead who refuse to 'die' or do the living have trouble letting them go? The evidence of ghosts suggests a little of both, and perhaps the ghosts of the famous hold some of the clues. Many famous people have been held to have 'returned' after their death, sometimes to locations they loved in life, sometimes to people dear to them, and sometimes to people who held them dear but who never actually met them in life. If Elvis Presley is really doing everything in death that is attributed to him, his work schedule now is more than anything Colonel Tom Parker ever worked out for him in life.

The emotional outpouring that accompanied the death of Diana, Princess of Wales, is evidence of the powerful emotions that people invest in the famous, meeting some need in their own lives. Within days of Diana's death, her apparitions were reported seen in pictures in her former London home. It is likely that often we seek to see these famous people because of that personal investment we have.

But at the same time we must ask ourselves what makes famous people famous. It is clear that there are special qualities in many of the famous that made them so; a special drive, a special depth of passion perhaps, emotional challenges in their personal history that formed powerful characters.

For the more materialistic, perhaps they have gained so much so quickly they find it especially difficult to let go of it in death. And perhaps their stronger, enhanced emotions make it all the more easy for them to return, or remain, after death.

How we perceive the famous as ghosts may also tell us something about 'how ghosts work'. Do the dead come back as ghosts or do the living 'generate' ghosts? Elvis has been reported in the white jumpsuits he wore in his last years, but was that how he saw himself or is that just how he is remembered by his fans? General Custer is seen with his long flowing hair, though he had had a crew-cut just before his death. Several ghosts have been seen in the same clothes they wear in portraits in the houses they are seen in. Are ghosts seen in their most popular image because they choose to be, or because they are a projection of the sighter?

Name: Fred Archer
Location: Hamilton Stud Lane, Newmarket, Suffolk, eastern England
Date: 1927
Source: Various

At the age of 29, in 1886, the famous jockey Fred Archer died. He was a leading jockey, the winner of over 2,000 races including five Derby wins, but became depressed and violent following the death of his wife. He himself died within two years; they are buried together.

In 1927, a local woman claimed that she had seen the ghost of Archer galloping on a grey horse from a copse on Hamilton Stud Lane towards her and her daughter, who also saw the apparition before it vanished. The woman had known Archer and was certain that it was his ghost she saw. Her report brought other people forward who said they had seen a ghostly horse and rider in the same place.

In addition to riding the local roads, Archer's ghost is said to haunt the racecourse itself and is credited with having caused several horses to shy or stumble during races. Certainly there have been many instances of horses acting strangely, slowing or stumbling for no apparent reason. For example, in 1950, the jockey Charlie Smirke claimed that his mount, Kermanshah, fell unexpectedly at precisely the same point where a horse the previous year had fallen. Apparently, at that point people have seen a white ghostly shape in the air at about the height of a horse's head. Whether Archer's ghost was to blame for this is unclear, but it is known that Archer was intolerant and unpleasant towards fellow jockeys.

Name: Blackbeard
Location: Okracoke Inlet, Pamlico Sound, North Carolina, USA
Date: 1718 onwards
Source: Various

Edward Teach (sometimes reported as Tache or Thatch) is known through history by his more famous nickname, Blackbeard. He was born in Bristol, England, and employed as a privateer against the Spanish during the War of Spanish Succession. He later turned to piracy, attacking Spanish and French ships in the West Indies from his warship, *Queen Ann's Revenge*. He achieved an alliance with the Governor of North Carolina and the State Collector of Taxes, giving them a percentage of his stolen loot in exchange for their protection. Blackbeard hid much of his money at Jake's Hole on the eastern shores of Maryland, sinking heavy treasure chests to the bottom of the cove, 15 fathoms down.

He was a distinctive character, tall and overbearing, most of his face concealed by a beard and with dark, sinister eyes. He fostered an air of evil by such tricks as tying small bones into his beard and golden trinkets into his hair, and wearing a cap adorned with burning cannon fuses. Another trick was to add amounts of gunpowder to his rum and then set it on fire and drink it, flaming. He was violent and malign, performing many unnecessarily cruel acts. Conversely, he was noted for a certain chivalry, not usual amongst pirates. In particular, he was courteous in his dealing with female captives at a time when other pirates were known to rape their victims.

On 22 November 1718 he was shot dead and decapitated by a Lieutenant Robert Maynard of the Royal Navy who had been hired by the Governor of Virginia to capture Blackbeard. Blackbeard's ghost has been seen at many of the locations he favoured in life, several times at Jake's Cove where 'spook-lights' are also attributed to his presence. He has also been seen at Okracoke Inlet where he died, and at Teaches Hole on Okracoke Island, which was his favourite look-out point. Local rumour is that Blackbeard is searching for his head and there are even reports of a deep, booming voice shouting, 'Where's my head?' (Though how he is capable of speech in that condition is unclear.) Fishermen regard seeing Blackbeard's headless corpse as a good omen and likely to result in a successful day's fishing.

Name: Emily Brontë
Location: Haworth, West Yorkshire, northern England
Date: Up to the 1960s
Source: Various

Emily Jane Brontë, who died at the age of 30 in 1848, is believed to be the spirit that has haunted the village of Haworth through the decades. Forever associated with her only novel, *Wuthering Heights*, written in the year before she died, her ghost has been seen walking the old packhorse route from Stanbury to the farm at Top Withens, which is said to have been the source of inspiration for the book. It is said that Emily, of all her sisters, was the most passionately attached to the moorlands around Haworth. Her ghost is said to haunt the paths around the Brontë waterfall. It is also said that her ghost appeared at Weaver's Restaurant, to the proprietor, climbing a staircase long since removed.

Name: Charles Cornwallis (First Marquess Cornwallis)
Location: The Spy House, Port Monmouth, New Jersey, USA
Date: 1800s to the present day
Source: Various

Charles Cornwallis (1738-1805) was the British General and statesman whose defeat at Yorktown, Virginia in 1781, after a decisive confrontation with George Washington's forces, virtually ended the American War of Independence.

After the war, Cornwallis returned to Great Britain, and later took up an appointment as Governor-General and Commander-in-Chief in India, later still becoming Viceroy of Ireland. He died on 5 October 1805, just after having been re-appointed Governor-General of India.

Cornwallis is said to be one of no less than 24 ghosts, many of them famous, seen at what is known as The Spy House in Port Monmouth, New Jersey. The Spy House, referred to by ghost hunter Arthur Myers as 'one of the most haunted places I have ever visited or heard about', has had a chequered history: as a colonial centre, a tavern, a bordello, a refuge and an inn. It is said that Cornwallis frequented the building when it was a tavern and that his ghost is still seen wandering the halls in a drunken manner and, according to W Haden Blackman in *The Field Guide to North American Hauntings*, it is said to be 'quite boorish when encountered'.

The Spy House is also alleged to contain the ghosts of native Americans; Thomas Whitlock, who developed the site in 1648; and a British spy and cut-throat known as Captain Morgan (not the more famous Captain Henry Morgan of the 1600s).

Name: Oliver Cromwell
Location: Various
Date: Since 1658
Source: Various

Given the impact made by Oliver Cromwell on the history of Britain, it is perhaps unsurprising that his ghost has been reported in several places. Cromwell, who lived between 1599 and 1658, was the leader of the Puritan revolution in England, having joined the Puritans to preserve Protestantism against what he saw as the tyranny of King Charles I's monarchy. He became Lord Protector of the Common-wealth of England, Scotland and Ireland in December 1653, holding that office until his death. Born in Huntingdon, Cambridgeshire, on 25 April 1599, the son of a wealthy farmer, he entered Cambridge University at the age of 17 but left early when he inherited his father's lands the following year. In 1620 he married Elizabeth Bourchier, the daughter of a London merchant. At the age of 29 he was elected to Parliament, but the following year the King dismissed Parliament and for 11 years ruled without the democratic chambers. In 1640 Charles was forced to call Parliament again, with Cromwell still one of its members.

A move to overthrow the King gradually grew and early in 1642, when civil war was apparent, Cromwell returned to his home to raise troops and equipment for the anti-monarchy cause. Cromwell invested in his troops his own passion for religion; each soldier carried a Bible as part of his equipment. Although Cromwell forbade Roman Catholics in his army, he accepted people from all the Protestant churches which, at that time, was considered a very tolerant position. His bravery and determination gained him the nickname 'Ironside', bestowed on him by Prince Rupert after Rupert's defeat at Marston Moor, near York, in July 1644.

Throughout the Civil War Cromwell became more and more prominent. In June 1645 Charles, defeated at the Battle of Naseby, fled to Scotland hoping that the Scots would support with him – he was a Scot by birth – but they turned him over to the English. England was now effectively ruled by an army under Cromwell and a small remnant of Parliament loyal to Puritan ideals, which became known as 'The Rump'. Both 'The Rump' and the army believed that Charles had to be eliminated and convinced Cromwell of this. In 1649 the King was tried and beheaded. The British Isles was declared a republic under Cromwell, now Commander-in-Chief of the army. Cromwell dismissed 'The Rump' in 1653, taking the title of Lord Protector. His rule was one of religious tolerance towards all

Protestants. He also allowed back into England Jews, who had been banned for over 300 years. He strengthened the Navy and the British Government gained great respect overseas.

In one sense, Cromwell's rule was in isolation; on his death, the title of Protector passed for only a few months to his son Richard before the monarchy was re-established. However, the development of more liberal views in both church and state, which have formed the basis of what many hold to be a tolerant society from then to the present day, are held by many to be the result of Cromwell's influence.

Cromwell's ghost has been said to haunt Ghost Hill in the flat fenlands near Murrow in Cambridgeshire, some miles to the north of his birthplace. He is also said to haunt the Old Hall at Long Marston in North Yorkshire, which was his headquarters during the Battle of Marston Moor. On the roads near this battle site in 1932, motorists were shocked to drive through the spectral echoes of what appeared to be stragglers from the defeated Royalist army; one of several examples of ghost armies from the Civil War.

In 1960 Cromwell's decapitated head was placed into the ante-chapel of Sidney Sussex College in Cambridge. In 1967, two undergraduates in Chapel Court saw the floating apparition of a yellow head .

Name: General Custer
Location: Battlefield Museum, Little Bighorn, Battlefield
   National Monument, Montana, USA
Date: Since 1876
Source: Various

General George Armstrong Custer (1839-1876) was born in Ohio, trained at Westpoint and served with distinction throughout the American Civil War. He became a Brigadier General at the age of 23. From 1866 he commanded the 7th Cavalry against the native American Indians of the Great Plains. In 1874 his expedition found gold in the Black Hills which were sacred to both the Cheyenne and Sioux and were protected by treaty. However, the Goldrush that followed massively escalated an existing conflict between native Americans and white settlers and prompted the United States government to be more aggressive in its resettlement policies. In 1876 Custer was ordered to lead the 7th Cavalry against an alliance of Cheyenne and Sioux organised by Sitting Bull and Crazy Horse. On

25 June Custer and 647 soldiers encountered thousands of Indian warriors in the valley of the Little Bighorn river, where Custer ordered an immediate attack without waiting for reinforcements. Custer and 264 United States soldiers were killed when the 7th Cavalry was massively overwhelmed. This event has come down through legend as 'Custer's Last Stand'. Historical analysis of the attack has varied between a belief that it was expedient in the face of necessity to the alternative belief that it was vainglorious, foolhardy and suicidal.

The battlefield is reportedly haunted by many of the dead soldiers, according to psychics and mediums who have visited it, and there are many reports of ghost-lights moving aimlessly around the site, particularly at night. Many have felt a sense of pain, sadness and despair at Last Stand Hill, the spot where Custer is said to have fallen, and at the Battlefield Cemetery, where many of the dead were buried. Near the Battlefield Cemetery is the Battlefield Museum where, over several years, many employees have reported apparitions near their beds in the apartments there. The apparition of Custer has been seen several times in the museum, apparently walking the hallways late at night.

Classification of Custer's ghost is unclear. He has all the elements of a recordings ghost, i.e. non-interactive and a figure apparently deep in thought, but on the other hand the building is a modern construct and was not there when Custer was alive. Some believe that Custer's ghost is a protective spirit, checking the building for intruders.

Another interesting aspect of the slaughter was that it appears to have been foretold by omen. In May 1876, a month before the Last Stand, Custer and the cavalry left Fort Abraham Lincoln, watched by many who cheered them on. (It was also from Fort Abraham Lincoln that they marched for their final confrontation.) Many of those present to cheer the troops on apparently saw half of the regiment lift up into the sky and disappear. The general feeling was that the phenomenon was an omen of death; one which came to pass on 25 June.

Name: Benjamin Disraeli
Location: Hughenden Manor, Buckinghamshire, southern
    England
Date: 1881 onwards
Source: Various

Benjamin Disraeli was a statesman and novelist who twice held the office of Prime Minister of Great Britain. Born a Jew in 1804, he converted to Christianity in 1817, which enabled his political career to develop. (Jews were excluded from Parliament prior to 1858.) Educated in Law, he gave up his studies to write and in 1837 first took his seat in Parliament. He was a dramatic, flamboyant man, dressing in the manner of a dandy and using dramatic speech and gestures. Indeed, his first speech in the House of Commons, traditionally one politely received, resulted in his being ridiculed, to which he replied, prophetically, 'I shall sit down now but the time is coming when you will hear me.'

Disraeli was, in effect, an instigator of British Imperialism. He purchased shares in the Suez Canal for Britain, thereby safeguarding England's trade routes to India, and he proclaimed Queen Victoria, Empress of India in 1876. In 1878, his ingenious strategies in the Congress of Berlin blocked Russia's progress in the Balkans and saved Turkey from Russian domination. For this Victoria rewarded him with the title of Earl of Beaconsfield and translated him to the House of Lords.

With the generous assistance of Lord George Bentinck and his brothers, who lent Disraeli two-thirds of the purchase price, he acquired the Hughenden Estate in 1847. He and his wife, Mary Anne, lived there until their deaths; hers in 1872 and his in 1881. The beautiful house, which was the centre of Disraeli's political and social life, is presently in the care of the National Trust and every room is still imprinted with some reminder of Disraeli and his friends. The staircase and hall display the Gallery of Friendship, the portraits of statesmen he held most dear. The library contains an autographed copy of Queen Victoria's only published work and, of course, copies of his own novels. In his study, the black-edged, notepaper that he always used after his wife's death can still be seen.

His own portrait is displayed on the staircase and it here where Disraeli's ghost, apparently clutching a sheaf of papers, has been seen. Visitors to the house have told staff of the unmistakable sighting of the charismatic figure. Certainly the house was central in his life; perhaps it is still so in death.

Name: Georgie Porgie
Location: The Cock and Bottle Pub, York, northern England
Date: 20th century
Source: Various

George Villiers, the second Duke of Buckingham, who died in 1687, achieved a certain kind of immortality by becoming the lead character of the children's nursery rhyme, Georgie Porgie. He suffered several disappointments in his life. In 1673 he met his downfall in Parliament, immortalised in the nursery rhyme: 'When the boys came out to play, Georgie Porgie ran away.' Another disappointment, perhaps, was his wish to be buried in York being ignored; he was buried in Westminster Abbey.

Perhaps that is why his ghost appears in York. Not surprising is his return to a pub, as in life he was known to lead a scandalous and wild lifestyle, which apparently his ghost continues to do. His shadowy figure has appeared near the fireplace in the bar, but disappears when approached. Upstairs he appeared to one former landlady while she was in the shower. She watched the apparition then walk up the stairs to the attic, but after her cries had brought her husband, the two of them searched the upper floors and could find no-one there. There are also reports that his 'presence' has stroked or fondled younger women in the pub.

Descriptions of his apparition are fairly consistent, and consistent with known likenesses of Buckingham; tall, long flowing hair and embroidered clothing, though such a description could fit a number of people from the same era.

Name: Matthew Hopkins, Witchfinder General
Location: Mistley, Essex, southern England
Date: 1991 to the present time
Source: *Ghosts Along the Border* by Wesley H. Downes

Matthew Hopkins, Witchfinder General, was in his day one of the most hated and feared people in Essex and Suffolk. His headquarters were in Manningtree and Mistley and it is here that he is thought to have returned as a ghost. Several fishermen at a lake in the grounds of Mistley Place have apparently seen the apparition of a man some 5 ft in height wearing old-fashioned clothes, a tall hat, and knee-high boots, fitting the description of Hopkins. This figure was reported more than ten times between 1991 and 1993, and in several cases by more than one person at a time.

One 22-year-old man, fishing at night with a companion, told how the figure manifested itself in the moonlight, ten feet away from them. To quote from Downes's report: 'The figure remained station-ary for about 30 seconds, then began to drift towards them; at this move the fisherman swung his fishing rod round and the end joint passed right through the figure, at which both of [the witnesses] turned and ran, only returning the next morning to retrieve their gear.'

Hopkins's ghost has also been reported in the Thorn Hotel at Mistley, and in two public houses in Manningtree where it is believed he interrogated victims during his witchhunts.

Name: Percy Lambert
Location: Brooklands racetrack, Weybridge, Surrey, southern England
Date: 1913 onwards
Source: Various

From 1907 to 1939 Brooklands racetrack was one of the most prominent in Britain. Perhaps its most famous driver was Sir Malcolm Campbell, holder of many world land speed records. Brooklands predated the famous Indianapolis track by one year and is regarded as the birthplace of motor racing on enclosed circuits. The racetrack is currently under preservation by the Brooklands Society, who care for the track and the surviving cars and aircraft housed there.

There have been reports of both apparitions and the sound of racing cars when the track was known to be empty; manifestations of the track's glorious days of over half a century ago. Specifically, the apparition of a man wearing old-fashioned racing goggles and helmet has been seen. Many believe that the apparition is of Percy (Pearley) Lambert, who was one of Brooklands's prominent early racing drivers. Witnesses to the apparition have included mechanics and workers occupying the track and buildings, in particular the building known as 'The Vatican' in which Lambert's car was once garaged. Other reports have come from general visitors and racing enthusiasts.

Lambert died from a fractured skull in 1913 on the track during a record-breaking attempt when a tyre burst at the end of the 'railway straight', resulting in him and the car being hurtled across the track. The crash was shortly before his planned wedding. Many ghost researchers lean towards the view that some restless spirits are so because they have been cut off in their prime, or have left unfinished business behind at death; perhaps this is so in this case.

If the apparition is not Lambert then the other candidate is Vincent Herman, who was the first driver to die at Brooklands in its opening year in 1907.

Robert Titherley, the Brooklands Society director, told us another story, of an apparition of a driver who had died crashing over the banking. This bloodstained, ghostly figure terrified a young boy in his garden, causing him to run into the house calling for his parents. This house is built on the exact spot where the driver died.

Name: Emperor Nero
Location: Santa Maria Del Popolo, Rome, Italy
Date: AD 68
Source: Various

It is said that Emperor Nero, remembered for his decadence and excesses, for his huge mansion in Rome and his persecution of Christians, committed suicide in AD 68 where the church of Santa Maria Del Popolo now stands. After his death, his bones were buried under a walnut tree on the site and thereafter his evil ghost – and indeed an entourage of evil spirits – haunted the area, tormenting the citizens nearby.

In 1099 the people requested the help of Pope Paschal II, who instigated three days of prayer and fasting, resulting in his receiving a vision of the Virgin Mary and an instruction that the walnut tree was to be cut down and the bones disinterred. The Virgin then indicated that the bones should be burned and the ashes thrown into the River Tiber. These instructions were followed and Nero's ghost was put to rest.

Name: Pausanias
Location: The Temple of Athena, Greece
Date: Fifth Century BC
Source: Various

Pausanias was a Spartan general who had a leading role in the war between the Greeks and the Persians and defeated the Persians in the naval battle of Plataea in 479 BC. He went on to capture Byzantium but, according to the historian Thucydides, became so arrogant that he was asked to return home to explain himself. So angry was Pausanias at the demand that he approached the Persian King Zerzex with an offer to betray Greece. After proof of this treachery came to light, Pausanias fled to the Temple of Athena and hid in a small building next door, where his pursuers walled him in. He starved to death there.

According to the chronicles, his ghost haunted the temple and made such frightening noises that the priestess called for a magician and finally the ghost was forced to 'go away'. The account may sound like the stuff of legend, and perhaps it is in part, but it is worth remembering that paranormal sounds and exorcism are as much a feature of modern-day accounts.

Name: The President
Location: Helsinki, Finland
Date: April 1957
Source: *Modern Mysteries of the World* **by Janet and Colin Bord**

On 19 April 1957 two women, Mrs E. Sinisalo and her aunt, Maja, were walking towards the elevator in an apartment building when they saw Finnish President Dr Juho Kusti Paasikivi standing by the elevator door. The President had died four months earlier. Mrs Sinisalo opened the door and the President ushered them in first, saying, 'After you, ladies, please!' They all went in and travelled up to the fourth floor, the door opened and the President began to leave. As he did so, he said to the two women, 'Ladies, you must certainly be wondering why I am here when I should be in the grave. But it is really so!' The door closed and the lift carried the women higher, but they could look down and see him through the glass door as they ascended. They noticed that never did the President operate the lift; they had opened the doors and selected the floors. Mrs Sinisalo commented: 'He looked a little younger and thinner than when I had last seen him. But he still spoke in the big, almost raucous voice for which he was famous.'

Strangely, the fact that they were in the lift with a man they knew to be dead did not occur to them at the time, almost as if the experience had left them in a slightly entranced state. Mrs Sinisalo said: 'I did not quite realise that he was a dead man until he announced it himself . . . but I still think it is curious that neither Aunt Maja nor I remembered when we were in the elevator with him that we knew Paasikivi was dead.'

And what of Paasikivi? He apparently knew he 'should be in the grave' and seems to have been almost as astonished as the women were to find he was not. But why did he appear? For all his astonishment, the deceased President imparted nothing of significance to the women.

Name: Superman

Location: California, USA
Date: 1950s onwards
Source: Various

There have been many claims of a curse for principal actors involved in recreating the adventures of America's foremost comic-book hero, Superman. The actor Christopher Reeve, who played the lead in four major blockbuster movies, was disabled during a riding accident, and his co-star Margot Kidder, who acted the part of his 'love interest' Lois Lane, suffered a highly publicised breakdown.

But before Christopher Reeve, George Reeves was the television incarnation of Superman in 104 episodes over six years in the 1950s. His death remains a mystery. The coroner believed the evidence indicated suicide; many of Reeves's friends believe he was murdered. A Los Angeles detective claimed: 'Frankly, the evidence seemed to support that Reeves was murdered.' He was found with a bullet having shattered his skull, fired upwards; the bullet was located in the ceiling. No suicide note was found. Those who believe he was murdered hold that it was revenge for an affair he had been having with a Hollywood executive's wife. His will left his entire estate to her. But others say Reeves was despondent at the cancellation of *The Adventures of Superman* and was virtually penniless.

Mrs Bessolo, Reeves's mother, certainly was not penniless and she was so sure that her son was murdered that she hired Hollywood barrister Jerry Giesler to discover his murderer. The investigation discovered that two bullets had been fired from the gun. As Giesler asked: 'Since when do suicides get a chance to shoot twice?' Giesler also discovered that Reeves had almost been killed three times prior to his eventual death, in three different road incidents which some believe were murder attempts.

'He took his Superman role seriously,' said a fellow actor. 'He really worked hard at being Superman.' This is perhaps reflected in his memorial. Reeves was buried in the Pasadena Mausoleum in California, with the inscription 'My Beloved Son SUPERMAN, George Bessolo Reeves: January 6, 1914 – June 16, 1959.'

But that, apparently, was not the end of 'Superman', nor perhaps of his love for the role. The house he lived and died in has had several residents since; one couple heard a noise in the bedroom and, when they entered, apparently saw an apparition of Reeves dressed in his 'Man of Steel' costume. As they watched, the apparition disappeared in front of them.

Name: Alfred Lord Tennyson
Location: Farringford Hall and Tennyson Down, near Freshwater, Isle of Wight, UK
Date: 1893 onwards
Source: *Ghost Encounters* by Cassandra Eason

In youth Tennyson received considerable criticism for his poetry, but the publication of *In Memoriam* in 1850 sealed his reputation as one of the greatest poets of all time. His most famous works include *Morte D'Arthur* and *The Charge of the Light Brigade*. He succeeded Wordsworth as Poet Laureate, which brought prosperity and the ability to buy Farringford Hall, which he used for prominent entertaining. He is known to have loved the Hall (later a hotel), and the Downs nearby.

He would walk the Downs overlooking the sea wearing his dark top coat and wide-brimmed black hat, sometimes wearing a black cloak. In particular, Tennyson would stop on the wooden bridge crossing the path from Farringford to the Downs in the early evening and recite poetry to local people. If he felt ill at ease at Farringford or wanted to avoid unwelcome guests, he would often slip out to walk over the Downs.

After his death in 1892 he was deeply mourned in the locality. When a figure thought to be impersonating Tennyson was seen walking over his favourite paths and the bridge, a local posse set out to apprehend the impostor, presumably with a view to impressing on him a greater respect for Tennyson's memory. In January 1893 the figure was seen striding across the Downs and one of the watchers attempted to seize him. The figure, however, walked straight through his potential assailants towards Farringford Hall, where the apparition disappeared into thin air. Since that time Tennyson's ghost has been seen many times on the Downs, on the bridge and on the walks around the Hall. The site now sports a granite monument to Tennyson.

Name: Lucy Walter
Location: Roch Castle, Dyfed, Wales
Date: 20th century
Source: Various

To anyone other than a historian the name Lucy Walter, or even the other name by which she was known, Lucy Barlow, is probably relatively unfamiliar. Nonetheless, in her brief life of 28 years, she played a key role in British history. She was born at Roch Castle in

1630. At the age of just 14 she met the future King Charles II in the Channel Islands where he had fled from England during the Civil War. At the age of 19 she bore him a son, James Scott, later to become the Duke of Monmouth. Although he was illegitimate, Charles II acknowledged him as his son, particularly as he had no legitimate offspring. English Protestant leaders tried to force Charles to name Monmouth as his successor but Charles instead named his brother James, a Roman Catholic, and he banished Monmouth from England. On the death of Charles in 1685, Monmouth returned to England to attempt to claim the crown for his own. The subsequent rebellion was known as the Duking Days and its destruction resulted in the trials known as the Bloody Assizes. Monmouth was executed at the Tower of London.

It is Lucy's ghostly form that is alleged to be the lady in a white dress running noisily through her birthplace at Roch Castle. She is said to move through locked doors and the sound of her running footsteps is held to have disturbed the sleep of many guests at the castle. Her apparition has allegedly been seen by Viscount St Davids and many other people present at the castle, including staff and visitors.

Name: H.G. Wells
Location: Spade House, Sandgate, Kent, southern England
Date: Present
Source: *Haunted Shepway* by Paul Harris

H.G. Wells had Spade House built on the coast at Sandgate, in Kent, in 1899-1900. He wrote many of his most famous works there, including *Kipps*, *The War in the Air* and *The History of Mr Polly*; plaques at the house commemorate his presence there. Since his time there the property has been developed; it has been a restaurant and a residential nursing home.

Night staff of the nursing home have reported odd occurrences. One said, 'We all smell strong pipe tobacco along the corridors between rooms three and five.' Another commented, 'I've also noticed [the same thing] between rooms 18 and 20.' Staff have tried to investigate and found no-one smoking a pipe, and there is a warm feeling that it might be the presence of Wells, who was known to have smoked a pipe when he lived there.

An apparition seen in the building by a member of staff is a lady in Victorian-style dress walking up the stairs and along the landing, which is speculated to have been his wife or a close friend of Wells. Certainly the dress is from the right period.

Paul Harris's analysis does point out that since the place is a nursing home and does have many elderly and infirm people, some of whom have died there, any ghosts, if ghosts are connected with the dead, could relate to any number of people.

Name: Gilbert F. White
Location: The Wakes, Selborne, Hampshire, southern England
Date: 1793 onwards
Source: Various

> Now climb the steep, drop now your eye belong
> Where round the blooming village orchards grow;
> There, like a picture, lies my lowly seat,
> A rural, shelter'd, unobserved retreat.

Lines from *Invitation to Selborne* by the 18th-century naturalist and poet Gilbert F. White (1720-93). Probably his most famous work was *The Natural History of Selborne* published in 1789, which recorded in fine detail his observations of the flora and fauna of that part of Hampshire and showed his love both of Selborne and of the environment generally. He is regarded by many as the first true English ecologist.

What is believed to be his ghost has been seen in the gardens of the house he loved dearly.

White lived at The Wakes most of his life. The house is now open to the public and is beautifully maintained in 18th-century style with many of his furnishings, embroidered bed hangings and portraits of his family. The garden of The Wakes is being restored according to his writings; already in place are his 'Quincunx', a wooden ha-ha (sunken fence) and some of the flower beds to display the plants he knew and wrote about. Perhaps Gilbert White is still enjoying the tranquil beauty of the house and grounds that he loved in life.

Name: William Wordsworth
Location: Rydal Mount, Lake District, north-west England
Date: 1909
Source: Various

There are many reports of relatives and friends appearing in chairs they loved while alive; some ghosts even 'move house' with a fondly loved chair. So it is, apparently, for one of England's most famous poets.

Rydal Mount in the Lake District was William Wordsworth's home from 1813 until his death in 1850 at the age of 80. In 1909 a Miss Ward was staying there, sleeping in what she later discovered was the room of William's wife, Dorothy. She woke up during the night and 'saw perfectly clearly the figure of an old man sitting in the armchair beside the window'. He was sitting with both hands on the chair arms, leaning back and looking downwards, the moonlight coming through the window lighting up the top of his head. She recognised him immediately as Wordsworth, found the sighting 'solemn and beautiful' and not at all frightening, and watched until the figure gradually faded away.

Haunted Objects

While there seem to be no limits to what objects can be haunted, from a specially loved watch or ornament to an ordinary everyday item around the house such as a radio, there seem to be two front-runners: armchairs and mirrors. Armchairs are for some a sanctum sanctorum, a place to end the day in peace and tranquillity and think through the emotions, good and bad. Perhaps that is why so many seem to be the favoured haunts of their former occupants. Most of the ghosts so reported seem content. Mirrors on the other hand seem to be haunted with a less content form of spirit; many haunted mirrors leave their owners ill at ease, sensing a malign presence, and so on. Perhaps what is seen in a mirror is akin to the technique of 'mirror or crystal scrying' − using the reflective surface as a form of mediumistic channel. And perhaps in so doing, people tune in to their fears and doubts as much as to their hopes and dreams.

Name: Huaska
Location: New York, USA
Date: 20th century
Source: Various

The American researcher of the paranormal Hans Holzer recorded an extraordinary story of a chair that came into the ownership of Bernard and John Simon of New York. When they bought it they were told that it was of Mexican Indian origin; and apparently so it turned out to be.

After just a few days in their home, Bernard woke up in the middle of the night, found himself drawn to the chair and saw an exceptionally tall man sitting there. He began to call out to the apparition but the figure disappeared. Holzer arranged a seance and contacted an entity calling himself Huaska who claimed that Bernard

Simon was his reincarnated son. The chair had apparently once belonged to Huaska and he had influenced John and Bernard to buy the chair as a way of making himself known to them. Having done this, Huaska indicated that he would not be troubling the brothers again. The figure was not seen again.

Commenting on the case, Peter Underwood makes the point that while Huaska's spirit may be at peace with the chair now residing with his reincarnated son, what would happen if the chair moved on into other hands?

Name: John Naden, 'In Stile'
Location: Bosley, Macclesfield, Cheshire, north-west England
Date: 1880s
Source: Various

In the 1880s John Naden murdered his employer Robert Brough while in cahoots with Brough's wife. Murder did not apparently come easily as he needed 'Dutch courage' from a bottle before committing the crime. Naden left his knife at the scene of the crime, which formed the basis of a prosecution and conviction that led to his being executed by hanging on the gibbet that stood on Gun Hill, near Bosley. His body was then left hanging in chains on the gibbet as a warning to others.

The gibbet was eventually demolished and the wood used to build the stiles on the field borders. It is believed locally that the stiles are haunted by Naden's ghost, a vicious and menacing figure that approaches people out of the darkness, reeling and gesturing as if still drunk, as he was during the crime that he died for.

Name: Radio Ham
Location: South London, England
Date: 1990s
Source: Colin Croft (witness) / authors' own files

Colin wrote to us having read our book The Poltergeist Phenomenon: 'It reminded me of one or two experiences which I had some years ago, although these must be classed as very "low-level" happenings, perhaps they should be called "unconscious psycho-kinesis".

'Several years ago I shared a ground-floor flat in South London with two male friends. During the three years we shared together, there were three occurrences: money was removed overnight from where it had been left; chess pieces, left in position overnight for the continuation of the game, were subsequently found to have swapped around; and a paperback copy of *The Lord of the Rings* disappeared without trace. All three of us made light of these occurrences, which could, of course, have been put down to human forgetfulness or simple malobservation.

'Some years later, however, I had two experiences which I find difficult to explain. At that time I was sharing with a friend from work, and I had the back room. One day, I returned home from work feeling unwell. I made up a bed in the central living room, which had a solid fuel boiler. I had slept for three hours or so and decided to get up. I took the bedding into the back room to put it away. I was surprised to hear the sound of a radio, which I thought was coming from the room above mine. This room was occupied by a normally quiet person. In any case, it was odd that he was at home in the early afternoon. The sound got louder, and I was on the point of going upstairs to remonstrate when I realised that it was my radio that was on. This was an old valve radio, with bakelite knobs. It was on a short flex and was on the floor, on top of a wool carpet. I had to turn it some way to switch it off. I tried to work out how it had come on. I wondered if I had switched it on with my foot, but it was impossible to get my toe under the on-switch.

'I wondered if the radio had in fact been on all the time and that a loose connection was responsible. I switched it back on and to the lowest possible volume, but soon realised that, in the dead of night, even that low volume would have been audible. Also, it had been at least three weeks since I had used the radio. I had it examined by an electrician for possible faults, but none were found. I came to the tentative but unsatisfactory conclusion that the radio had been switched on, but that a loose connection had prevented any sound coming through until it had been reactivated by pressure from my footsteps as I walked past it carrying my bedding.

'However, about eight months later I had to abandon this theory. I came home from work with a severe, oppressive headache and decided to go into my room to lie down for a while. I had hardly been in the room a few moments when I hard a grating noise and the radio was on once again. To this day, I can offer no explanation to account for this. One factor common to both experiences was my poor state of health. All that can be said is that the radio was definitely on, and it had not been switched on by me.'

Name: Reflections
Location: Orpington, Kent, southern England
Date: 1982
Source: Mr D. Park of Orpington (witness) / authors' own files

Mr Park described to us in *Ghosts At The Time Of Death* the possible haunting of his grandmother's house after the death of his grandfather. But the house, which his grandmother told him was possibly built on the site of an old monastery, was also the subject of a quite different type of haunting. The following two reports from Mr Park may be unrelated, except for the fact that both involved mirrors – a not uncommon claim in ghost reports.

'The event, which stills chills me, comes from the summer of about 1982, I think. I was standing in my gran's bedroom looking out of the window, in broad daylight. I turned and out of the corner of my eye noticed what looked like a black figure, a bit like a monk, standing in the shadows. My gran had an old dressing table with twin folding mirrors which faced the window, and this was what I saw in them. My brother, to my surprise, also saw the same thing at another time. This was why, when he got older, he didn't come over to the house so often.'

Mr Park's second account also relates to a mirror. 'My mother told me that when she got married she was given an antique mirror as a gift; 3ft high, 1½ft wide, with a large frame. She put the mirror in the bedroom. One day, when she was moving it to another room, she saw what seemed to be a second, distant reflection of a figure in the mirror. There was nobody else in the room that could account for this. This shook her up a lot and she put the mirror in the spare room, out of the way, so that she could forget about it. She regarded the mirror as evil, and bad luck seemed to follow her after she had seen this figure. It so worried her that she broke the mirror and put it in the shed, where it stayed for some years until finally being disposed of. I can only say that I remember when I saw the mirror in the shed it gave me an odd feeling of dread. Once it was gone, she told me, things improved a great deal.'

Name: The Stones In The Fireplace
Location: Airdrie, Lanarkshire, Scotland
Date: 1990s
Source: *Haunted Scotland* by Norman Adams

A couple occupying a new council house in Airdrie saw, one night, the apparition of an elderly lady standing beside an ornamental stone fireplace in their home. Considerably frightened, they contacted the Scottish Society for Psychical Research, who investigated the case. The investigation at first uncovered no obvious associations for the building nor the land it stood on. However, it was then discovered that the couple had built the fireplace themselves with stones they had recovered from a derelict house. According to a medium, Albert Best, in transferring the stones to their home they had also transferred the earthbound spirit of a lady who had owned and lived in the former house.

Name: TV Appearance
Location: Hunslet, Leeds, West Yorkshire, northern England
Date: Christmas 1997
Source: *Daily Mail*, 14 February 1998

At five o'clock in the morning on Christmas Day 1997, five-year-old Liam Plummer was photographed opening his presents by his grandparents at the traditional Christmas family gathering. In the room at the time, apart from Liam, were both grandparents, their daughter Jane (Liam's mother) and Liam's brother, Christopher. The room had a television in it, but it was not switched on at the time. They had an enjoyable Christmas and noticed nothing untoward.

Some weeks later, they took the photographs to be developed and when they received them back discovered that behind Liam, clearly visible on the family's television screen, was the face of a woman, laying down with eyes closed, looking either asleep or dead. None of the family recognised the woman nor could they account for the image on the TV screen from their own actions in the room. As Liam's grandfather said, 'We were all facing the TV but we saw nothing at the time.' Analysis of the pictures indicated it was not a double exposure. A medium, Tress Connor, commented in the newspaper, 'There is such a thing as a spirit photograph, and they are very precious things.'

Recordings And Replays

The most commonly known form of ghost is the apparition, the favourite of Hollywood films for decades. Many are reported walking through, say, walls where doors used to be. The Roman legion walking through the Treasurer's House appears to have been walking where the road used to be. As such they seem to be a 'video' laid down in former years, triggered occasionally and viewed by lucky – some would say unlucky – witnesses. However harmless such a 'video' would presumably be, there can be no doubt of the effect such sightings have on some of the witnesses.

Name: The Bearded Sailor
Location: Sandwood Bay, nr Cape Wrath, Highland Scotland
Date: Several reports to the present
Source: Various

A bearded figure in brass-buttoned reefer jacket, sea-boots and a sailor's cap has been seen many times here. Witnesses have included visitors walking the faintly pink sands of the Bay, fishermen familiar with the location, and crofters of the area. Some reports have included the same figure being seen in an uninhabited and partly ruined cottage nearby. One Edinburgh woman who had a piece of wood from the staircase of that cottage suffered haunting phenomena in her home including the sounds of footfalls, the smells of alcohol, and rattling of crockery, and also saw the apparition of the bearded figure.

One witness was climber Ian Strachan, who was alone at the location in the 1980s, the rest of his party having set off to walk to Kinlochbervie. He suddenly saw the figure of a man 'in a black or navy hip-length jacket . . . it was almost as if he had appeared from nowhere'. For several minutes Strachan saw him walk on the beach and then disappear. Never did the figure seem to see or respond to him. Strachan commented: 'I felt as if rooted to the spot, not in the least nervous, but there was a strong feeling of unreality, not fear, in the scene.'

Name: Clanking Knight In Armour
Location: Bamburgh Castle, Northumberland, north-east England
Date: Early 20th century
Source: Various

The Anglo-Saxon Chronicle states that Ida, the first king of Northumbria, built a fortress in Bamburgh in 547. It was the seat of power from which northern England and Scotland were ruled. It features a stone keep built during the Norman period. The castle was surrendered to William Rufus in 1095 by Robert Mowbray, Earl of Northumberland, after a siege, and was the scene of many Border battles in the 14th century and a stronghold during the Wars of the Roses. King Henry VI ruled from Bamburgh for a time. It was the first English castle to suffer battery from artillery. Over time it deteriorated badly until, in 1894, the first Lord Armstrong of Cragside bought the castle and rebuilt it for private use, during which time there were apartments there. He demolished much of the former structure and replaced it with a castle-cum-mansion. It is from this time that the ghost report comes.

One apartment was occupied by Sylvia Calmedy-Hamlyn. She awoke in the night and saw the spectre of a knight in armour walking across her bedroom. She could also hear the clatter of chains, in almost too-good-to-be-true Hollywood style. She watched as he crossed the room and walked into the corridor outside, then descended a flight of steps. The identity of the knight is not known, though knights in armour would have been commonly seen in Bamburgh Castle during periods of its history. Indeed, there are suits of armour on display in the basement of the keep

Name: The Elderly Lady
Location: Nivingston Country Hotel and Restaurant, Scotland
Date: At least 1980s to the present
Source: Allan Deeson (proprietor) / authors' own files

The building dates back to 1725, picturesquely placed at the foot of the Cleish Hills near Kinross. Allan Deeson came to the hotel in

1980, by which time reports of an elderly lady were already locally famous. In Allan's own words: '. . . we have received many reports from guests about "strange" noises and sightings. The comments always come from guests in the same part of the hotel. The noises relate to footsteps and doors closing, when nobody is present, and there have been three "sightings" of an old lady dressed in night-clothes exiting one bedroom, and entering another bedroom which was formerly a bathroom. The room from which she exits was one in which a former owner shot himself in the 1900s.'

Is the lady related to the former owner? Are guests seeing a recording of when she used to go nightly from her bedroom to her bathroom to get herself ready for bed?

One story of the haunting is that the tales of the ghost – though not, we understand, the elderly lady herself – somewhat disturbed the players of Raith Rovers Football Club in 1994 just before an important match. No harm was done though; they won.

Name: Ghostly Fires
Location: 'Tanrahan's Town', St John's, Newfoundland, Canada
Date: Mid to late 20th century
Source: Dale Gilbert Jarvis, researcher and folklorist

Downtown St John's occupies an area that was once known as Tanrahan's Town, all of which burned to the ground in the fire of 1855. The neighbourhood was rebuilt from the ashes only to be destroyed completely 37 years later in the Great Fire of 1892.

With its history of destructive fires, it is fitting that one of the more unique hauntings in Newfoundland occurs in a house within the limits of what was once Tanrahan's Town. The building was constructed shortly after the Great Fire of 1892. For most of the middle part of the 20th century the house was occupied by an old woman who lived alone. She eventually died there and the house stood empty for a while before it passed on to new owners, who began to notice a very strange phenomenon.

An upstairs room at the back of the house contains not the ghost of a person or animal but rather of a ghostly fire. Different people have reported seeing a fire burning in the fireplace, but upon closer examination the fire has disappeared and there was no noticeable heat, the stones there being cold to the touch.

In the 1980s, as a tenant lay in his bed in a different room on the same floor, his door swung open. Looking from his bed out into the hall, the man saw the flickering of firelight reflected on the walls. Knowing himself to be alone in the house, he left his bed to investigate and found nothing. He closed the door and returned to bed. The door swung open again, revealing the same strange light. He got up to check and again found nothing, the light disappearing as he left his room. He returned to bed and again, just as he was drifting off to sleep, the door swung wide, the firelight flickering on the opposite wall.

While this type of haunting is rare, it is not unique. A similar spirit fire was reported in a small seaside community on the south coast of Ireland by John D. Seymour in 1911. According to reports, a large family house in the community was known to be haunted by a variety of spirits. Two sisters occupied one of the upstairs rooms, where they shared a bed. The two girls on numerous occasions awoke to find the floorboards of the room engulfed in flames, flames which produced neither smell nor heat. The first time this happened, the girls ran from the room, convinced that the room underneath was ablaze. This fire would be witnessed two or three nights in a row and then would disappear for some time before suddenly blazing forth once more. While it was witnessed on occasion in other parts of the house, it occurred chiefly in the room where the two girls slept.

Name: A Headless Figure?
Location: Oakhill Park, Barnet, north London, England
Date: 1950s to the present time
Source: *Barnet Press*

Oakhill Park in Barnet has a reputation for several hauntings. In 1985 Jill and Malcolm were walking in the park after midnight when they saw a black form floating around a foot above the ground. Their impression was of a hovering headless figure with slow-moving legs, though they could well have been seeing one of the more amorphous lights associated with marshlands and open spaces and attributing some element of shape to it. The couple were alarmed, particularly when it seemed to turn towards them and look at them. They left in haste. Jill said, 'I know it sounds really strange and I'm sure a lot of people don't believe it's possible, but we've never forgotten it. We crouched down low and tried to get a good view of the ghost but when it turned and confronted us about 50 metres away, it was really frightening and we . . . ran for our lives.'

Another witness, Valerie, had a different experience in the same park in the 1950s. She was there with a friend in the early evening, after dark. They were meeting other friends on the first bridge and had come down East Walk and through the gates in Parkside Gardens. On the other side of the path they saw a man sitting on a bench. He was wearing Victorian- or Edwardian-type clothes and what was described as an 'Oscar Wilde-type' hat. They could see him clearly, as he was illuminated by a street lamp nearby. As they approached him and they were just some ten feet away, he suddenly vanished. 'He just disappeared,' Valerie said. 'It was like a light being switched off. My friend screamed and screamed and then collapsed onto the floor.'

Valerie remembered the incident some 20 years later when she heard from another couple who had been taking photographs in the same spot in the park. When the photographs were processed there was a figure on them, someone who had not been there when the photographs had been taken. The figure matched the description of Valerie's sighting years before.

Name: In Its Former Glory
Location: Hastings Castle, East Sussex, southern England
Date: 12th century onwards
Source: Various

Hastings Castle, on the East Sussex coast, may have been built on the site of a very ancient church. Certainly in the 12th century it was used as a monastery, which is believed to account for the ghostly sounds of organ music heard there occasionally. There are church ruins in the grounds and it is thought that the church held an important position; Archbishop Anselm is thought to have preached to King Stephen there; Thomas á Becket probably preached there also. Becket's ghost is reputed to haunt the ruins, walking the grounds on autumn evenings.

The castle also has an anonymous ghost, thought to walk the cliff edge. The Curtain Wall of the castle ends where the cliff has eroded and clairvoyants have reported to the custodians that they have felt a 'presence' there. Most famously, local fishermen say that they have sometimes seen the castle, on sunny, misty mornings, in full glory, with pennants flying from the turrets.

Name: The Last Ride Of Lieutenant B.
Location: Murree, Punjab, India
Date: Summer 1854
Source: Various

In 1854 a young officer, R. Barter, and his wife were posted to a hill
station at Murree in the Punjab and stayed in a house known as
Uncle Tom's Cabin. The house had been built a few years earlier by
Lieutenant B., who had since recently died in Peshawar. Barter had
known Lieutenant B. but had not been in touch with him for some
years prior to his death.

One night Barter was alone with his dogs on the road just outside
Uncle Tom's Cabin when, 'I heard the ring of a horse's hoof as the
shoe struck to stones.' Barter watched as a rider approached, a man
mounted on a pony, in full evening dress, white waistcoat and tall
'chimney pot' hat, and accompanied by two servants. The two dogs
with Barter crouched by his side, whimpering. Barter called out to
the figure, asking who it was and then recognised the rider as
Lieutenant B. He was, however, changed from when Barter had
known him years ago. He was now fatter and had a beard. Barter
approached him but tumbled while climbing the bank to the road.
'Recovering myself instantly, I gained the road . . . there wasn't a
trace of anything; it was impossible for them to go on, the road
stopped at a precipice about 20 yards beyond . . .' He could see
nothing on the road and could hear nothing. When he got home he
found his dogs had fled there.

Barter later discussed Lieutenant B. with someone who had known
him at the end of his life, a Lieutenant Deane. Deane commented, 'He
became very bloated before his death; you know, he led a very fast
life, and while on the sick list he allowed a fringe [beard] to grow, in
spite of all we could say to him, and I believe he was buried with it.'
Deane was also surprised that Barter knew about the pony that he
described. 'How do you know anything about all this? You hadn't
seen B. for two or three years, and the pony you never saw. He
bought him at Peshawar and killed him one day riding him in his
reckless fashion down the hill to Trete.'

In the six weeks that Barter and his wife stayed at the cabin they
several times heard the sound of a 'a reckless rider', though they never
saw anything again.

Name: The Leather Shoe
Location: Thorington Hall, Stoke-by-Nayland, Suffolk, eastern
  England
Date: To the present day
Source: *Stories of Ghosts and Hauntings Along the Essex and Suffolk Border*
  by Wesley H. Downes

There are two ghosts reported from Thorington Hall, which is now
in the care of the National Trust. One ghost is a little girl, in a plain
brown dress tied around the waist with a cord, seen and heard on
the landing at the top of the stairs by several witnesses. She is locally
thought to be a child from the Umfreville family who once lived
there, though there are no records of a child dying.

The second ghost is that of a heavily built man whose footsteps
have been heard climbing up and down the stairs or walking across
the floor in several of the upstairs rooms.

Interestingly, while plasterwork was being repaired in 1937, the
builders discovered a lady's shoe buried in the wall. It was taken to
Colchester Museum, dated as 16th-century and is still on display
there. In Elizabethan days it was common to build items of leather
into the walls of a building as a form of protection against ghosts
and evil spirits, so perhaps the house already had a reputation for
haunting when it was undergoing the earlier repair or renovation.

Name: Man In A Top Hat
Location: New Court, Trinity College, Cambridge, south-east
  England
Date: 1922
Source: *Ghost and Ghoul* by T.C. Lethbridge

T.C. Lethbridge, a well-known Cambridge archaeologist and
researcher of the paranormal, started his book *Ghost and Ghoul* with an
account of an apparition he had seen. Lethbridge was one evening
sitting with a friend, G.W., at Cambridge, in rooms that were said to
have been previously occupied by 'generations of Buxtons, but, as
there were no Buxtons in the college at the time, G.W. had them.'
After a discussion in front of the fire, Lethbridge stood up, passed his
friend and walked past a table in the room to go out of the door. As
he got up, but before he had said good night to his friend, the door
opened and a man came into the room. The man, wearing a top hat,
walked up to the table and stood with his hands resting on it.
Lethbridge thought it must be a college porter who wanted to talk to

his friend and therefore he bid his friend good night, said good evening to the other figure (who did not reply) and then left the room.

The next morning, when Lethbridge met his friend again, he asked him why the porter had come in. He was concerned that perhaps there had been a complaint about them talking, though he was sure they hadn't been making unreasonable noise. His friend, however, was quite adamant that nobody had come in the room and Lethbridge became convinced that he had seen an apparition of some sort.

As to who he was, Lethbridge was very open-minded and considered a thought projection from anywhere, perhaps from G.W., perhaps from someone sitting sleepily in a chair in a London club, or the ghost of one of the Buxtons who had occupied the rooms formerly.

Name: A Monk-like Figure
Location: Deer Abbey, Aberdeenshire, Scotland
Date: 1929
Source: Various

In 1929, Mrs Margaret Robertson and a friend were walking on the A950, near Deer Abbey a few miles from Dunshillock and Old Deer, when they stopped at a stone parapet of a bridge to chat to each other. They heard a swishing noise and saw, walking down the middle of the road, a tall, dark-cloaked figure of a man with a hood over his head. Mrs Robertson said, 'His face was just a grey blur.' She described the figure as walking silently and disappearing into the dark. Both companions were alarmed by this and even more so when a car appeared shortly afterwards which should have illuminated the figure in its headlights but in fact showed the road to be completely deserted. Mrs Robertson believed the figure could have been the ghost of a monk from the nearby abbey and commented that she never again sat on that bridge and always cycled very fast past it.

Name: A Murdered Servant?
Location: Heysham, Lancashire, north-west England
Date: 1960
Source: M. Walker (witness) / authors' own files

Mr Walker contacted us after reading one of our books to tell us of his own experience of seeing a ghost: 'During 1960, when I was 15,

I was living in a semi-detached bungalow with my parents and our cat. I was an only child. The bungalow had been built just the previous year. Some time later, my parents started to complain that now and again they heard knocking in the walls of the bungalow. The cat's hair stood on end while this knocking was taking place. Now, my mother is a strong-headed Yorkshire woman and my father was a purser in the Merchant Navy and had been at sea throughout World War II; he was a very tough man. If they said they heard knocking, then they heard knocking.

'Up to that time I had experienced nothing out of the ordinary. But that was about to change. One night, I was lying in bed when I looked up and, standing half in and half out of the door, I saw a very pretty young woman. Her hair was tied at the back in a bun and I can remember she was wearing a white blouse. She had an hour-glass figure. I realised from the clothes she was wearing that she was from a different period in time; either Victorian or Edwardian. I called to my mother and the woman disappeared. Yet she had been so real and solid. I remember that I was not frightened.

'I am now 54 and what I witnessed that night is just as clear to me now as it was then. It certainly was not a dream; you just do not remember dreams that happened nearly 40 years ago. Later, my mother's uncle discovered that our bungalow had been built on land belonging to a large house further down the avenue. In around 1903, a servant, a young woman, had been found murdered there.

'I never experienced anything again in that house up to the time I left to get married in 1968. My parents still heard knocking in the walls, but it certainly did not upset them. I believe in the afterlife and that certain spirits become trapped at the time of death.'

Name: The North Portland Library
Location: Portland, Oregon, USA
Date: 1990
Source: H. Michael Ball / Ghosts of North Portland website

Located at the corner of N Killingsworth Street and N Commercial Street, the North Portland Library was built in 1913. The second-floor meeting room can accommodate 150 people. Unless it is in use, the entire second floor is closed and secured. Security cameras are mounted at three outside locations, at the main entrance and inside the meeting room. The monitor views frames from the output of each camera in sequence.

One day in 1990, a library assistant who was viewing the monitor from the main desk noticed a man sitting in a chair on the second floor. But there was no meeting scheduled for that day and therefore the room and the floor were sealed off. The assistant called her supervisor and together they watched the monitor: outside shot, outside shot, one more outside view, shot of the main entrance; upstairs shot and there he was – a man seated in one of the chairs. He was dark and motionless.

Together they unlocked the door to the ascending stairwell and climbed until the meeting room was in view. There was nobody there; the room was completely empty. They returned to the main monitor downstairs and when the frames came round to the meeting room they could see the man sitting in the room again. This time the supervisor went back upstairs while the assistant watched on the monitor. The apparition on the monitor vanished before the supervisor could make it into the room.

After that, the apparition was seen quite frequently. It was only ever seen on the monitor, never directly in the room. Among employees there was debate whether the dark figure was a weird play of shadows or whether the sighting represented a haunting. More recently, the figure has been seen much less, and often even when it is present, by the time of the 'next round' of images the figure is gone.

If the figure is a haunting, is it connected to the strange footsteps reported from outside the building? One ex-employee suggested that if a person was to walk up the pavement on Commercial Street, heading from the library toward the doors of Jefferson High School at around one or two o'clock in the morning, they would be virtually guaranteed to hear footsteps walking towards and around them.

The same person also related a story from a spot less than 300 feet from the library. He had a friend that lived on the corner of the block there. He had stopped outside his friend's house while another friend went inside the house to talk; the correspondent remained waiting outside in his car for them to return. He had the window of the car down, when, all of a sudden, he heard heavy footsteps coming towards him, from behind and across Commercial Street. He turned his head, expecting to see someone approach but there was no-one there. He jumped out of his skin – his expression – rolled up the car windows, started the car and pressed on the horn to get his friend out of the house. When he arrived, 'I told him what I'd heard and [he told me] he's also heard the footsteps before. It freaked him out, too, and he jumped in the car and we got the heck outta there.'

Name: The Old Printer

Location: The Offices of the Edinburgh Evening News, Edinburgh, Scotland

Date: 1994

Source: Esther Harward of The Scotsman Publications Ltd/Edinburgh Evening News (Article by Simeela Khaliq)

These offices are in a building almost 100 years old. In 1994, page make-up artist Scott McKirdy was in the basement printing hall and had just finished work for the day when he encountered the silent figure of an old printer in the corridor.

In Scott's words: 'I saw a man purposefully striding along the corridor below. He was wearing matching brown trousers and jersey and was wearing a blue apron tied at the back. In his arms he had a big wooden tray filled with bits of metal the size of matchboxes and it looked really heavy. He didn't look like a shadow at all – he looked very solid – but he didn't make any noise at all, not even with the metal. It was like a silent movie.' Scott ran away as fast as he could, fearful of the sighting. 'Everything was a blur,' he said.

When Scott arrived back among his workmates, sweating and his heart pounding, he convinced three of them to join him in the basement area. Together they discovered a door a few feet from where the man had appeared, though it looked as if it had been locked for 'at least a month'. As Scott said, 'It didn't make sense, as I would have heard him put down his tray and fumble with keys to open and close it. He could never have opened the door and come through because I definitely would have heard it open and close. And when I saw him he was walking briskly as though he had just walked through the door – as though nothing had been in his way.' Scott was certain that he had seen a ghost; he could think of no other explanation.

Scott is not the only person to have encountered a ghost at the newspaper's offices. The mischievous spirit of a blonde-haired woman dressed in black has been seen by staff walking towards the staff entrance, but it then disappears as people approach it. In another encounter a security guard came face to face with the ghost of an employee who had been dead for several years.

The newspaper interviewed clairvoyant Inez Hamilton from Stockbridge in Edinburgh. She was certain that Scott had seen a ghost. 'There is no doubt that he saw a spirit. That's a fact. There were very strong spiritual vibrations down in the area and there's more than just the one person still working down there. The spirit had a job to do and he was just getting on with it – he is very contented and there is no badness in him. I felt a powerful awareness, a feeling. The spirit loved doing what he did and he probably worked the twilight shift. He really loved his job. Spirits like this mean no harm, there is nothing to fear.'

An investigation by Alex Wallace of the Edinburgh branch of the Scottish Society for Psychical Research concluded that, 'Scott is a very down-to-earth young man and his approach to his sighting was both natural and accepting. I would consider there is a definite link between him working in the paste-up room, involved in making up pages, and the apparition he saw, who worked with the old-fashioned metal blocks and etchings. It must have been almost like master meeting apprentice and it's a clear case of a crossover in time dimensions, when past meets the present. No-one can explain why these happen but they definitely do.'

Identifying the type of ghost that Scott saw is unclear. Inez Hamilton is referring to a spirit inhabiting the building after death; Alex Wallace is perhaps considering the possibility of a timeslip, a bridge between time when Scott has seen into the past. Perhaps the printer is a 'recordings' ghost – a natural replaying in the present of an event from the past.

The newspaper recorded the 'spooky comments' of some of the staff at the *Evening News*. Andy MacDonald, a supervisor, commented, 'If he's been working here all these years, there's going to be a hell of an overtime bill!' But the prize for tongue-in-cheek must go to Ricky Armstrong, the caretaker in the building, who reacted to the suggestion that the old printer was a chap called Bob. 'It couldn't have been old Bob because the guy looked like he was working!'

Name: One Man And His Dog.
Location: A small lane between Tarporley and Tiverton, Cheshire, north-west England
Date: September 1971
Source: Various

A tiny lane connects Tarporley and Tiverton, two small villages near the Delamere Forest. It is rumoured to be haunted by the shades of a man and his dog.

In September 1971, Mr A. Pressick was driving in the area and found himself on the lane when he saw the figures ahead of him of a man walking with his dog. Slightly lost and disoriented, he stopped alongside them to ask for directions. The man was dressed in khaki and a rain-proof hat. Pressick noticed that although the night was calm and windless, the two seemed to be pressing into a strong wind, the man's body tensed as if fighting the force of wind. Pressick even noted that the dog's saliva was blowing backwards.

His request for assistance at first received no reply, not even a response; the figures kept on plodding. Pressick shouted his request again. He only noticed the man looking towards him with glaring eyes, yet ignoring him and walking on. Pressick began to hear the sound of wind, yet he could not feel any. Prudently, he decided to drive on, and as he did so he looked back to see the lane empty, the figures having disappeared. Pressick could see nowhere that they could have gone; there was an unbroken line of hedges bordering the road. Some years later, a local farmer told Pressick that a man walking his dog had been knocked down and killed in the lane during a night of violent storms.

Name: Oscar
Location: Department store in Bolton, north-west England
Date: Winter, around 1990-1992
Source: Researcher Maxine Glancy

Maxine interviewed the witness, Jackie Davenport. What is important about the geography of the room Jackie worked in is that her view of the area around the lift, from her desk, was obscured by a 5ft wall known as a 'keep safe'.

Jackie said: 'On this particular day, the lift opened around four o'clock. As I stood up from my desk, I could see a man standing there. I could see him from his chest upwards. He had dark clothes on. I couldn't really see any colour, just black. Tall hat with a brim on it. I can't really remember any features on his face or anything, just that he was an older, middle-aged man. So when I saw him and walked round, I thought "customer". You always had to pick up a pen, so I didn't think anything else, just picked up my pen and, from looking down to see where the pen was and walking round, which was probably two seconds, there was nobody there. It was only when I walked round [the keep safe] that I thought, "Where's he gone?" I thought, "Well, the lift is on the ground floor, he couldn't have gone down [in that time], there's nobody gone down the stairs because I would have seen them." '

Jackie, when thinking about what she had seen, also realised that she should not have been able to see so much of the man from where she was. 'At best, I would have seen the top of his hat if he was very tall,' she said. 'In order for me to see what I saw from where I was stood, he must have been about 8 or 9 feet tall.' She later speculated that he could have been floating above the ground.

'I didn't want to go back and work on that floor, I was really scared. I got straight on the telephone to downstairs and [told my colleagues] what had happened. They just said, "That will be Oscar from the basement." There was this so-called ghost in the basement called Oscar that a few people had seen, but I don't remember a description of him. As far as I knew he was either in my mind or there's no other explanation I could give other than it was a ghost of some sort. But nobody had given that description of the clothes or the hat or anything at all. The Oscar thing seemed to be a "touchy" thing rather than a visual thing.

'I don't really know why I didn't think "Why is he dressed like that?" or "Why has he got that hat on?" because you get all sorts in [the store]. I just didn't really think until afterwards, when I realised that it was not really something that people would wear, a tall hat with a brim on. I definitely didn't imagine it, it was too real for me to have imagined it. There was the sound of the lift which I cannot explain because the lift was on the ground floor. It was a normal lift opening and shutting, and the figure that stood in front of me was as solid as you are now. It was a man stood there smiling at me. He was pleasant, just a man stood there waiting to be served. Not a stern look or anything like that. If I hadn't heard the lift, I wouldn't have looked up because he didn't speak or make a sound.

'I had no choice in where I had to work, so I continued working on the second floor. It never happened again but I was never 100 percent [comfortable]. I was always "looking round".'

Name: The Romans
Location: The Treasurer's House, Minster Yard, York, northern England
Date: 1953
Source: Various

The Treasurer's House's own literature sets the scene: 'While other towns may challenge the claim of York to be the most haunted town in Britain, Treasurer's House is the most haunted house in the city and its ghosts are the oldest in the country . . . During the 800 years of its history Treasurer's House has been the home of many interesting characters, so it is hardly surprising that succeeding generations have felt that the presence of some of them still remains.'

It is most famous, internationally so, for sightings of Roman armies in its cellar. The most famous case is the sighting by Harry Martindale, a retired policeman who in 1953 was an 18-year-old apprentice plumber working in the cellar. Martindale first heard a trumpet sound and then saw the top of a soldier's helmet emerging through the wall he was working on. He was so shocked that he fell off the short ladder he was standing on and 'scuttled back into the corner of the cellar'. The soldier who was wearing the helmet emerged through the wall, carrying the trumpet, marched across the cellar and disappeared into the opposite wall.

Even more extraordinary, following him was a huge carthorse and then at least 20 soldiers in double file. Martindale noted that they were at a lower level than him, their knees almost at floor level. The old Roman road is around 18 inches below the present level; they were apparently walking on the old level, not the present one. The soldiers were carrying lances, round shields and short swords. Throughout the whole experience Martindale heard the trumpet blowing, even though the trumpeter had long disappeared into the opposite wall. The soldiers, he noticed, were not marching but walking two abreast, and looking dishevelled and unshaven.

Martindale ran to the curator, who commented immediately: 'By the look of you, you've seen the Romans, haven't you?'

The round shields Martindale described were a source of interest. It was long believed that Roman infantry carried rectangular shields, but it was discovered that during the fourth century the Sixth Legion was withdrawn from York and reinforced by auxiliary troops who did use round shields. Perhaps these were the troops Martindale saw.

As the comment by the curator indicated, the Romans were a well-known phenomena at the Treasurer's House. In 1946 a previous curator saw something similar and in the 1930s a visiting American professor reported the same thing.

In 1957, not long after Martindale's report, a caretaker at the Treasurer's House, Mrs Joan Mawson, was walking through a low tunnel towards the cellars when she heard the sound of horses and saw a troop of Roman soldiers just a couple of feet away from her. She also described the soldiers looking tired, dishevelled and dirty. She saw them on occasions after that and each time noted how dirty and mud-splashed they were. On a third occasion she saw mounted soldiers so tired they were almost resting on their horses' necks from exhaustion.

The old Roman road known as the Via Decumana, which led from the north-eastern gate of York to the legion headquarters, precisely follows the description of the direction given by Mrs Mawson.

The Romans may be the most famous ghosts of the Treasurer's House but they are not the only reported manifestations. It is also thought be haunted by one George Aislabie, who owned it in 1663 and died there in 1674 following a duel. Witnesses have reported his 'threatening presence' at the Chapter House Street door of the Treasurer's House. There are also reports of the apparition of Lady Beaumont in the drawing room, recognisable from her portrait on display in the building, and the ghost of an unidentified man, 'a tall young man with long, fair hair tied back at the nape of the neck, wearing a scarlet tunic trimmed with gold, black trousers and buckled shoes,' seen in the Lower Hall.

Name: The Silent Man
Location: Bangor, Wales
Date: 1997
Source: Brian Pritchard (witness) / authors' own files

Brian told us of experiences he had had in a house in Wales during his student days, when he was lodging there with others. As he described it: 'In my third year, I lived in a house that was a very interesting place: built into the hillside, it had been at various times a nursery, a party house and a brothel. My room was on the ground floor, above the kitchen, and if I had thought it was haunted when I moved in I would certainly have fled the country! But in a short time I became accustomed to the idea. It started first with the feeling of a presence. There was a spot – just near a side window – at which I sometimes got the impression that a person, about 5½ft tall, was standing. I make no claims to being psychic. Actually, I'm rather unobservant, but over time I got to "know" my "ghost". I believe he was about 50, had lived in the 1950s, was Welsh and his name was Ewan Evans. Don't ask me how I know this – I have no evidence that any such person ever existed – but I just seemed to know.

'But after a while I began to catch glimpses of him in that spot, particularly in dim lighting. He would disappear if the lights were bright. He wore a grey cardigan, had thick, dark hair swept into a side parting, and was short in stature.'

Though not afraid, Brian decided he would rather not share his room any more and came up with a method of exorcism unique in our experience. As he told us: 'One day, on the advice of my father, I announced to him that if he wasn't going to pay rent, he could clear off – and I never noticed him again!'

It is unclear whether the apparition in Brian's bedroom was a recording-type ghost or not. He never interacted and seemed to be staring out of the window, though Brian formed the impression that he was not really looking at anything. Recordings ghosts do seem sometimes to be deep in thought; perhaps in life the man had stood there wrangling with some emotional problem that had left an impression.

But interestingly, the house may also have been haunted by another ghost. As Brian described it: 'The other ghost was downstairs in the kitchen, which connected with the lounge though there was no door. My friend and housemate Helen, when alone and busy in the kitchen, would often sense that someone had entered behind her and, generally assuming it to be me, would say something, only to find herself alone. Like me, she wasn't afraid, although we would both assert that the idea of ghosts generally terrifies us. Eventually, she got into the habit of referring to her "ghost" by the name Paul. I asked her why she had chosen the name and she said that she simply knew that this was his name. I was present once when this experience occurred to Helen. I was sat in the lounge watching television (facing the kitchen doorway) when she started talking to herself. From my chair I asked her what she meant, and she was surprised to see where I was, as she had the impression that I was standing by her.'

Name: Sparkling Monks
Location: Welwyn Garden City, Hertfordshire, southern England
Date: 1965
Source: Jim Ferguson / authors' own files

When Jim Ferguson was with his girlfriend near a golf course on the Great North Road, he was hardly expecting to see the extraordinary sight that they both shared one evening.

'This was in 1965, I was about 17 or 18, and I was sitting with my girlfriend on the golf course near Sheriff's Wood one summer's evening around 9pm. It was not dark but it was gradually getting darker. We were sitting with our backs to the tree-line looking towards the Great North Road. We were both alerted by quite a lot of sound behind us; we turned round and saw a group of tall individuals dressed in cloaks and hoods, the cloaks drawn at the waist. They walked in a line, one behind the other. We looked at each other and said: "They must be going to a party, we'll follow them." We were following them parallel at about a road's width distance, so we had a very clear sight of them.

'They were all kind of very light grey, maybe they were white but they appeared light grey in that light. They looked like monks, but I've no idea what they actually were. They were talking between themselves. We couldn't hear what they were saying at that distance, but there was a lot of conversation going on. We could hear their cloaks rustling as they moved along and we could hear their footsteps.

'We began to realise that something wasn't quite right. They weren't actually solid; they were kind of sparkling. You know how you begin to distrust what you are seeing, so we decided to run on a little bit, crossed the little stile and got into the road so that we would see them head-on. We were able to stand there for a few seconds, watching them come towards us. You could see a face but you couldn't make it out. But it did not look real; it looked sparkly. When they got to the edge of the woods where the road intersects, they simply disappeared. The sight stopped, the sound stopped, they were gone.

'At that point my girlfriend and I looked at each other and I think instinct just told us to run down the road, so we did. We ran down the hill, stopped at the bottom and looked back, and I said, "What did you see?" She described exactly what I had seen. So we both saw it, no doubt about that. It was definitely there.'

We asked what Jim thought he might have been seeing. 'They were walking down a well-trodden path and appeared to do so with ease. We don't know whether we were looking into the past or the future, do we? I did have a feeling they were walking above ground level, not actually floating, but slightly off the ground.'

Name: Victim Of A Duel
Location: Lafayette Square, Washington DC, USA
Date: 1820 to the present day
Source: Various

A plaque on the wall of a house in Lafayette Square states that it 'was the home of Commodore Stephen Decatur, who died here March 22 1820 from wounds received in a duel with Commodore Barron'.

In 1820 Stephen Decatur was America's most prominent naval champion, a hero of four wars who was looking forward to his retirement. However, he had helped to court-martial a naval officer years before and the man had now challenged him to a duel. Decatur, on the night before the duel, stood gazing out of his window in deep reflection. Just before dawn the duel was fought and later Decatur was brought to the house fatally wounded.

Within a year, his face was seen looking out of the window as he had done on the night before his death. The window was walled up but still there were reports of his transparent image gazing out from that spot. There have been other reports of a figure seen slipping out through the house's back entrance carrying a small black box under its arm, just as Decatur did with his duelling pistol on the day of his death.

Name: The Walnut Girl
Location: Armona, California, USA
Date: 19th century onwards
Source: Rachelle Erickson (witness)

In the San Jouquin Valley of California, the Armona Southern Pacific Depot was built in 1931. The old train station stands derelict today and strange events happen there. Rachelle reported that: 'One time when I was nine years old, I went in there late at night. I was shining the flashlight around the room when the light fell on someone else who was in there. It was a girl my age, about nine years old, totally nude, and with a Victorian hairstyle. I was so surprised I dropped the flashlight. When I picked it up again, she was gone.

'Later my mother told me that when she was a little girl she had once seen this same girl in an orchard. As it turned out, other people had seen her, too, described as about nine years old, always in the nude. She usually appeared near large concentrations of walnuts, such as a walnut orchard, a warehouse full of walnuts, or even the walnut section of a grocery store.'

As the girl is non-interactive, it is possible this is a recordings-type ghost. However, there is a legend to this story and some believe the girl is attracted to walnuts for a purpose. As Rachelle explained: 'In the 19th century, several young girls were skinny-dipping in a canal. All of a sudden, boys showed up. Most of the girls tried to hide themselves by running into a nearby walnut orchard. One girl tried to hide by ducking under the water, and staying under until the boys had left. Unfortunately, she drowned. She now realises that if she had opted to go to the walnut orchard, she would have lived. She now tries to be near large quantities of walnuts in order to make up for her mistake, although it's too little too late. She almost always appears to females because she doesn't want males to see her in the nude. She's particularly attracted to girls her own age, which would explain the incidents of me and my mother.'

Fights And Battles

If emotion is one of the factors that creates the lasting impression we call a ghost, then war must be one of the most emotional times for many people. No surprise, then, that wars throughout the ages have created all sorts of ghostly manifestations, from individual warriors apparently still haunting the scenes of their victories, defeats or deaths, to whole armies apparently still 'in situ' in some form.

Name: Cavalier
Location: Malvern, Worcestershire, central England
Date: 1978
Source: N. Sweet (witness) / authors' own files

Mr Sweet was at boarding school in 1978, at the age of around 12 or 13, when he had a sighting that frightened him then, and remains with him to the present day.

'There were about 10 or 11 of us. It was about eight o'clock at night, a clear, cold night. We had just gone back into the main school building for our baths – the matron was very strict about that. Just as I finished, one of the boys shouted, "There's someone on our cricket pitch," which was over the far side of the main sports field. "Let's go and see who it is," said someone else.

'Only three of us went out; I went somewhat reluctantly. We had a small torch and made our way to the site. The sight that greeted us is one I shall never forget; it was man kneeling beside a white horse, his head was bowed and in his hands, and his shape shimmered an unearthly gold colour. He was wearing what I now believe to be the outfit of a cavalier from the English Civil War period. We stood a few yards from the figure for several minutes, then we approached nearer. He turned his head and glared at us; two of the boys ran, I stood there as if glued to the ground. His eyes looked sad, and a sort of smile appeared on his face. Then he reached down, picked up a wide-brimmed hat, placed it on his head and turned away, leading the horse. He only walked three or four steps and was gone. I followed, but there were no hoof-marks or anything; I never saw the figure again. I left the school the next year. I was later told there were several small skirmishes between Cromwell's troops and the King's army on that site during the English Civil War. Perhaps he had been killed on what was now our cricket pitch.'

Name: A Cut On The Head
Location: Naseby, Leicestershire, central England
Date: 1990
Source: *Ghosthunter* by Eddie Burks and Gillian Cribbs

Retired schoolteacher John Wellens had lived in his 16th-century cottage in Naseby since 1964. Naseby was the site of Cromwell's most significant win over the Royalist forces during the English Civil War in June 1645, which effectively gave the Roundheads overall victory. There have been local claims of ghostly re-enactments of the battle seen in the sky, and apparitions of dishevelled and defeated-looking soldiers seen in the fields.

In 1990, Wellens found that guests staying in a bedroom they had called the 'haunted room' claimed they were having nightmares. Apparitions were seen and rattling and scratching noises had been heard. Wellens called in ghost researcher and psychic Eddie Burks to investigate the house.

Eddie sensed the presence of a Roundhead trapped in the house since the 17th century. He had died 'by a musket ball that hit his skull. He died shortly afterwards in considerable pain,' as Eddie described. Eddie went on to say the soldier was trapped by a sense of purpose. He had arrived at the house originally to search for something in that room and he was continuing to search for it even after his death. Eddie believed that he had originally arrived because a King's messenger was there with an important document and he was shot and died in the attempt to retrieve it.

What was fascinating – although, as Wellens said, 'It cuts right across my logic' – was that some days before Eddie arrived, Wellens had discovered a deep gash, seven inches long, on his forehead, which had required stitches. Wellens explained, 'I felt nothing at the time, but then I saw blood dripping onto my face and hands. It just happened. No, I had not been drinking. But I felt no pain until the nurse put in the stitches.'

Eddie believed that the spirit had projected the injuries onto Wellens and that by sharing the pain, Wellens had helped the spirit to be freed.

Name: The Legacy Of 'Butcher' Cumberland
Location: Culloden, Scotland
Date: 1746 onwards
Source: Various

Visitors to Culloden, to the east of Inverness, and particularly to the battle site, have often reported it being a sombre, despairing place. If so, then it reflects the tragic events that took place there in 1746, in the last major battle ever fought on British soil.

On 16 April 1746, 5,000 Highlanders under Charles Edward Stuart ('Bonnie Prince Charlie') were routed by 9,000 disciplined, highly-trained troops under the command of the Duke of Cumberland, supported by ships of the Royal Navy in the Moray Firth. The Jacobite forces were devastated, with over 1,000 lives lost in the battle and in the ragged retreat to Inverness. The battle effectively ended the hopes of the Scots for a return of a Stuart to the throne of Scotland. The fiercely fought encounter lasted barely 60 minutes but the Highlanders – more used to fighting in the hills – were overwhelmed. Cumberland acquired the nickname 'Butcher' from his order that no prisoners should be taken, greatly increasing the death toll.

The clansmen who died in the engagement were buried around the battle site, their graves marked by stones. Seventy-six of the few hundred English who died were buried in the 'Field of the English'. During the 19th century the site was marked by the building of a large memorial cairn.

Since that time, there have been many reports of ghostly armies, their battles replayed in the sky. The sounds of the battle have often been heard; clashing swords and the cries of the combatants. There have also been a number of reports of individual ghosts of Highlanders marching, or covered in blood, and even of the ghostly images of corpses around the field. Lily Seafield in *Scottish Ghosts* reports the shade of one tall young Highlander seen wandering the battlefield, sad and dejected, and muttering what sounds like the word 'defeated'.

The highest numbers of reports come from the anniversary date of the battle, 16 April. Norman Adams in *Haunted Scotland* recalls that during the 250th anniversary gathering at the battle site in 1996, a photograph was taken by one woman there which appears to show the spectre of a bonneted Highlander. That same woman, he reports, suffered some poltergeist activity in her home afterwards, though whether the experiences were connected is unclear. A clairvoyant called to her house suggested that the house was haunted by the ghost of a Highlander who had been killed helping Bonnie Prince Charlie escape, and who was 'aggrieved at being ignored by history'.

Bonnie Prince Charlie escaped the scene, but nearby Culloden House, where he spent the night before the engagement, is said to be haunted by his shade.

Name: Major's Leap
Location: Wenlock Edge, Shropshire, central England
Date: 1965
Source: Various

In 1645, Wilderthorpe Manor in Shropshire was owned by Major Smallman, a Royalist who came under attack by the Parliamentarians. When Wilderthorpe Manor was besieged, the Major escaped on horseback along Wenlock Edge. He reached what is now known as Blakeway Coppice and leapt over a cliff edge leading to a 100ft drop. Assuming he was dead, the attackers called off the chase, though in fact the Major survived. The area became known as 'Major's Leap'.

At Easter 1965, Eva and Alick Knight were driving in the area when they saw the grey and black shapes of a rider on horseback standing on a track ahead of them. The rider wore a wide-brimmed, large-plumed hat, cloak and breeches. As they watched, the horse and rider leapt off the track and into a nearby field. Mr Knight thought that the figures had leapt over the brow of a hill.

The site where the apparitions were seen is some nine miles away from the believed site of the major's flight, but some historians have proposed that the route the Knights saw the figures pursuing is a more likely route for the Major to have taken.

Name: Missing Comrade . . . Not Missing.
Location: Cranwell, Lincolnshire, eastern England
Date: Summer 1919
Source: Navy News (the newspaper of the Royal Navy), May 1996 /
    J Roberts of Taunton, Somerset

When the HMS *Daedalus* Maintenance Group lined up in the Transport Yard in 1919 for an official photograph to commemorate the disbanding of their unit, there would have been the usual mixed emotions; old friends parting, looking forward to a world free of war, and so on. One of the emotions was of sadness, because missing from the official photograph would be their colleague Freddy Jackson. He had died just three days earlier, on the same patch of tarmac where they were now lined up, when he stumbled into a whirling propeller. Some of the people now lined up for their photograph had formed part of Freddy's entourage at his funeral.

A photographic firm of good repute, Bassano's, was brought in to take the group photograph. When it was developed, the photograph was pinned up for all to see. Wren Bobbie Capel, later married to Air Vice Marshal Arthur Capel, remembered the gasps of astonishment when the group could clearly see, on the photograph, Freddy standing just behind the back row. 'I have thought and puzzled over it for years,' said Mrs Capel, 'but I can think of no explanation other than it is a picture of a ghost.'

'There he was, and no mistake, although a little fainter than the rest,' wrote Air Marshal Victor Goddard in his book *Flight Towards Reality*. 'Indeed, he looked as though he was not altogether there, not really with that group, for he alone was capless, smiling; all the rest were serious and set, and wearing service caps.' Goddard confirmed that the company used to take the photograph were reputable and that there would have been 'no hanky panky in the darkroom', and also that the negative was examined for signs of faking and there were none.

The photograph was the subject of an Australian TV documentary and was the only one of several to stand up to scrutiny in a British television examination of 'spirit photographs'.

Name: The Phantom Army
Location: Conygar Hill, Dunster, Somerset, south-west England
Date: 1951
Source: Various

In 1951, Joyce Nicholls and Frances Robinson were on holiday in Dunster and visited Conygar Hill, a steep tor. Atop the tor is a small tower that was built in 1760. The couple climbed the tor, entered the tower and climbed to the top. The day was warm and sunny, but as they reached the top they felt the atmosphere change, becoming cold, darkened and like winter. Then the couple heard, coming from the north, what seemed to be the sound of a huge group of people marching towards them. They believed they were hearing a ghost army approaching them. Furthermore, they believed that the army was approaching them horizontally, at their own elevation, although they were raised above any surrounding land. When they felt the army was close to them they panicked and frantically ran from the tower, cutting themselves on thorns and twigs as they fled.

What the ghost army related to is unclear, though just 20 miles away to the east took place the most crucial battle of the 'Duking Days'. The battle of Sedgemoor took place on 5 July 1685 when the Duke of Monmouth's 'Peasant Army' was finally confronted by King James II's forces. The Duke had challenged the legitimacy of the King, and indeed had himself proclaimed King in Taunton Market Place. He was captured at Sedgemoor, taken to London, and beheaded on 15 July. Since that time the sounds of the battle have been reportedly re-enacted at the battle site, and there have been sightings of apparitions of tired, routed, defeated soldiers there. Perhaps an echo also reached the couple at Dunster.

Alternatively, Dunster Castle was, during the English Civil War, occupied by both sides at different times; perhaps what they heard related to the engagements that had happened there.

Name: The Soldier
Location: Leyton Road, Harpenden, Hertfordshire, southern England
Date: 1970s
Source: *Harpenden 1st* newspaper

Harpenden housed several units of soldiers during the First World War. There are several reports from various areas of the town of the ghosts of those soldiers still appearing from time to time. One such report arose from a cottage near the Silver Cup public house where a boy living in the cottage told his mother about a man in his bedroom. Apparently, the mother took little notice at first, presumably believing the boy to be describing an imaginary friend, but started to take an interest when the boy described the uniform of a First World War soldier. When enquiring among the neighbours, she discovered that a 19-year-old soldier, who had been killed in the war, had once occupied the boy's bedroom.

We interviewed a local woman from another part of the town who also had a similar experience. Her son, around three years old, had started to tell her about a friend he met in the garden whom she believed was an imaginary companion. However, her son continued with his description of 'Thomas' as he called him, telling his mother, 'He is a soldier.' What convinced the mother that her son might have been talking to a ghost from the First World War was her son's description of the Battle of Arras, a name which she felt would mean nothing to her child but which was one of the most significant battles of the Great War. As Arras was the administrative centre of the département of Pas-de-Calais and a strategic railway junction, it became the centre of five major battles of the war.

The Wicked And The Cruel

We said in the introduction to the previous chapter that emotion might play a part in creating ghost phenomena. If so, then even more emotion – at the individual level – is probably felt by the victims of wicked and cruel acts. Many of those who have been such victims would have felt not just the frustration of being cut off in their prime, or deprived of the chance to say goodbye to a loved one, but would have felt the indignity and the injustice of evil killers and social systems that allowed wickedness to flourish. As such, it is hardly surprising that some areas seem to be drenched in emotion – and reflected in ghost and spirit reports.

Name: Axed To Death
Location: Overwater Hall, Overwater, Cumbria, north-west
   England
Date: To the present day
Source: Stephen Bore (one of the hotel's proprietors)

The ghost of Overwater Hall is said to be a very chilling sight, a woman tapping on the windows or passing through a door, characterised by her severed stumps of arms and no hands. According to Stephen Bore, the original owner of the house, Joseph Gillbanks, had a mistress who caused him great embarrassment when she turned up at what was then his family home. She told him that she was pregnant and he rode her out to Overwater Tarn and drowned her. It is believed that as she tried to clamber back into the boat, he chopped off her hands with an axe. This would be the origin of the gruesome spirit that has been seen in the hotel.

Name: A Fateful Affair
Location: Corvin Castle, Transylvania, Romania
Date: To the present
Source: Various

Transylvania is the central province of Romania, surrounded by the Carpathian Mountains. Though much associated with the legends of Dracula, the region has plenty of other dark history.

Corvin Castle holds part of that darker side. It is thought to be Transylvania's greatest fortress, a 14th-century edifice decorated with grotesque gargoyles, built by the warlord Prince Iancu Corvin.

The apparition of a woman dressed in white, and dripping blood, is said to haunt the main tower of the castle and has been reported right up to the 1990s by staff and visitors. Her story is said to be that she lived in the 15th century and was a lady of the household who fell in love and had an illicit affair with a lowly manservant. For punishment she was stripped naked, tied to a pillar in the Knight's Hall and killed by having a nail driven through her head.

In 1873, during restoration work, evidence showing this was not all legend was unearthed. A female skeleton was found buried under a staircase, the skull split in two by a spike.

Name: The Field Of The Burned
Location: Montsegur Castle, Pyrenees foothills, southern France
Date: 13th century
Source: Various

In the 13th century there was a religious revolution from which came the Cathari, meaning the 'pure ones'. The Catholic Church grew alarmed at the popularity of this rival and in 1208 Pope Innocent III demanded a crusade against the Cathari, who were hunted down throughout France, tortured and massacred in an attempt to destroy the sect forever.

When it first became apparent that they were to be victims of persecution on a scale rarely seen before, the Cathari created a central base and headquarters at Montsegur Castle where they could secure their secrets and artefacts, turning it into a fortified stronghold protected by a garrison.

In May 1243, 205 Cathars, and their soldiers numbering some 300, were besieged in Montsegur by a force of some 10,000 men. After around ten months, on 1 March 1244, Pierre-Roger de

Mirepox left the castle under the flag of truce to negotiate a surrender. The soldiers were to be allowed to go free, but the Cathari had to renounce their faith and come back to the Catholic Church to seek forgiveness for their heresy. If they did not they would be burned alive; huge bonfires were lit at the foot of the mountain as a clear indication of their fate if they did not surrender. The soldiers left except for a few who had converted to the Cathar belief, and then on the morning of the 16 March 1244, 216 Cathars, singing together, marched down the mountainside and into the flames below.

The site where they went to their deaths is known as the Field of the Burned and is marked by a simple memorial cross. Many people have reported feeling the intense strange energy of the area, and a white ghostly mist has often been reported rising from the Field of the Burned and up to the castle ruins. Of the 'Perfecti' – the most devout of the order – it is said that their ghostly forms are seen at their stronghold, perhaps still trying to protect their secret treasure.

Name: Gibraltar Point Lighthouse
Location: Toronto Island, Canada
Date: 1800s
Source: Toronto Ghost and Hauntings Research Association /
   Matthew Didier

The plaque on the wall of the Gibraltar Point Lighthouse is a rare one; it warns visitors that the site is supposed to be haunted.

The first lighthouse keeper is believed to have been John Paul Rademuller, who used the site to brew bootleg beer in the years immediately after the 1812 war. Two drunken soldiers went to the lighthouse to get some of the beer but were refused by Rademuller. Angry after their journey, they killed him, dismembered his body and buried it all around the building. In 1893 bones were unearthed from around the lighthouse. It is said that on dark, stormy nights Rademuller's apparition can be seen going up to light his beacon.

Name: Katharina
Location: Lauenstein Castle, Bavaria, southern Germany
Date: Unknown
Source: Simon Marsden, *The Journal of a Ghost Hunter*

Berg Lauenstein (Castle Lauenstein) is one of Bavaria's fairytale-like castles. Resplendent in blue and white, it is not dissimilar to the internationally famous Neuschwanstein Castle at Fussen, one of King Ludwig II's extravagances. Berg Lauenstein is thought to have been built by King Konrad I in around 915. It is in the northernmost point of Bavaria in the hills and is presently state-owned and used for various functions.

It was once owned by the lords of the family Von Orlamünde. Berg Lauenstein's ghost is thought to come from the time when this family occupied the castle. It is said that Graf Otto Von Orlamünde died fighting abroad, leaving his widow Katharina and two children alone in the castle. Over time she fell in love with Albert Von Nürnberg but to win his affections believed that she would have to be rid of her children. Senseless with love for Albert, she inserted thin needles into the brains of the children and then circulated the story that they had died mysteriously in their sleep of some illness. Given her position in society, this went unchallenged.

However, the legend has it that she was then overcome with grief and decided to work out her guilt by committing herself for the rest of her life as a nun to the monastery where her children's bodies were buried. After her death it was said that her ghost, a pale white apparition, sad and sighing, haunts the corridors and rooms of the castle, and in particular a stairway to the main tower.

Name: Lady Glamis
Location: Glamis Castle, Scotland
Date: To the present
Source: Various

Glamis Castle was built as a hunting lodge in Scotland and is the ancestral home of the Bowes Lyon family. After John, the sixth Lord Glamis, died, his wife Janet, Lady Glamis, was imprisoned on a trumped-up charge of witchcraft. King James V had hated her family and was determined to see it ravished once the sixth Lord was gone. James seized the castle and he and Queen Mary moved in, ransacking the building in an attempt to diminish the inheritance of Janet's son. Lady Glamis was in time burned at the stake. Janet's son was to be executed after he had become of age, but was saved when the King died prior to that. Eventually, he was restored to his home and title.

Janet's ghost, exhibiting a glow, has been seen floating above the Clock Tower. A sighting of a 'Grey Lady' ghost, seen by many walking along the corridors in the castle, has also been attributed to her. Glamis has been the scene of a great many sightings over time, some allegedly affecting the present Queen Mother, the most famous surviving member of the Bowes Lyon family.

Name: The Lady Of The Manor
Location: Frendraught House, Aberdeenshire, Scotland
Date: 1630
Source: Various

Frendraught House in the 1630s was the home of the Crichton family, a powerful family controlling a large area of north-east Scotland. In 1630 a boundary dispute between Sir James Crichton and a member of the Gordon clan resulted in Crichton shooting Gordon, Laird of Rothiemay. Sir James was fined heavily for his crime and shortly afterwards was again before the High Sheriff for shooting Leslie of Pitcaple in another dispute, though this time the ruling was in Sir James's favour. Leslie swore revenge on the House of Crichton. Sir James was escorted back to Frendraught with an armed party including John Gordon of Rothiemay and the Marquis of Huntly's son, John Melgum, Viscount Aboyne. Once they had returned to Frendraught House, the visitors were put in the Old Tower to stay the night by Lady Crichton, an active participant in her husband's disputes and described once as 'somewhere between Medusa and Lady Macbeth'.

During the night the tower burned down and many people burned to death. The commission investigating the fire concluded that 'the fire could not have happened accidentally but designedly' and suspicion rested on Lady Crichton. Although she was cleared of the charge on appeal to the Privy Council, Sir James and his wife were apparently severely changed by the fire. Lady Crichton later began to support Presbyterianism and was excommunicated by the Catholic Church into which she had been born. She died 'without benefit' of clergy and was buried, like her husband, in an unmarked grave.

Frendraught is said to be haunted by Lady Crichton because of her guilt. There have been sightings of a 'dark woman in a white dress' as far back as the 18th century when a Victorian clergyman reported seeing the apparition in the house and in the grounds. In 1938, when the house was empty, one teenager reported seeing a face watching him from a window. When he alerted a keeper, who also saw the intruder, the house was searched but no-one was found.

The house later came into the possession of Yvonne and Alexander

Morrison. Mrs Morrison encountered the ghost in the 1940s and several of their guests cut short visits because of disturbances that made them uncomfortable.

Name: Love Triangle
Location: Bristol, south-west England
Date: Spring 2000
Source: Lionel and Patricia Fanthorpe

Reverend Fanthorpe is an investigator of the paranormal who will be known to many readers for his lively, leather-clad, motorbike-touring presentation of Fortean TV. He and his wife told us the following account, reproduced here in their own words.

'We were called in to investigate the Bristol Odeon Cinema, where a young usher had felt unable to continue with his work because of what he felt were the hostile psychic manifestations taking place there. We have been enthusiastic but objective investigators since the 1950s, but neither of us is noticeably psychic. We like to take reliable and sensitive friends with us on these investigations, to get their views on what can be seen and heard at a particular site. For our visit to the Bristol Odeon, we were very glad to have the expert psychic services of Rosie Malone, an author who had worked with us very satisfactorily on several previous occasions, including on some of our TV programmes.

'As we entered the building, Rosie's first encounter was with a spirit who told her he had been on the site for centuries, long before modern Bristol became a city. In her view, he was not hostile or evil but was merely territorial and defensive. We passed his apparent area of influence without undue incident, and the young former usher told us that we were now approaching one of the areas where he felt particularly frightened and vulnerable. He showed us a line in front of one of the screens where he was certain the apparition had walked. He also told us the background scenario to the alleged hauntings.

'At some time in the mid 1940s, either during the closing stages of the Second World War, or immediately after it ended, a returning serviceman became involved in a love triangle and shot his rival in the Bristol Odeon. The young usher who had been so disturbed by what he had seen and heard felt that it was either the spirit of the killer or that of the murder victim who walked that particular line immediately in front of the screen. I duly walked it, saying prayers of exorcism as I went.

'We then proceeded to the corridor outside, and here I was aware of something anomalous. It is very rare indeed for me to see or hear anything paranormal, but in this corridor I became aware of a foul stench of decay. I checked carefully with the cameraman and sound recordist, who both confirmed that they could smell it, too. At this point things took a sudden dramatic turn. The young usher complained of severe pain and said that the evil psychic presences in the corridor where we now stood were attacking him. I was several paces away, exploring the far end of the passageway. Rosie was very close to the distressed young man. She called to me for assistance – as she does on these occasions – and I then stood between the usher and the point where Rosie said she could see his psychic attackers. I began a prayer of exorcism and added the famous words attributed to Saint Columba when he allegedly defended a distressed fisherman on Loch Ness, by calling out to the fabled monster: "Touch not thou that man!" As I, myself, couldn't see the effect which both Rosie and the usher assured me I was having on the "attackers", I had to rely totally on their word for what happened next. "They're terrified of you. They're retreating fast," they both assured me, which I felt was rather more than I deserved. If we assume that exorcism works, and that evil psychic entities can be routed by an ordained priest, we must always remember that he or she is only a channel for God's unlimited power. It is omnipotent goodness which blasts evil away, not the mere priest who calls for that divine aid.

'What I did notice very strongly for myself, after Rosie and the young usher assured me that the negative, hostile presences had gone, was that the foul smell had gone, too. Once again, I checked with the cameraman and sound engineer and they confirmed that the air now smelled fresh, clean and wholesome again.'

Name: Machbuba
Location: Bad Muskau, Saxony, Germany
Date: 27 October 1840
Source: Simon Marsden, *The Journal of a Ghost Hunter*

The solemn spectre said to walk the roads between the village of Bad Muskau and the castle that dominates the village is thought to be the Abyssinian girl known as Machbuba who died at the castle on 27 October 1840. The inscription on her tomb, copied from the church register of 1840, describes her fate.

'At midday on 27 October the Abyssinian virgin Machbuba died at Bad Muskau Castle. The Duke Herman Von Pückler-Muskau had brought her back with him from one of his journeys to the Orient, where she had been living in the high mountains of Abyssinia at the source of the Nile. She was the daughter of a servant of the Abyssinian royal family and became a slave of a neighbouring country who were at war with her rulers . . . then Machbuba was sent to Khartoum in the Sudan, where the Duke bought her. She was 11 years old. He felt sorry for her and took her back to Bad Muskau as an orphan, where she died of a broken heart at 16 years of age. Her funeral took place on the evening of 29 October in the village cemetery. All the Duke's servants took part in the ceremony, lining the pathway from the *schloss* (castle) to the graveyard, each man and woman holding a flaming torch for the child they had come to love.'

Simon Marsden in his *The Journal of a Ghost Hunter*, comments that on visiting the castle and speaking to the curator, he was told that although publicly the Duke claimed he had brought the girl up as a daughter, when he was drunk he boasted of her beautiful young body, implying a more carnal relationship.

Name: The Murdered Housemaid

Location: Robert Gordon's College, Aberdeen, Scotland
Date: 1780s
Source: Brian R. W. Lockhart, headmaster of Robert Gordon's
    College

There is no written account of the ghost in any of the histories of the college, but the story has been passed down over the years. One Sunday in around 1780, when the pupils and masters had gone to St Nicholas Kirk for a service, two burglars broke into the hospital to steal Robert Gordon's collection of coins from the Governors' Room. The burglars thought there would be no-one in the building but a housemaid surprised them and they stabbed her to death. They fled without stealing anything. The scene is dramatised in the play *The Auld Hoose* by Walter Humphries and John Mackintosh, performed at the first Founder's Day in 1934. The date of the murder is given as 13 October 1781, the maidservant is called Betsy and the thieves do not stab her but hit her over the head with a chair.

However, the housemaid is supposed to haunt the college. The bloodstain on the floor in the north-west corner of the Governors' Room remained until the early 1950s when the floor was replaced

Oliver Cromwell's ghost has been sighted in numerous locations throughout England (*National Portrait Gallery*)

After his death in 1892, Alfred Lord Tennyson has been spotted walking over his favourite paths near his home on the Isle of Wight (*National Portrait Gallery*)

William Wordsworth's ghost was seen sitting in a chair at his former home in the Lake District, Cumbria (*National Portrait Gallery*)

The Foran's Hotel, Newfoundland: the death of a guest was accompanied by strange knockings which persisted until the body was removed (*Newfoundland Historic Trust*)

'I carved that. Do you like it?' asked a figure to a tourist in York Minster in York admiring the stonework shortly before disappearing. The ghostly return of a proud craftsman? (*John and Anne Spencer/Paranormal Picture Library*)

Reverend Lionel Fanthorpe exorcised an attacking evil presence from this cinema, using the words of Saint Columba when he defended a fisherman from the Loch Ness Monster: 'Touch not thou that man!' (*Lionel and Patricia Fanthorpe*)

Alan Broe is convinced his dog Tina, who had been killed in a road accident, appeared to him in spirit afterwards (*Alan Broe*)

Now a radio station, Merritt House has been under the intensive study of the Toronto Ghosts and Hauntings Research Society, with several paranormal results (*Toronto Ghosts and Hauntings Research Society/Matthew Didier*)

A ghostly World War Two airplane still roams the skies over Ladybower Reservoir in the Peak District (*John and Anne Spencer/Paranormal Picture Library*)

Oakhill Park, north London: a figure in turn of the century clothes and an 'Oscar Wilde' hat seen here by witnesses suddenly disappeared (*Jennifer Spencer/Paranormal Picture Library*)

Several hauntings associated with World War One relate to Leyton Road in Harpenden, Hertfordshire, including the ghost of a soldier and a deathly omen (*Jennifer Spencer/Paranormal Picture Library*)

A timeslip in Scotland: there were no structures seen in front of the camera when this picture was taken at Balmakeil – a photograph of a time past or future? (*Malcolm Robinson/Strange Phenomena Investigations*)

Verulanium: a timeslip that occurred here may have shown a glimpse of St Albans' Roman imperial past (*Jennifer Spencer/Paranormal Picture Library*)

The sounds of Al Capone's banjo are one of many ghostly echoes heard and felt at Alcatraz in San Francisco, now a major tourist attraction (*John and Anne Spencer/Paranormal Picture Library*)

The Chase Crypt, Barbados: The 'moving coffins' case is a well-known and still unexplained haunting phenomenon (*Lionel and Patricia Fanthorpe*)

Hermitage Castle, Scotland: This foreboding structure has been the scene of many terrible events in its long history. Some at least seem to have left an enduring echo into the present in the form of hauntings (*John and Anne Spencer/Paranormal Picture Library*)

The authors' long series of ghostly 'stake outs' at Dover Castle in Kent have produced several paranormal results - a rewarding site for the aspiring ghostwatcher (*John and Anne Spencer/Paranormal Picture Library*)

because of woodworm. A member of staff who was then a pupil at the school at that time recounts that until that time boys received medical injections in the Governors' Room and, if they were brave, the carpet was rolled back and they were allowed to see the stain.

Name: Presence In A Room
Location: Cheltenham, Gloucestershire, south-west England
Date: May 1996
Source: Gloria Dixon, researcher

Gloria Dixon, a well-known researcher of the paranormal and editor of *Strange Daze* magazine, interviewed Patricia, who had a tale to tell of a possible haunting at a hotel in the Cheltenham area.

From Gloria's report: 'Patricia is well-known to me; she has had many unusual experiences during her life. She neither dwells on these unusual experiences, nor does she discount them. She appears to integrate them into her life and just gets on with day-to-day living. She was married to an RAF officer and has travelled extensively because of this.'

Patricia told Gloria: 'I was invited to join some American friends of mine as their guest. I was to stay with them at a hotel just outside Cheltenham in Gloucestershire in May 1996. It was a very old building, dating from the 13th century. When I arrived in the afternoon I was given my room number, 19, and made my way up the stairs to unpack my luggage, etc. It was on the second floor, but there were no lifts. As I walked up the stairs, which seemed to be very bleak, being so old and in stone, I sensed someone was behind me and I wasn't very happy. I thought 'This is ridiculous' but there was some kind of pressure as I walked up the stairs. You couldn't dash up the turret stairs because they were awkward to climb.

'I went into my room to unpack all my things and I can't explain exactly in words . . . but . . . I was uneasy in the room. I didn't know the reason why, as there was nothing there to upset me, but I just felt very uneasy, which was unusual for me. I unpacked all my things then came downstairs and we went out and had our dinner. When I went upstairs later in the evening to retire, I still sensed something peculiar. I went to open the wardrobe door and I hesitated before opening it, which was rather strange because I thought, "Why am I hesitating, it's only a wardrobe?" But I felt as though there was some presence there. I opened the wardrobe and there was nothing there, so I put my clothes away, shut the door and went to bed.

'My bed was against the wall; a single bed. I went off to sleep. When I awoke I was turned towards the wall in the bed and I woke up with this terrific pressure on my back, forcing and pushing me in a very unpleasant way. I was really frightened and thought, "Dear me, what is going on?" It took great courage, I have to say, to find the light and put it on, because I was petrified to turn around because of the pressure in my back, which was really hurting me. I put the light on and very reluctantly turned round . . . and there was nothing there. After I put the light on, the pressure dispersed. I had definitely been awake, and I am sure it was that pressure that made me awaken. From then, I could not get back to sleep, as one would appreciate, for quite some time. I left all the lights on in the room all night long and I was most unhappy about it.

'However, the following morning, I went down to join my American friends and during breakfast I told them about my experience. They insisted I should change my room. I then went to the reception area and asked the receptionist if he could enlighten me with any information about the hotel because of the bad experience I had during the night in my room. He said to me, "Your room number, was it 19?" I said yes, 19. "Oh," he said, "the maid who changes the beds would not go up to that room because whenever she went up the turret stairs there was the marching of heavy feet behind her and she was petrified and ran down and would not go back there . . . to that room . . . anymore."

'Although my friends felt I must move rooms, I felt rather embarrassed that there would be all this performance to try and find another room, and I said just to leave it and I would try and cope with it. That night I did not go to sleep at all without all the lights on and I even had the television on. I hesitated and went towards the wardrobe again and I had a terrible sense that there was somebody there. It was as though . . . almost as though . . . the spirit or whoever it was that was there was out more or less to injure you, not to be pleasant. I never felt at ease in that room at all, but it was something very strange that I experienced. I hadn't experienced that type of thing before and I was really quite shaken.'

Name: Robin Redcap
Location: Hermitage Castle, near Hawick, southern Scotland
Date: 13th century onwards
Source: Various

The brooding-looking Hermitage Castle was built in the 13th century. It is said to be haunted by an early occupant, William de

Soulis, who is believed to have practised black magic under the master wizard Michal Scot. Local rumour has it that he was aided by his assistant and 'familiar' Robin Redcap, who is also said to haunt the castle. There are stories of blood-curdling screams heard from within the ancient walls.

The castle certainly has had a known violent history. In one area is a pit where prisoners were left to die; one lasted for 17 days, having kept himself alive that long on bits of grain dropped accidentally from above. The castle also has a 'murder hole': two portcullises with a space between. People trying to gain entry who were not in favour could be trapped between the two gates and killed from above.

On one of the ruined walls within the castle appears to be a carving of a face, an image that apparently changes according to the light. Perhaps it is a carving, perhaps a simulacrum; local stories believe it to be a likeness of de Soulis himself which cannot be checked as there are no known likenesses of him.

Research indicates that possibly the stories of William de Soulis may be a combination of two previous owners' histories. One early owner was Nicholas de Soulis, known to have been brutal and villainous. A later owner, Sir William Douglas, is known to have starved Sir Alexander Ramsey to death in the obliette.

The castle was also later owned by James Hepburn, Earl of Bothwell. One of his visitors at the castle was Mary, Queen of Scots, whom he married after he helped murder her husband Lord Darnley. A previous custodian claims to have seen Bothwell's ghost walking across the courtyard. Another ghost locally believed to haunt the castle battlements is a solitary figure thought to be John Stenhouse of Hawick.

Outside the castle, in the grounds, is an area of the river, Hermitage Water, known as 'the drowning pool', where it is believed murders took place in earlier centuries. In July 1996 a visitor reported that she was pushed from behind there, when there was no-one anywhere near her.

One workman reported seeing a figure standing in an upper-floor window when the castle was locked and empty – a fascinating claim as there are no floors in that area of the Hermitage and the figure would have been around 30 feet from the ground!

On 28 September 1990 the custodian, Jenny Much, was closing up the castle for the night. It was around 7.30pm. The key would not turn and oil brought to lubricate it had no effect. A replacement key would not work either. Jenny's dog, usually at ease in the castle, was agitated. As she drove away that night she was convinced she could hear 'laughing' and she was very frightened. Six years later to the day, 28 September 1996, Jenny was closing up again when the batteries in her torch suddenly failed and again the door could not be locked. No-one knows if there is any particular significance to the date in the castle's history.

Name: The Spectral Horseman
Location: Wycoller Hall, Wycoller, Lancashire, north-west England
Date: 1929 and earlier
Source: Peter Crawley and Colin Veacock of Ghost Quest / local newspaper coverage

Wycoller Hall is said to be the reality behind Fearndene Manor in Charlotte Bronte's Jane Eyre. Indeed, the Hall has been abandoned and decaying since the days when the Bronte sisters would walk down from Howorth to Wycoller over 150 years ago. The ruins are now open to the air. Perhaps its most dramatic feature, now clearly visible from outside, is the huge fireplace, today surrounded by shrubs and vegetation.

It is said that one of the Cunliffe family, who owned the Hall, murdered his wife by beating her to death with a horsewhip after he had returned to find her in the arms of a lover. In another account, the lover is discovered to be a long-lost brother of the killer, the murder condemning him to a spectral existence. Certainly, one of the main ghostly legends of Wycoller Hall is one of a horseman who gallops on a spectral steed across the moors up to the packhorse bridge at Wycoller Dene. The ghost dismounts and climbs the steps of the Hall, within which the screams of the murder are heard re-enacted before the horseman gallops off again into the night. The spectral horseman, consumed with remorse, became condemned to return to the scene every year as penance, so the local legend goes.

Another famous ghost of Wycoller Hall is the Black Lady, or Black Bess as she is known. In that legend, perhaps even derived from the story related above, it is said that a squire, Simon Cunliffe, chased a fox into the Hall pursued by the hunt and the hounds but, on seeing this, his wife Bess screamed and Simon Cunliffe whipped her to death with his horsewhip for her extreme sensitivity. E.W. Folley, in his book *Romantic Wycoller*, states: 'Simon Cunliffe swore a great oath and cursed her chicken-heartedness.' The story is that she re-appears in the rustling black dress she wore on the day to occasional frightened visitors. In other accounts the Black Lady is seen wandering wistfully by the village stream. She is known to have frightened off at least one pair of young lovers she encountered.

James Carr in *Annuls and Stories of Colne* reports that in the early years of the 20th century a young girl and her lover were seated in one of the decaying rooms of the Hall, locked in each other's arms, when the pair heard the sound of footsteps and the rustling of a woman's dress. 'Suddenly they held their breath; nearer and nearer came the footsteps, the door opened noiselessly, and in glided a lady clothed from head to foot in black silk. She uttered not a word, but casting one long, anxious look around the room and seeing only the frightened lovers, withdrew as quietly as she had entered.' To her dying day the girl who had witnessed it said she could never forget the apparition of the 'Lady in Black'.

E.W. Folley is said to have been one of the witnesses to the ghost, though he never officially recorded the fact in his writings. Local historian Geoff Crambie believes that Folley, who died many years ago, saw the ghost in 1947.

It appears that sightings go back right through the 20th century and probably even earlier. There is an account in the local *Daily Telegraph* of Saturday 2 February 1929 written by Elliott O'Donnell, who set out the account of Mr Lebrun, from the Channel Islands, who was on a walking tour in the north of England and took shelter under a hedge near Wycoller Hall: 'Suddenly distinct above the roaring of the elements came the sound of horses' hooves. There was something curious about them, something that puzzled the listener, something he could not define. As they drew nearer the rain suddenly ceased and the moon, which had hitherto been hidden behind a thick bed of clouds, shone forth illuminating the road and a field beyond with a cold white glow. Lebrun was about to continue his walk and was already stamping on the ground to restore his circulation when the sound of the hooves drew close and the next moment a man on a big black horse dashed frantically past him in the direction of Wycoller. He was gone so quickly that Lebrun had not even caught a glimpse of his face. He only noticed, much to his surprise, that the horseman wore a very wide-brimmed hat with what looked like a plume in it, high boots belonging to a bygone day, and a long, loose voluminous coat; and that the horse's accoutrements also appeared to be of a very antique and picturesque description. Indeed, so struck was Lebrun with the altogether strange appearance of the horse and horseman that he commented on it the following day to someone in the neighbourhood. This person immediately told Mr Lebrun about the haunting and was genuinely surprised when he learnt that Mr Lebrun had never heard, until then, of the Phantom Horseman of Wycoller Hall.'

Echoes of the haunting may well still exist at the Hall. Peter Crawley and Colin Veacock, of Ghost Quest, have studied the ruins of Wycoller Hall since 1995. On 26 July 1996 they were about to leave the outlines of the scullery when they heard a sound similar to that of a riding crop.

Name: The Stonemason And Others
Location: United States Capitol, Washington DC, USA
Date: From 1793
Source: Various

The domed Capitol building in Washington DC, the seat of government, has many alleged hauntings. The first is probably the stonemason who, legend tells us, during the building's construction had an argument with a carpenter who then beat him and walled him into the structure, using the mason's own trowel to seal his tomb.

Other ghosts include Presidents John Quincy Adams and James Garfield, an unidentified First World War soldier, and a huge demon cat supposedly prowling the halls at night. But the most frequent reports are of the spirits of House of Representatives Speakers Joseph G. Cannon and Champ Clark, who had a heated debate in the chamber and who, Capitol guards have said, have been seen still arguing in the chamber long after their deaths.

Name: The White Lady Lover
Location: Wolfsegg Fortress, River Danube, Bavaria, southern
  Germany
Date: 14th century onwards
Source: Various

The Bavarian fortress of Wolfsegg was built in 1028 and is said never to have fallen to its enemies. However, there is a story of conspiracy dating back to the 14th century, which is alleged to have created a White Lady ghost that haunts the present ruins. It is said that a baron of the castle married a woman and that his relatives contrived to convince him that she was having an illicit affair. Convinced by their machinations, he killed his wife and her supposed lover, who had been set up by the relatives. Then the baron himself was murdered by the relatives, who claimed that their act was one of justice and revenge and they inherited his property. The slain baroness in luminous white has been reported walking the rooms of Wolfsegg. Several people have seen the apparition and have heard her phantom footsteps.

Name: The Witchhunts
Location: Salem, Massachusetts, USA
Date: 1692 onwards
Source: Various

Outside of Europe, probably the most famous witchcraft persecution was in Salem (now known as Danvers), Massachusetts, in 1692.

A few young girls in Salem started playing games of divination – not unlike schoolgirls and schoolboys have for centuries – and as the stories spread so hysteria began to affect the Puritan community. Some of the girls acted as if demonically possessed; we would probably recognise it today as clinical hysteria. This bizarre behaviour spread from Elizabeth Parris and her cousin Abigail to their friends.

It was Mary Sibley, aunt of one of the friends, who first invoked the subject of witchcraft. She asked a Caribbean slave to bake a witch's cake, supposedly resulting in the children being able to name those responsible for their condition. Arrest warrants were then issued.

The accused were brought before magistrates John Hathorne and Jonathan Corwin. In the manner of so many witchhunts, the girls accused others. By the end of the summer 141 people had been accused. Ultimately, 19 'witches' were hanged on Witch's Hill and one man, Giles Corey, was pressed to death.

Common sense took some time to return to the town. Around five years later all 12 jurors of the trials signed admissions of error: 'do hereby declare that we justly fear that we were sadly deluded and mistaken . . . and do humbly beg forgiveness . . .' The judge of the trials similarly expressed his sorrow.

Many believe that the horrors of the witchhunts have left their impression on the town in the form of hauntings. Those executed are said to have returned to various locations in 'Old Salem'; on Witch's Hill, where one claim is that all 19 victims have been seen 'swinging' from invisible gallows, and in the former home of Jonathan Corwin, which became known as the Witch House. The most fearful haunting would appear to be the echo of the screams of Giles Corey as he was slowly crushed beneath a weight of rocks piled up on his chest until he could no longer breathe. The appearance of Corey's ghost near the Old Jail is also held to be a bad omen for the town.

Perhaps the sense of injustice the witchhunts caused is part of the reason for the hauntings in the town.

Name: A Wizened Face
Location: Dublin, Republic of Ireland
Date: 1959
Source: Strange Phenomena Investigations (SPI)/Malcolm Robinson

At the age of 22 Ms Teresa Fleming moved into her new flat unbelieving of her good fortune. She loved the flat and her first few weeks there were ideal. But shortly after that she began to experience phenomena she could not explain. As she described: 'As I was watching television I heard footsteps coming up the stairs, and as the flat was over a shop and the building was detached and I had my own separate entrance, I knew something was wrong. But on investigation I discovered nothing and I put it down to my imagination.

'However, as I arrived home from work the next evening, I was climbing the stairs and there appeared to be a small "wizened" face of a man wearing glasses looking at me. Then it disappeared as I reached the top. That same night I heard what I thought were chains being dragged along the landing as I lay in bed and [they] stopped outside my bedroom door.

'I borrowed a friend's alsatian dog who knew me well and whom I had looked after many times. He started crying and throwing himself at my door. The next day he couldn't wait to get out, and he never again would come and stay with me.

'From then on things got worse. Lights turned on in various rooms and the phone would ring during the night with no-one at the other end. I had the wiring for both checked but nothing was amiss. Still the dragging noises continued. I was very frightened by this time but as I had put my savings into furnishing the flat, I was unable to move.

'Not content with scaring me, the ghost not only kept up his dragging sound along the corridor until it reached my bedroom, but the door would suddenly open about 12 inches, then the wardrobe door would swing open and the key which was always in the wardrobe door disappeared. Then one day I arrived home from work to find that my wardrobe had been pushed to the other side of the room. I put it back in place and went to take a bath, and just as I was about to leave the bathroom, the whole ceiling fell and missed me by a hair's breadth. On looking up, I again saw the wizened face of that old man.

'That same night, just after I went to bed, my door was suddenly thrown wide open with such force that it hit the wall. I was literally stuck to the bed with fear, and after five months in my home I decided that I couldn't take any more of these "happenings" and moved out, selling what I could and leaving the rest.'

Although Ms Fleming had had paranormal experiences as a child, and indeed did so later after she left the flat, she commented, 'Never will I forget the awful five months at the flat which I had envisaged as being my home for life.'

Ghosts With A Message

A sense of purpose or duty characterises people the world over. The classic studies of motivation show that after the basic requirements of food, shelter and safety have been met, the next human need is to feel valued, to know that what we do has worth to ourselves, others and the world at large. If there is a 'return' from beyond the grave, then it is hardly surprising that some come back to fulfil a mission not completed, to impart some information they might regret not having done in life. For some it is to give a warning, for others to say goodbye; sometimes it is for reasons which seem to be almost trivial – like the case of Mimi's Jewellery below – but perhaps not trivial to the person involved. And always we have to ask ourselves who creates the ghost or spirit; is it the deceased with a sense of purpose, the living with a sense of need, or a combination of factors? This chapter may hold a few of the clues we need to answer the mysteries of hauntings.

Name: Alex Scott
Location: The Derby, Epsom, Surrey, southern England
Date: Saturday 10 June 1995
Source: The Mail on Sunday, 11 June 1995

Several racecourses in Britain are reputed to be haunted, usually by former jockeys or trainers. The most recent addition to the list was Epsom Downs during the first Derby held on a Saturday in 42 years. The winning jockey, Walter Swinburn, believed that he was helped in his victory by the spirit of murdered trainer Alex Scott.

Scott had been murdered in 1994 in a shooting incident at his home in Cheveley, near Newmarket. He had said before his death that he believed his horse Lammtarra would one day win the race. Scott's widow, Julia, commented, 'His horse meant so much to Alex. It was the apple of his eye.' She did not attend the 1995 Derby, saying, 'I don't need to go to Epsom as I know Alex will be there in spirit. I can feel him looking over my shoulder, even as I say this.'

Swinburn, after winning the race, commented, 'He was helping me from above . . .' He added, 'I know he was helping me from above because from everything going wrong in the first two furlongs, just everything went right after that, then I know he paved the way. I got chopped at the mile-and-a-quarter gate and had to make the inside rail. When we came down the hill, I said, "Please give me daylight. Please, God. Please, Alex." Sure enough I got daylight, like Moses in the Red Sea. Once I got that daylight, once he was into overdrive, I knew the race was ours.'

Name: Alis
Location: St Pierre de Lyon, France
Date: 1526
Source: Various

In 1526 (or 1528, according to researcher Harry Price) an 18-year-old sister at the nunnery of St Pierre de Lyon, Anthoinette de Grollee, had a strange experience that was to lead to an early account of poltergeistery. She was alone in her room when she felt a presence lift her veil, make a sign on her forehead and kiss her. She opened her eyes to see who had intruded on her isolation and found that she was alone. Rationally, Anthoinette dismissed the experience as a dream.

But within just a few days she started to consider other possibilities. She heard rapping noises coming from the floor beneath her, sounds which other nuns also heard. The noises followed Anthoinette as she moved about, and they were never heard if she was not present.

Adrian de Montalembert was asked by the bishop if he would investigate the reports. He wrote of the noises: 'I have often heard it,' and 'It would rap as many blows as I demanded.'

Anthoinette decided that it might be communication from a former nun, Alis de Telieux. Alis had left the nunnery some years before, after she had been found stealing. She had died, destitute and diseased. Anthoinette and Alis had been close friends and Anthoinette often dreamed of her.

The rapping was used as a form of communication in much the same way that the Fox sisters would do 300 years later; and through the rapping it was confirmed that the spirit in the nunnery was indeed Alis. She wished to be buried in the abbey. The Abbess agreed and Alis's body was exhumed from its grave and brought to the abbey. During a service for the deliverance of Alis from purgatory, Anthoinette apparently took on the personality of the deceased and asked for absolution.

Shortly after the service Adrian de Montalembert returned to the abbey and, again by rapping, Alis indicated that she was free of purgatory. There is a report that during this communication Anthoinette levitated. The final act in this extraordinary tale came shortly afterwards on the feast day of St Benedict when 33 loud raps were heard, followed by an 'unendurable' bright light which 'burned' for eight minutes. St Benedict had been Alis's patron saint.

Name: Aunt Leah
Location: Weston, North Yorkshire, northern England
Date: 1910 onwards
Source: *Man's Survival After Death* by Reverend Charles L. Tweedale

The Reverend Tweedale's Aunt Leah died on 13 August 1905. Having seemingly been at peace for a number of years, her apparition was seen and through several other manifestations she began to make herself known, apparently with a specific purpose in mind. There had been one manifestation of something seen as 'a winged figure, something like a cherub in appearance'. There were poltergeist-like noises, scratching sounds that seemed to belong to a bird and the growling sound of an animal which was believed to be Aunt Leah's terrier who also came back with her from 'beyond the veil'. The dog, which had died years before Aunt Leah, apparently would return and on one occasion sprang at Mrs Tweedale while she was walking upstairs. Mrs Tweedale and their servant, Ida, also watched once as the dog jumped up and rang the dinner gong.

Aunt Leah's most dramatic apparitional appearance was on Christmas afternoon 1910 when, clad in white, she appeared from behind a curtain and passed physically through the Christmas tree without disturbing it or displacing any of the ornaments hanging on it.

Aunt Leah's ghost also had the habit of shouting the Christian names of members of the family from the top of the stairs 'in a most wonderful, indescribably sad, wailing tone'. She disturbed objects in bedrooms, startled servants on the stairs and had long conversations with Mr Tweedale's mother Marie, her sister in life. The Reverend

Tweedale heard her voice but never actually saw her. Nonetheless, his wife, his mother, three children and two servants saw and heard Aunt Leah and he wrote: 'The witnesses signed the various statements in my presence, and on oath, which I am also prepared to do independently where my own testimony is concerned.'

Aunt Leah, now communicating by rapping, apparently explained that she was unhappy because her name had not been carved on the family vault. She later confirmed this in voice to her sister Marie, 'her wonderful voice seeming to come from the ceiling'. The family did indeed carve an inscription on the vault, presumably expecting this to bring the sighting to an end. But Aunt Leah had not yet finished with the material world. As the Reverend Tweedale wrote: 'My Aunt Leah continued to manifest wonderfully for several months, appearing to the various members of the household, and also speaking in the direct voice, audible to all present. She was last seen and heard on 9 February 1913 when, appearing suddenly, tall and white, her face plump and clearly visible, she took out of my wife's hand an article she much used when in Earth life, saying: "It's Leah's, it's mine." The dog continued to be seen from time to time, notably on 25 December 1911 (another sociable Christmas visit!) when it was seen in our bedroom, and again on 8 October 1914.'

Name: Bell Farm Apparitions
Location: Beaminster, Dorset, southern England
Date: 1998
Source: Stephen Hall, national investigations co-ordinator for
ASSAP, and investigator Ian Percy

There is a ghost report which relates to the parish church of St Mary in Beaminster. It first appeared in *The Gentleman's Magazine* in 1774 and is recalled in the current official literature of the church. During the spring of 1728 the body of a local boy, John Daniel, was found in a field near his home. His mother testified that he suffered from fits and he was buried without inquest. At the time the parish church of St Mary was being used as a school room. On 27 June 1728 some of the boys were playing in the churchyard, while some were inside the church, and they heard something that sounded like the striking of a brass pan. The boys searched the building but found no-one.

As they were ending their search they heard the sounds of a religious service followed by singing. When these sounds had stopped, one of the boys, looking for a school book, entered the school room and was shocked to see, in the room, a coffin lying on a bench. He called the others and five boys together returned to the room where they all saw the apparition of the dead John Daniel sitting some distance away from the coffin. He was holding a pen in his hand and had what looked like a book next to him. Four of the five boys had known him in life. In fact, one of the boys was Daniel's half-brother and immediately recognised him and the coat he was wearing. This boy picked up a stone and threw it at the apparition; immediately the ghost, the pen, the book and the coffin disappeared.

Colonel Brodrepp, a local magistrate, investigated the boys' claims and found that their stories agreed even to the minutest detail, and that their description of the coffin was accurately like the one that Daniel had been buried in. Even the account of the one boy who had not known Daniel in life was corroborative. This boy, however, added one piece of information. He said that there was a white cloth around one of the hands of the apparition. It later transpired that the woman who had laid Daniel out for burial had indeed removed such a white cloth from the boy's hand – he had apparently suffered a small injury days before his death.

The body of Daniel was exhumed and it was discovered that in fact he had been murdered by strangulation, though there is no record of anyone having been brought to justice for the crime. If that was the ghost's intended message, it was indeed a dramatic one.

In 1998 it appeared that the story was to take on new 'life'. Stephen Hall led the investigation into haunting phenomena at neighbouring Bell Farm for ASSAP. The following is extracted from the ASSAP report in Stephen's own words: 'The *Bridport News* of 27 August 1998 carried the story of a local farmer, David Potter, who had reported seeing two ghosts in his fields. I spoke at length with him about the incidents that had been occurring, then arranged for a formal interview for Sunday 6 September at his farm.

'Ian Percy and I visited Bell Farm and interviewed the witness and his wife. David Potter told us how it started. On 18 August at 4.45am Mr Potter went out into his field, which is abutted by the Daniel family burial ground, to check on some cows which were close to calving. He did not have his torch switched on at the time, but he had a strange feeling he was not alone in the field. One of the cows had already calved and Mr Potter switched on his torch to see where the cow was. He located the cow, but to his astonishment he saw two figures standing by it (just as if they were watching it calve). They were about ten paces away from Mr Potter. One of the figures he thought was a woman, because she was wearing what appeared to be a long white gown "coming off from her head about ear level", which appeared to be flowing. She seemed solid in appearance. The other was (he believed) a child wearing a dark outfit. He thought it was a young boy but could not be certain because he could not see the child's face, as it was slightly distorted. Mr Potter observed that it went very cold as he watched the couple, and he commented that it was an indescribable sensation.

'As he shone his torch on the couple, the woman turned and faced Mr Potter and her eyes shone bright pink in a way he could not describe, which fixed him to the spot he was standing on. He was unable to move. The couple moved across the field and a cow which was lying down on the ground got up as if to move out of their way. Mr Potter then heard the graveyard's gates open and close. This really spooked him and he panicked, quickly leaving the field, and he was still shaking several hours later. Mrs Potter commented that she had never seen him so frightened. Mr Potter later checked the graveyard but found nothing unusual.

'We examined the family burial plot where the apparitions had moved towards. The first thing we noticed was that the gate was in very good state of repair, which we found somewhat unusual considering the rest of the plot was in such a generally bad state. It appeared as if it had been freshly painted and oiled, which defied explanation, as we were led to believe that no one had paid any attention to it for a number of years. We also noticed that the gate lock opened very easily, as if it had also been freshly oiled. It seemed odd that the gate had been so well maintained while the remainder of the plot had been left in decline and in a general state of disrepair.

'Mr Potter informed us that the activity seemed to coincide with the visit of an elderly relative of the Daniel family requesting a visit to the grave site. Mr and Mrs Potter believe that she wishes to be buried there when she passes on. It should be noted that this elderly relative had paid a visit to the grave, and from the conversations we have had with Mr Potter, it would seem that these occurrences started at the same time as her visit.'

Stephen and Ian believe it likely that the apparitions were of Daniel and his mother. It would seem possible that the hauntings were 'triggered' by the visit to the grave of one of their living relatives.

Name: Chain Rattling
Location:Athens, Greece
Date: 1st century
Source: Various

The chain-rattling ghost of Athens is argued by some to be the very first story of a haunted house. It was recorded by the Roman author Pliny the Younger.

Pliny noted that a large house in Athens had remained empty for some years because it was apparently haunted by the ghost of an old man who rattled chains and made moaning noises. Then the philosopher Athenodorus visited Athens, saw the house and decided that it would be the right place for him to do some contemplative study. He paid a low price for the rent as the owners were quite honest with him and told him that it was because the house was haunted. He claimed he was not afraid of ghosts and set himself up for his studies. He did, however, remain awake throughout the first night, perhaps nervous, or more likely curious. During the night he heard the sound of rattling chains approaching him and when he looked up saw the apparition of an old man beckoning to him. Athenodorus ignored this and the ghost moaned and rattled still further. Unable to concentrate, Athenodorus followed the apparition through the corridors and into the garden, where the ghost disappeared in a dense clump of bushes. Athenodorus noted the spot and then returned to the house to sleep.

The following day, Athenodorus reported the incident to the local authorities and magistrates arrived at the house to dig in the place indicated. There, under the earth, they found a skeleton wearing chains and shackles. The body was exhumed and buried with proper respect and the haunting ceased.

Name: A Change Of Heart
Location: Davie County , North Carolina, USA
Date: June 1925
Source: Various

James L. Chaffin died in 1921 leaving all of his estate to his first son, Marshall Chaffin, and ignoring his other three sons and his wife. No doubt they were disappointed but the will was not contested.

Four years later, in June 1925, one of the younger sons, James Chaffin, dreamed that his father was standing by his bedside wearing a black overcoat. The apparition told him, 'You will find the will in my overcoat pocket.' The following morning James told his mother about the incident and asked where his father's black overcoat was; it was with his brother John. At John's house the coat was found and examined thoroughly. Sewn into the lining was a slip of paper stating: 'Read the 27th chapter of Genesis in my Daddy's old Bible.' With a neighbour to witness events, James returned to his mother's house, looked at the Bible and found a will in the pages of the 27th chapter of Genesis. This will divided the property evenly between the wife and four sons. Although Marshall at first suspected the new will was a forgery, he came to believe it was his father's handwriting, something which was also attested to by ten witnesses. The property was therefore divided according to the new-found will.

The 27th chapter of Genesis tells the story of how Jacob tricked his blind father into granting him the estate of his brother Esau; perhaps James L. Chaffin had had some doubts about the integrity of his son Marshall. The speculation is that the father had expected the will to be discovered when the Bible was used but that after four years it had not been so discovered and therefore his spirit had set out to draw attention to his dying wishes.

Name: Cured Of Fright?
Location: Inverurie, Scotland
Date: Mid 1900s
Source: Strange Phenomena Investigations (SPI)/Malcolm Robinson

Ms Christine Ramsay contacted SPI to report a comforting apparition which, as it turned out, harked back to an incident in her childhood.

One day Christine was lying in bed because of an illness and associated pain. Just after her husband drove off to work, she heard her bedroom door open and then close, and she heard footsteps walking towards her bedside. She knew intuitively that it was her grandmother who had died of cancer some five years earlier. 'I sat up straight in bed and asked my gran to show herself, which she did. She was sitting on the edge of my bed. She looked incredible, so beautiful. Her hair was glossy and her skin was a very healthy-looking pink. She wore her glasses and a coat buttoned up to her neck.'

Her grandmother asked her immediately, 'Are you frightened, are you frightened now?' Christine told her grandmother she was not frightened and hugged her. As she commented: 'She was warm and

as solid as you or I. She told me about my deceased Aunty Betty who
for the last 20 years of her life had been without the use of her legs.
My gran said she was now walking perfectly. Gran also spoke about
other relatives, living and "dead".' Apparently they talked for around
an hour and then Christine lay down on her bed, put her hand over
her eyes and fell asleep. As Christine said: 'It was the best sleep I'd had
in weeks.'

Christine then went to see her mother to tell her of the encounter.
Her mother told Christine a story from the day before her grandmother had died. The family had gone to visit for the last time, going
into her room in pairs. Christine and her sister had been the first in,
but Christine soon ran out, disturbed because the person lying in the
bed had not looked like the grandmother she knew; in her illness she
had become thin and pale. Apparently the grandmother had then
called for her daughter (Christine's mother) and said to her, 'I've
frightened Christine, I've frightened Christine.'

It seems to have brought peace to both surviving generations, and
perhaps the grandmother as well, to know that that fright had ended
and that Christine was now at peace with the image of her
grandmother.

Name: Father's Warning
Location: Duffryn-Rhondda, Glamorgan, Wales
Date: Approx 1970
Source: T. Llewellyn (witness) / authors' own files.

'About two years after my father, John, died, he came back to me. I
was at that time about 24. My father had not been a well man, having
suffered from heart problems for many years, and unfortunately he
contracted Asian flu during the epidemic in the 1960s. He passed
away at a hospital in Swansea.

'On the night in question the events started as a prank. My
brother-in-law, Dennis, was apt to playing the odd trick and on this
night he took the pull cord of my bedroom light, hid behind the
door and then switched the light off. He then shook me awake and I
woke to find the room in total darkness. I turned round to face the
wall and there standing with his back to the wall was someone who
looked as if he had a dark sheet wrapped around him. Thinking it
was Dennis up to his old tricks I swore at him and at that moment
this person slowly walked up to my bed and when he came close I
could see it was not Dennis. My father stood there looking at me.

When he moved, a kind of phosphorous light came from him. I lost
my voice and my heart was racing and my hand went through him.
I ended up on the floor of the bedroom in shock. I believe he came
to warn me of something.'

Name: Fisher's Ghost
Location: Fisher's Ghost Creek, Australia
Date: 20th century
**Source: Georgina Keep, Local Studies Librarian, Cambelltown
City Library**

On the road from Sydney to Melbourne, near Cambelltown, is
Fisher's Ghost Creek. Frederick Fisher was the name of a murder
victim whose body was not located during the investigation into his
disappearance. The ghost of Fisher was said to have been seen sitting
on the bridge at the Creek, and pointing to a particular location. By
working out the exact spot the ghost had been pointing to, from the
eye-witness testimonies, Fisher's body was located. The murderer was
found, tried, prosecuted and hanged for the crime; after that, the
ghost was apparently laid to rest and was seen no more.

Many elements of the story appear legendary to us, though the
story is strongly believed locally. Frederick Fisher and his ghost are
commemorated in a street parade called 'Fisher's Ghost Festival',
which is a two week celebration of the legend held every November
since the 1950s.

Name: The Green Briar Ghost
Location: Green Briar, West Virginia, USA
Date: 23 January 1897
Source: Various

On 23 January 1897 the body of Zona Heaster Shue was found on
the kitchen floor of her home in Green Briar, West Virginia, by an
errand boy, Andy Jones. Her body was examined by a doctor who
declared that she had died naturally, and she was duly buried. The
doctor, it transpired, was restricted in his examination by Edward
Shue cradling his wife's head and crying with grief throughout; he
prevented the doctor from studying the back of her head. There was
a good deal of sympathy for her husband Edward (sometimes given

as Erasmus), the local blacksmith, who was regarded as a kind and virtuous citizen.

A short while after Zona's funeral her mother, Mary Jane Heaster, saw Zona's ghost on several occasions and spoke to her at least four times. Zona's spirit was insisting that she had in fact been beaten to death by her husband, apparently because she had not prepared meat for his dinner that night. Mary Jane demanded an investigation into her daughter's death and Zona's body was exhumed on 22 February and underwent an extensive autopsy. This revealed that she had indeed suffered a severe attack which had resulted in a broken neck and crushed windpipe. Edward Shue was arrested, convicted of murdering his wife and sentenced to life imprisonment. He died of natural causes in his cell three years later. Zona's ghost never reappeared, apparently having achieved its quest for justice.

An historical marker on the highway confirms that the case is the 'only known case in which testimony from ghost helped convict a murderer'. It has, however, been speculated that Mary Jane made up the ghost story to justify her suspicions; in the same newspaper that announced her daughter's death was a story from Australia about a murder case that had been solved by a ghost sighting – ironically one in which a man later confessed he had made up the ghost story to avoid having to admit to being a witness to the crime.

Name: Harry Perkins
Location: Northampton, central England
Date: Not specified (mid 20th century)
Source: Douglas (witness) / authors' own files

Approximately one month after moving into their Northamptonshire home, Douglas and his family began hearing strange noises in the early hours of the morning. After a few months they noticed that Caroline, Douglas's nine-year-old sister, was speaking to someone that was apparent to her. She could see and hear him and was apparently fully interactive with him, he being able to respond to her questions. Douglas did not believe his sister but, as he explained: 'A couple of nights later, I was in bed and my brother was across the room from me – I always know when he is asleep because his sheets are off and he is "sweaty". I was just about to doze off when I felt a whack on my head; I found that it was a pillow from my brother's bed, but he was still fast asleep. I actually felt a presence in the room and from then on I believed; throughout the next occurrences we sort of accepted it. He is actually quite friendly.'

Douglas went on: 'My sister found out his name, which is Harry Perkins. He said he used to fly from Sywell Airport, which is the local airport here. He said he was flying after having a fight with someone – it might have been something to do with a girlfriend or something like that – and he crashed on the land near this house.'

Their mother, Margaret, has also seen Harry Perkins and described him as wearing a black polo neck; she has indicated that he appears to be about 25 and is very good looking. Apparently, every time she sees him he is smiling. Interestingly, Buddy (her partner) apparently also sees him but usually in a uniform. For some reason he appears to be 'not too pleased' with Buddy.

Douglas offered an interesting story relating to his brother Nicholas. The family believes that Harry Perkins tries to 'help us out'. Apparently, Nicholas woke up once feeling somebody trying to wake him and, just as he woke up, heard his car being broken into. The family believes that Harry might have been trying to warn him.

Douglas said: 'We have friends come in and they actually see Harry, walking across from the kitchen. You don't see through him, you see him like you would an ordinary person.'

Name: A Healing Apparition?
Location: Skegness, Lincolnshire, eastern England
Date: 1990s
Source: Steven Thomas (witness) / authors' own files

Silent apparitions can bring about many reactions in witnesses, from amazement through disturbance and even fear. This report, however, contains a rarer response: a belief that the apparition either had some healing capability or was perhaps calming enough to allow the witness to heal himself. Perhaps this visitation does not contain a message in the strict sense, but purpose.

The witness is Steven Thomas, and the apparition was of his father who had died some years before, on 12 March 1983. As Mr Thomas described to us:

'I was ill in bed suffering from stomach acid. I was in so much pain that the doctor told me that if the pain did not go away I would have to go into hospital.

'This is a bit hard to explain. I was, the next day, still in bed when suddenly I could see, in addition to my bedroom door, another, apparitional, door at the foot of my bed and my father came through

it into my bedroom. He didn't stay for long; he just came in and then
went out again. The pain had been just about killing me, but as soon
as Father went, the pain went. I was back on my feet.'

Name: High On Everest
Location: Mount Everest, Nepal
Date: 1993
Source: *Night and Day*, 11 June 2000

The actor Brian Blessed, arguably as famous for his mountain
climbing exploits as for his acting, related a story of an experience he
had while climbing Everest in 1993. 'My grandfather appeared to me
as a young man and said: "You'll climb it later, Brian, but for the
moment you have to go down, lad." I said: "I will, Grandad, I will."
I turned away but when I turned back, he was in exactly the same
position. He wasn't in my mind. He was as tangible as you are.'

Blessed added, presumably thinking of a time after his own death:
'I think the lines are very well connected between the living and the
dead, so I will certainly keep an eye on my daughter from wherever
I am.'

Name: In The Car Park
Location: Ealing, west London, England
Date: Friday 10 December 1999, 9.30am
Source: Judith Ja'afar (witness), as related to the authors

Judith is a valued colleague of ours, a leading UFO investigator and
researcher of the paranormal. But sometimes researchers find themselves on the 'other side of the camera'; this is Judith's own story of
a ghostly encounter. The joy of this, as the reader will appreciate, is
that Judith has the experience and knowledge of the subject to
question her own sighting and analyse it for the reader. She is also
able to articulate the extraordinary feelings that such encounters
impress in the witness.

'This puzzling encounter took place outside my office at 9.30am, as
I pulled into the front car park. The layout of the car parking area is
important: there is an open parking area in front of the building
directly as you pull in from the road, with spaces marked out to the
right and left. Directly in front is the entrance to a steep ramp that takes
you down underneath the building, where there are several covered

spaces, and leads out into a larger open car park at the back. I always park in this open area at the back. There are no exits in either the covered area or the open area at the rear, and the outside is completely walled-in. The only way in is down the ramp, and the only way out is back up the ramp. The entrance to the offices is to the right as you drive in, about 40 feet behind the beginning of the ramp. It is a fairly wide plate-glass frontage, which leads to an entrance lobby with a door in the rear wall leading to stairs and the lift. Anyone entering or leaving the building can be clearly seen from the outside.

'As I pulled in, I immediately noticed a woman walking towards me from the direction of the entrance doors, and just near the tall lamppost that is situated at the top of the ramp. I did not see her coming out of the building. She was leaning over to her left side, with her left arm up at the left side of her head. My immediate thought was that she had come out of the building to use a mobile phone. I saw that she was wearing unseasonably lightweight clothing on such a cold morning – a long, black, floaty kind of skirt, black heeled shoes and a cream and black horizontally-striped top with short sleeves and a drawstring waist. She was not wearing a jacket or overcoat.

'As I drew level with her, just before going down the ramp, I realised that she did not have a mobile phone, but appeared to be holding her head in pain or discomfort. By this time she was no more than six feet away from me and I managed to get a good look at her face. She was very pretty, with shoulder-length blonde hair, and appeared to be in her late twenties. Why I felt compelled to take in so much detail about a stranger "just passing" didn't make any sense to me until a moment later. As I was making these "in an instant" observations, she raised her head and looked directly at me. What I saw in her clear blue eyes shook me to the core – such a profound sadness and desolation, a pleading for help, the like of which I have never seen before and which I find I do not have a suitable vocabulary to adequately describe.

'All this was happening while I was slowly approaching the ramp (I didn't stop the car at any time), and I had been so sorely affected by this puzzling encounter that I made a mental note to rush back up after parking the car, approach the woman and offer my assistance. To my surprise, as I reached the bottom of the ramp and was emerging into the back car park, through my rear-view mirror I saw that the figure had followed me and was walking quite smartly down the steep incline. I then decided that she must be feeling so unwell that she had decided to get a breath of the clean, cold December air. But why wasn't she wearing a coat or jacket?

Then I reasoned that she must be making her way to a car, possibly to retrieve something she had forgotten. But if she worked in the building, why hadn't I seen her before (or since)? I knew everyone that worked in the offices. Visitors to the building are not permitted to use the parking facilities and must leave their cars in a public lot across the road.

'I was considering all these things as I pulled into my parking space, trying to make sense of something that I already knew, in the very core of my being, was "all wrong". After I had parked my car, but before I had switched off the engine, I glanced out of my right-side window to check her location and found her just about to emerge into the open area, about ten feet away from me. Her gait was very determinedly carrying her forwards. She was, this time, looking straight ahead, as if oblivious to my close presence. But there was nowhere to go, except into a parked car. I knew then that I would easily be able to approach her and ask if she needed any help. My compulsion to offer assistance was by this time overwhelming. Why had this woman affected me so deeply?

'I switched off my car engine, reached over for my bag and opened the car door, at the same time looking out for the figure which had a moment before been almost within touching distance. There was no-one there! She had disappeared, it seemed, into the thin, cold air. I jumped out of the car with unusual alacrity and cast about looking for the woman. Nothing. I looked back up the ramp, telling myself that she must have done an amazingly fast about-turn in the couple of seconds when I wasn't watching her, but saw nothing. I then ran up the ramp myself, looked over to the entrance doors and into the lobby, scanned the small front car park and even ran out onto the street, looking both right and left. Nothing. Perhaps she had collapsed and had fallen under or behind one of the cars on the lower level? I ran back down and scoured the area, looking under and around every vehicle. Nothing. And nobody pulled out of either of the car parks. She had just "gone".

'I toyed with every rational explanation I could think of over the next few days, but I knew they were all impossible. I even reported the strange incident to my colleagues in the hope that one of them could come up with a sensible solution, or perhaps even recognise the description I gave of the woman. No joy.

'At no point during the episode did this woman appear to be other than a normal, if somewhat distressed, human being. She did not walk through walls (at least I don't think so), nor did she glide several inches above or below ground level. She negotiated obstacles in her path in a normal way. But it was the deliberate eye-contact she made with me that elevated the whole experience out of the mundane, and even out of the recording ghost category. There was purpose to this encounter, and that's what exercises my mind to this day. Why, and why me? If I had been a few minutes earlier or later, would the same episode have taken place, or did I just happen to be in the right place at the right time? Would it have happened to any other person who chanced to be coming into the office building, or was this reserved solely for me? I tend to believe that things happen for a reason, but for the life of me I can find no reason for such a strangely unsettling and ultimately frustrating experience.

'For someone who has not experienced such things, it is almost impossible to articulate the feelings that such encounters induce. Puzzlement, consternation and fear are common, accompanied by a "knowing" that supersedes all rational thought. A strange sense of immediacy and urgency invades the mind, telling the percipient that what is happening is important in a way that may not be understood, but sufficiently strongly to induce the brain to send out alarm signals to the adrenal glands, and to set the brain to search mode, looking for comfortable precedents. Analytical thought and physical movement are speeded up and enhanced as the body slips into fight or flight mode, the heart beats faster and excitement wells in the pit of the stomach. All these physiological reactions can be caused by normal, mundane fear, but when a person encounters something "other", for want of a better word, another dimension altogether is entered, metaphorically speaking. The sense of knowing is indisputable and unlike any other form of instinctive or intuitive response.

'My instincts had told me right from the first moments of the encounter that something was untoward about this whole situation. I believe we all have receptors that tune in from time to time to things "other", a faculty over and above our five senses which immediately tells us that we're dealing with something outside the norm. But I don't believe this is some airy-fairy "psychic" ability, rather a product of our human biology, and one day it will be scientifically identified as such.'

We have included this account in this chapter on the basis of Judith's speculation that the figure seemed to be interactive and seeking Judith out. But if she sought to give a message or a plea, what was it?

Name: 'Jim And Karen'
Location: Knebworth, Hertfordshire, southern England.
Date: Not given
Source: Jim Ferguson (witness) / authors' own files

A small example of unusual phenomena comes from Jim Ferguson, who described to us several events in his life. Some are recorded elsewhere in this book.

'One afternoon I was in the lounge and the stereo was turned off, though plugged in. This male voice came over the speaker. It said "Jim and Karen". I would say it was almost like a "broadcast-standard" voice. It had a positive and calm approach to it. When I checked the system, it was definitely turned off. I thought it was my wife, Karen, playing a joke and wondered, "How's she doing that?" At that point Karen came down the stairs and looked at me, suspecting that I was up to something. She had heard it from upstairs. It was very loud and kept repeating our names, "Jim and Karen". I said, "I'm not doing it. I just don't understand it at all."

'Then I began to feel slightly frightened because something was going on that we couldn't explain. I played around with the stereo but it didn't make any difference. Eventually I pulled the plug out and at that point, or just shortly after, it stopped.'

We suggested that sometimes police radios and the like come through speakers and telephones, though usually when switched on, unlike in this case. But Jim pointed out that such an explanation did not account for one thing: 'The voice was addressing both me and my wife by name.' He went on: 'It was somebody trying to attract our attention. That's what it sounded like. What he expected us to do, I've no idea.'

Name: Keith
Location: Massachusetts, USA
Date: 1990 onwards
Source: James (witness) / authors' own files

This story contains several of the oft-reported 'haunting' elements that follow a death, but with a persistence on the part of the deceased rarely experienced. The story is told in James's own words, related to us in 1997.

'I am a soon-to-be 35-year-old American man of Irish and German background. I pursue an "alternate lifestyle" – in other words I'm gay, which I mention only because it is pertinent to the tale.

'My first lover, with whom I lived for several years, came from a very dysfunctional family. So you can imagine I was quite surprised when after being diagnosed with AIDS in December 1988, Keith opted to return to his home. I accompanied him to help take care of him, but his family and I did not get along and they asked me to leave after only two months and forbade me to ever see him again. I was crushed, but left. At this point, AIDS-related dementia had set in and Keith was acting much like a child.

'In the summer of 1990, I was trying to get on with my life. I had met someone else, Brian (whom I still live with), and we were spending the summer in Massachusetts. Keith was now in a nursing home without a room phone, and I could no longer speak with him. On the morning of 30 July, I discovered that the watch Keith had given me for my birthday had stopped the night before at 11.20. On 1 August I received a phone call from Keith's home town telling me that Keith had died on 29 July. I was hardly surprised to discover that he had died at exactly 11.20pm.

'Later that year, around Christmas, I felt an awful need to get in touch with Keith's sister, the only member of his family that had treated me with any kindness whatsoever. We talked and she told me, "I know this is going to sound crazy, but when I got home from the hospital the night Keith died, all the clocks in the house had stopped at 11:20. I was so frightened I threw all the clocks out." When I told her about my watch she became quite agitated and begged me to change the subject.

'The following summer of 1991, Brian and I were again working the tourist season in Massachusetts. Around the anniversary of Keith's death, Brian and I were awakened at about 3am by the ringing of the phone (which was in the living room). Neither of us was awake enough to stumble out to get it, so we let the machine pick it up. Not being able to make out the voice from several rooms away, Brian said, "Who is that? I don't recognise that voice." Half-asleep, I muttered, "Sounds like Keith . . ." before dropping off again, not even thinking about what I had just said. Brian was off to work early the next morning, and so, alone with my cereal bowl, I sat down to play the odd message from the night before. Imagine my shock when, crystal clear, Keith's voice came over the machine, asking where I was, what I was doing, and why I was in Massachusetts instead of New York auditioning for Broadway. Then his voice left a number with the proper area code for his parents' home. I wrote down the number but then began trembling violently, tears coming to my eyes.

Then I made an enormous mistake. I was so stunned I didn't press "save" and the machine went into its automatic erase mode. Scientific proof – poof – gone! Still, I had the telephone number. I dialled. Keith's sister picked up and asked how I had gotten the number, as she had installed a new private line only a few days before and she was keeping it unlisted. I asked if anyone in her family could have been playing a trick on me by leaving me this number and told her about my late-night phone call. She was quiet for a moment and then informed me that her mother had also died a few months before, leaving her the house which she now lived in alone. No one could have called me from that number the night before she said, because she was staying at her boyfriend's home, and her house was empty.

'Though Brian, some friends and certainly Keith's sister believed my story, I had no proof. While I was inclined to believe that some part of Keith was "hanging around", I wondered if maybe Keith's sister and I had somehow just had some sort of telepathic connection that caused all these incidents. Then Christmas of 1991 rolled around. Brian and I were staying at my parents' home and on the afternoon of the 24th we were at church practising a duet for Midnight Mass. My choir director, a rational, serious man, interrupted our singing to inform us that a friend of mine would be singing with us tonight. "A friend of mine?" I asked. "Who?"

' "Your friend Keith just called to let me know he was coming to sing tonight. We can use a few more basses." Brian and I looked at each other. "Gordon, are you sure it was my friend Keith?" I asked. "Certainly," Gordon replied, "I couldn't mistake that accent anywhere. He said he was so excited about coming tonight, and how much he missed not being here last year." I turned white and sat down. Brian looked at Gordon and said, "Gordon, didn't you know? Keith's been dead for over a year." Gordon joined me in being pale, and has never quite recovered from the shock. To this day he prefers not to talk about it very much.

'That night, I approached the service with a little bit of trepidation. Would Keith somehow show up? But with the bright lights and grand music, heavy incense and warm, packed church, there was no trace of him that I could detect. If there was some sort of manifestation, it was overwhelmed. I have received no "messages" from Keith since.'

Name: Liam
Location: Deception Bay, Australia
Date: 1992 onwards
Source: James Richardson (witness) / authors' own files

James Richardson, whose account of seeing the apparitions of his stepfather and grandparents is related elsewhere in the book, had a quite different experience following the death of a young grandson.

'Five years ago I lost a little grandson, Liam, to a hereditary illness. He was born with a total allergy; there is no cure and he lived for just under a year. During this time he had to be held all the time and was totally dependent on his mother. Since then two girls have been born, one now a three-year-old extrovert and another just over a year old. This latest girl is very healthy but will not leave her mother and is very introverted and clinging.

'Recently I was sitting with the family on one side of the room and the youngest one was sitting on her mother's lap, clinging to her. Suddenly she turned her head and looked at me and smiled. And her face underwent a major change – and Liam was smiling at me. This definitely unsettled me and left me with a very eerie feeling because it was so real. This granddaughter is very well looked after and has a chubby face while Liam was emaciated like a famine-stricken child, so this was a major change of face and it shocked me profoundly. Unlike other experiences (related elsewhere in the book) which had occurred during times of trauma when my mind was otherwise occupied, this happened when my attention was fully concentrated on the family.'

Was Liam trying to communicate with his grandfather? Or perhaps to comfort him by telling him that he was 'alive' somewhere?

Name: Message To A Soldier
Location: A battlefield in France
Date: 1940s (Second World War)
Source: *Before the Colors Fade: A Biography of General George Patten* by his nephew Fred Ayer

General Patten described a time when he was in France during World War II, pinned down by heavy German gunfire. He told Ayer he had been 'lying flat on my belly and scared to death, hardly daring to lift my head'. When he did, he saw above him the heads of his grandfather and his brothers. 'Their mouths weren't moving, they weren't saying anything to me. But they were looking, looking not so much in anger as with unhappy scowls. I could read their eyes and they said to me, "Georgie, Georgie, you're a disappointment to us lying low down there. Just remember lots of Pattens have been killed, but there never was one who was a coward." ' Patten took courage, took command and won the battle.

Whether Patten was describing a vision generated from within himself or whether he believed it to be the spiritual 'presence' of his family members is not clear, though it is very clear from other writings that he was a believer in various areas of the paranormal. For example, he believed in reincarnation and that he had himself lived several times as leading soldiers in history. He also believed in ghosts.

It appears that he also believed in having received guidance from his deceased father. He described to his nephew how his father came to him in the evenings in his tent to encourage him to act bravely and to assure him that he would be successful in his campaigns. George said, 'He was just as real as in his study at home in Lake Vineyard.'

Name: Mimi's Jewellery
Location: Not given
Date: 1990s
Source: Stephanie Loveridge (witness)

Many people have tales of their loved one passing on, and how afterwards the dead contact them to gently let them know that they are fine. Stephanie's grandmother, Mimi, proved to be as unique in death as she was in life.

As Stephanie told it: 'I guess you could say Mimi was a 1990s woman who just happened to be born in the 1880s. She was a San Francisco newspaper journalist and an avid world traveller; she married an Irishman who owned a chain of movie theatres.

'After my grandfather's death, Mimi took over the business and was a force to be reckoned with, in Oregon as well as Hollywood. Her passions were nightclubs, travelling, Louis IV furniture, Sara Lee desserts and Chivas Regal scotch. Combine all those together and you wouldn't come close to the love she had for jewelery! She didn't care if it was costume or real, as long as it was unique.

'At the age of 82, Mimi was being cared for by my mother with the help of hired nurses. Even during her illness she was still a forceful presence. The week before her death, my mother's best friend Dodie came to visit. She and Mimi had been cohorts in several adventures and knew each other well, almost too well. Dodie had a passion for jewelery that rivalled my grandmother's.

'Towards the end, Mimi lapsed into a coma and they knew it was a matter of time. Mom and Dodie decided to remove Mimi's jewels as a precaution against theft. Even though they weren't sure Mimi could hear them, Dodie explained what they were doing and assured her that the jewels would be placed in a safety deposit box.

'As it was 2.30am, Mom and Dodie went home for a well-deserved rest and were sitting in the living room, quietly talking, when all hell broke loose! The large picture above the couch flew off the wall and hit Dodie on the head, and seconds later the rod in the bedroom closet, which held Dodie's clothing, fell to the ground, spewing her things all over the floor. At that point Dodie looked up and laughingly shouted, "I swear to God, Mimi, I didn't take your jewelery!" All of a sudden, they both felt a breeze go by and then all was quiet – especially Mom and Dodie.

'They checked the picture, the wall and the closet and found absolutely nothing that would have caused everything to go haywire. It was five minutes later that the phone rang and Mimi's nurse informed my mother that Mimi had passed on at 3.10, the exact time that the chaos began. Needless to say, neither of them were surprised as they had already got the message.

'One year later, as Mom and my sister were talking in the kitchen, they felt the air surrounding them still. Then the unmistakable odour of Joy perfume, the only brand Mimi would wear, floated by them and disappeared. I guess the time spent on the other side had mellowed Mimi's personality, or maybe she discovered that, true to her word, Dodie had not taken her jewels.'

Name: The Minster Spectre
Location: York Minster, York, northern England
Date: 1960s
Source: Various

In the late 1960s considerable repair and renovation took place at York Minster. One woman visiting the Minster was watching the workmen undertaking the renovations, dealing with the very intricate carvings that were being repaired. Suddenly she noticed, standing by her side, a scruffy-looking workman wearing a hat who said to her, 'I carved that. Do you like it?' Before the woman could comment, the figure disappeared.

The local speculation is that perhaps an ancient stonemason was keeping an eye over his work to ensure that the modern craftsmen respected it properly.

Name: The Pact
Location: Southern Scandinavia
Date: December 1799
Source: *Life and Times of Lord Brougham* (autobiography)

As a schoolboy Lord Brougham had made a pact with a friend that whichever of them should die first would return to the other to prove the question of life after death. But after school the two lost contact with each other, his friend having gone to India to work in the Civil Service while Lord Brougham remained in Edinburgh. Lord Brougham comments, 'I seldom saw or heard anything of . . . him . . . and I had nearly forgotten his existence.'

Lord Brougham was travelling in Sweden with friends in December 1799, going first to Gothenburg and then on to Norway, and at around one o'clock one morning they became tired and stopped at an inn for the night. Lord Brougham took a hot bath. In the bath he turned his head and saw, seated in a chair, his friend calmly looking at him. Brougham was shocked but immediately recalled the pact he had made with this friend. 'I could not discharge from my mind the impression that G [his friend] must have died, and that his appearance to me was to be received by me as proof of a future state . . .'

Soon after returning to Edinburgh he received a letter from India telling him that his friend had indeed died – and on the very night of the apparition.

Name: Proof?
Location: Dubai
Date: 1994
Source: Jonathan Stanyer (witness) / authors' own files

Although Jonathan has told us he has had several psychic experiences in England, this account is from a trip to the Middle East, perhaps bearing out his own belief that psychic experiences have as much to do with the individual as the location.

'I went out to work in Dubai with five other English teachers at the beginning of 1994. Stuck in our hotel while our house was being readied, we spent a lot of time in the lobby talking about this and that. I got talking with the oldest guy there (he was in his fifties) about the paranormal, as we'd both had psychic experiences. We ended the subject by jokingly deciding that whoever of us dies first has to contact the other to prove life after death. I thought nothing more of the conversation.

'However, a few months later this guy collapsed and died in the classroom of an oil complex. I was charged with getting his effects together as I was the only foreigner around. The next day I went away to Turkey for a holiday and after two weeks came back. I arrived back in Dubai late at night and stayed at the airport hotel. I had just lain down on my bed when there was a knock at the room door. I thought it was room service (which I hadn't expected) and went to open the door. Outside, the corridor was empty. I went back to lie on the bed and a few minutes later there was another knock at the door. Irritated, I got up and opened the door and again there was nobody there. The corridor was brightly lit and empty. I tried one or two of the nearby room doors but all seemed locked. I decided to wait near the door to try and catch whoever was knocking. A few minutes later the knock came again and I flung the door open in seconds. Again I was confronted by an empty corridor. By now I was a bit spooked and lay on the bed fully dressed waiting for the knock, resolved that I would then ask reception for a new room. There was no further knock and I fell asleep.'

Jonathan described it to us as 'a very weird experience'. While any message from his friend was unclear, it is possible that the friend sought to honour their pact to prove to the other survival of spirit after death. John considered this and commented: 'I have no other explanation.'

Name: The Red Barn Murder
Location: Polstead, Suffolk, eastern England
Date: 1827
Source: Various

Maria Marten was the attractive daughter of a farm labourer living in Polstead near Bury St Edmunds. She fell into a relationship with William Corder, a wealthy farmer four years her junior who had a reputation for being devious. When Maria became pregnant, Corder offered to marry her but did not. The child died, the couple argued and Corder was pressed to marry Maria by her parents. On 18 May 1827 Corder claimed he would take Maria to Ipswich to marry her. They would meet at The Red Barn, a property owned by Corder's father, and there a horse and gig would take them to Ipswich to be married. Maria left her home to meet Corder and was never seen alive again. During the course of that year Corder wrote to Maria's parents telling them that they were now married and living in the Isle of Wight.

Then for three nights running Maria's mother had a persistent recurring dream. It was so persuasive that she felt that someone or something was giving her a message: that Maria had been murdered and buried in The Red Barn. She persisted in demanding an investigation until her husband was able to go to the farm with a bailiff on 19 April 1828 and there they found the rotting remains of Maria's body in a shallow grave.

Corder was traced to London, charged with the murder and tried in August 1828. He pleaded not guilty, claiming Maria had taken her own life but he was found guilty and sentenced to death. He was hanged on 11 August 1828, after having made a full written confession of the murder.

This need not, of course, be a ghost story at all. However, one reason for including the story in this compilation is that there are many similar stories to this where the message imparted to the living is by an apparition or spirit of the dead. There has always been debate whether in such a case the dead return to communicate with the living or the living, having had a vision or telepathy of some sort, construct an apparition with which to 'communicate with themselves' in their minds. The case is therefore a good comparison, either because Maria did communicate with her mother in the dream or because apparitions, particularly with a message, may only be an extreme version of the same type of 'dreaming'.

Name: The Stillborn Baby
Location: London, England / Paris, France
Date: Early 1600s
Source: Various

In 1601 the 29-year-old John Donne had married 16-year-old Anne Moore without her father's permission and had suffered imprisonment as a result. To have risked such a penalty must say something for the powerful emotional bridge between the two of them.

Around four years after the marriage, Donne was forced to go to Paris with Sir Robert Drury as part of an entourage sent by King James I. His wife, near to childbirth, could not accompany him and indeed was very apprehensive of his journey, feeling that some bad fortune was to come of it.

Two weeks into the assignment in Paris, Donne told Sir Robert that he had seen the vision of his wife pacing in the room with a dead child in her arms. Although Sir Robert thought he must have been dreaming, Donne replied, 'I cannot be surer that I now live, than that I have not slept since I saw you, and am sure that at her second appearing, she stopt and lookt at me in the face and vanished.' Sir Robert sent a servant to England to investigate the position. When he returned, he reported that Mrs Donne was very sad, sick in her bed and had suffered a stillborn child after a difficult labour. The moment of birth had been around the same time that her husband had seen her apparition.

Name: Unfolding Medium
Location: Blenheim, South Island, New Zealand
Date: 1993 to the present
Source: Dawn Brighton (witness) / authors' own files

At the age of five, Dawn Brighton awoke one night and saw in the doorway of the bedroom she shared with her sister the figure of a man. He was dressed in army uniform, complete with a metal helmet. Her 15-year-old sister also saw the figure, which disappeared when they turned on the bedside lamp. 'Needless to say we were both very frightened,' Dawn commented, 'and spent the rest of the night in our parents' bed.' Dawn later discovered that the house had been used as a hospital for injured soldiers during World War II. It was the only psychic experience Dawn had until she was in her late teens.

At 18, Dawn moved into an old house in Blenheim, New Zealand. Within months a story unfolded that was quite chilling in its way. In Dawn's words: 'The house we rented had been divided into two flats, but the original house design was obvious. We had the original main bedroom, lounge, entry and kitchen, with a recently built-on laundry and bathroom. The other half of the house had the original bathroom and two smaller bedrooms, with a newer kitchen and a converted lounge. Our neighbours were a young couple with a small baby and severe marital problems. So all the slamming doors, bangs and thumps we started to hear we attributed to our noisy neighbours.

'However, we had been living in the house only a couple of months when I began to "feel" the presence of a ghost. One night I was lying with my eyes closed and I could "see in my mind" or rather "feel" the presence of this ghost. I was very frightened and woke my partner Martin up, but he couldn't see or sense anything.

'The next night the ghost was back and I could sense it as it went through the house. I could always tell where it was as I lay in bed with my eyes closed. I was very frightened. Every night, or at least most nights, I would wake up and feel this ghost entering the house. I could sense that it was an older female who appeared in white. She would pass through our front door, go into the kitchen then pass through the wall into the lounge of the other half of the house and into one of their bedrooms, then go back into the lounge and disappear out of their side door. Generally this was the way she moved through the house, very slowly, lasting about five minutes. Sometimes she would go into other rooms or linger in some but she never went into the newer parts of the house. All of this I could "feel" late at night in bed while Martin was asleep. He never has felt or seen anything.

'About a week after I first started sensing this ghost, late one night I woke up as usual and as always I was very frightened. On this night the ghost decided to enter our bedroom. She came through the closed door and went to the window on the far side of the room. She paused, looking out the window, then moved to the end of the bed and looked down at me. Then she moved around to my side of the bed and sat down on the bed. I was very scared and tried to scream but I couldn't. Martin slept on.

'Although I was very frightened, I got the feeling that she was not going to hurt me. She just seemed very sad. Then pictures started appearing in my mind. At first it seemed she was trying to show me something so I opened my mind just a little and "saw" two framed pictures, both of the same man. One was of a young man in his twenties with old leather pilot's headgear on and goggles on the top of his head. The other was of the same man dressed in some sort of military uniform. I had the impression that this was the woman's son and she was sad, I guessed, because he was lost or away or something.

'Then a scene began to run through my mind. It was like watching a movie only inside my head. It was of this lady that was beside me but she was being chased by a man. It was at this house but the house looked different, like I imagine it had before it was made into two flats. She was chased outside, but there it was different, too. There were paddocks around, not the houses that are there now. I watched in my mind as the frightened woman was chased into one of the paddocks and caught when she fell down. I saw the man had an axe, then the vision ended and I could just sense this very sad woman beside me.

'Then the most frightening thing *ever* happened. She lay down on the bed then just moved over so she was inside me! I tingled and buzzed all over. I was very scared. I couldn't move. I was screaming "No! No! No!" in my mind but not making any noise. Then my leg straightened and moved of its own accord. I begged the lady to leave me alone, I told her I was very scared. After a minute or two the sensation ended and she left the room and disappeared. I woke Martin and told him what happened. He comforted me but to this day he doesn't really believe me.

'The lady continued to haunt the house for the next eight months we lived there. She would often enter our room but she never contacted me again. She would just wander through the house, seemingly sadly. Eventually I had had enough and we moved out.'

From Dawn's description, to us it was clear that she felt that the experience had 'switched her on' to being sensitive to the paranormal. She has gone on to develop her mediumistic abilities.

Omens

One characteristic that psychologists identify in people is a need to control their environment. The passion for trying to predict the weather, for example, which in the modern Western world has little more significance to many people than in deciding what to wear, was of utmost importance in earlier centuries where crop failure could mean starvation for many. To try to predict – and control – the weather, a great deal of effort was put into 'identifying' gods that controlled it and appeasing them to earn their good favours.

Ghosts regarded as omens would appear to be a version of this – the idea that certain ghosts and hauntings give clues as to the future, and allow a certain measure of foreknowledge. How much of that is purely superstition with no rational basis is unclear. How much of the belief about an omen is attached after the event is equally uncertain. But what is clear is that omens are regarded as a part of the phenomenon of ghosts, and always have been.

Name: The Faceless Grey Man

Location: Pawleys Island, South Carolina, USA
Date: 18th century
Source: Various

The apparition of a faceless grey man has been seen on Pawley's Island many times. The identity behind it is unknown, though local stories attribute it to one of two people: either to Percival Pawley, who was the first man to settle on the island and name it, or the lover of a Charleston girl from the 18th century, when the grey man seems to have been interwoven with local legend.

According to the latter story, the girl was so beautiful she could have had the pick of any man she wanted but fell in love with her own cousin, who was regarded by her parents as something of a scoundrel. By family agreement the cousin was sent to France in order to break up the romance. He swore he would return and marry the girl but was said to have been killed in a duel.

The girl later married another man and the two lived on a plantation near Charleston, staying on Pawley's Island only during the summer months. Once, while her husband was away fighting in the army, a hurricane arose off the island's shore, sinking a ship, and one of the survivors found his way to her door. She discovered it was her cousin who had not, after all, died in France as she had been led to believe. Understanding she was now married, the cousin fled the island and later died of malaria. The woman's husband returned and they resumed their married life, but whenever they went to Pawley's Island she found herself watched by a faceless grey figure, haunting her from the dunes. It was said to be the figure of her dead lover.

The apparition has become associated with hurricanes generally and a sighting of the faceless grey man is thought to be an omen of an impending hurricane. The apparition is said to have been seen before the hurricanes of 1822, 1893, 1916, 1954 and 1955.

Name: The Ghost Ship
Location: Platte River, Wyoming, USA
Date: Late 1800s to the present time
Source: Troy Taylor of 'Ghosts of the Prairie'

One of the spookiest stories of ghostly omens is that of the ghost ship that sails the Platte River in Wyoming. It is an ancient vessel, broken and rotting, with tattered sails, and crewed by decaying phantoms. It is generally seen in the autumn. The ghosts are said to surround a corpse spread out on the deck and when witnesses see this they recognise the corpse as bearing a resemblance to someone they know. That someone is then said to die within a short period of time.

In 1862 Leon Weber, a trapper, saw the image of his bride-to-be aboard the ship and she was dead within 24 hours. In 1887, cattleman Gene Wilson saw his wife's apparition as the corpse on the ship and she died shortly after. In 1903 one Victor Heibe saw his friend's image on the ship and the friend died shortly after. There have also been many reports known to local ghost groups in the years since.

Name: Kit Crewbucket

Location: Trent and Mersey Canal, England, and other canals
Date: 1800s onwards
Source: *Ghost Encounters* **by Cassandra Eason**

The name Kit Crewbucket is a corruption of two words: 'Kitcrewe', an early form of the town name of Kidsgrove, and 'bucket', referring to a boggit (a ghost associated with mines and tunnels).

Kit Crewbucket was probably originally the name given to a ghost associated with Kidsgrove, on the Trent and Mersey Canal. A woman there was murdered by her jealous husband, a bargee working on the canal, and her headless body was carried by barge on the canal through the Harecastle Tunnel to where it was buried. Her ghost is said to return to the tunnel, an ill omen for those who see her. It is said that her face can be seen in the inky black waters of the canal as boats pass through the tunnel.

Similar ghosts have been reported elsewhere in England and Kit Crewbucket is now a name often applied to canal ghosts generally. A murder victim's body was dropped through a ventilator shaft into the Berwyck Tunnel on the Shrewsbury Canal and the white-faced Kit has been said to haunt there since the body was discovered. A similar ghost has been reported on the Grand Union Canal at Crick, near Leicester; again an omen of impending disaster.

Name: The Old Woman

Location: Leyton Road, Harpenden, Herfordshire, Southern,
  England
Date: Second World War
Source: *Harpenden 1st* **newspaper**

In the chapter on Fights And Battles we described several of the sightings of First World War ghosts seen in and around Harpenden, where many were billeted during the Great War. However, during the Second World War soldiers were also billeted in Harpenden in the Leyton Road area. There are many people alive today who recall the legend of the Old Woman in Leyton Road. Soldiers were billeted in a particular house and outside the house was a seat, Occasionally a soldier would describe having seen the Old Woman sitting on the seat which was regarded as a very ill omen indeed. Those soldiers who saw the woman did not return from the war.

Name: The Phantom Drummer
Location: Cortachy Castle, Angus, Scotland
Date: 1845
Source: Various

Cortachy Castle in Scotland is said to be haunted by a phantom drummer – the sound of his drumming is held to warn of the impending death of a family member. It is said that the original drummer boy was found having an affair with the countess and was thrown to his death from a high window, tied to his drum. Before dying he cursed the family in perpetuity as long as they lived at the castle. There are variations on this story, mostly involving clan rivalries.

In 1845 a Miss Dalrymple and her maid were staying at the castle when she heard the drumming sound. She told her hosts, Lord and Lady Airlie, who were distressed at this, knowing the story of the omen. Some months later Lady Airlie died, and it is said that she left a note explaining that she knew the drumming had foretold her death.

Name: Pope Alexander VI
Location: The Vatican
Date: 1503
Source: Time Life Books, *Phantom Encounters*

One of the most corrupt episodes of the Papacy was the reign of the Borgia Popes including Roderigo Borgia, Pope Alexander VI. His reign was marked by murder, incest, conspiracy and corruption. In 1503 the Pope, then 73, ostensibly died from malaria but there have been many rumours that he was the victim of a poisoning plot that backfired on him.

It has been suggested that Pope Alexander sought to kill a wealthy Cardinal in order to acquire his wealth. He invited himself and his equally corrupt son, Cesare, to his victim's home, taking wine with him which was poisoned. As he was heading to the rendezvous Pope Alexander realised that he had forgotten to bring with him the amulet that he believed would leave him unharmed by the poison and sent Cardinal Caraffa to get it. The Cardinal entered Pope Alexander's bedroom to see laid out a black draped bier supporting the corpse of Alexander VI. Alexander was, of course, at that time alive and heading for the banquet. At the banquet, however, either a mix up or possibly Alexander's belief in the power of his amulet, caused him to drink his own poison and a few days later he was dead; perhaps foreseen by Caraffa.

Name: Sir George
Location: The Millennium Dome, London, England
Date: 1960s – to the present?
Source: Daily Mirror, 28 April 1998

That the Millennium Dome in Greenwich, London, has had its fair share of problems will be known to anyone who has read a newspaper or turned on a television at any time since 1997 to the present day. Building work ran throughout to a tight schedule; when we were invited to visit the Dome just weeks prior to its opening in December 1999 it resembled a building site more than a Disney-like wonderland. Since opening it has failed to attract anything like the numbers of visitors it anticipated, and gossip in the Dome was that an unhappy spirit might be to blame.

In fact, this had been suggested in a Daily Mirror article of 28 April 1998. The ghost said to haunt the Dome site – and presumably now the Dome itself – was identified as Sir George Livesey. He was chairman of the South Metropolitan Gas Works Company which was once based on the site. Although he had been dead 90 years, employees of the gas company claimed frequent sightings of his ghost. One of the former employees, typist Pamela Wingfield, was quoted by the newspaper as saying: 'I was never a believer in ghosts until I worked there. The offices were locked overnight but when we came in the next morning they would be a real mess.'

A spiritualist, Maisie Flegg, apparently made contact with Sir George's spirit. It was believed that he was unhappy that the company he built up was to fold. 'He would be furious that the fruits of his labours were to disappear,' the newspaper quoted.

The company closed 30 years prior to the New Millennium Experience taking over the site for the Dome, and their spokesman told the newspaper that they were aware of his local legendary status. They commented: 'He has not been seen since we started building the Dome last June . . . But we would welcome him back in the year 2000. We would be delighted if he paid us a visit and had a look around.'

However, in the light of the events at the Dome since, perhaps it would be better if he were not there, particularly if he is showing his displeasure. As the *Daily Mirror* quoted Mrs Wingfield saying at the time: 'I wonder, as things haven't gone too smoothly with this venture, if Sir George isn't trying to make his unhappiness known.'

We might, tongue-in-cheek, speculate that Sir George even worked in a laugh at the expence of the newspaper itself. The page reporting his mischief was erroneously dated 1978, and not 1998!

Ghosts At Or Near The Time Of Death

The last desire to 'say goodbye', the need to make amends for wrongs in life, or the need to let a loved one know that 'it will all be okay' seem to form a major motivation for ghosts that appear around the time of their death. The original definition of a 'crisis apparition' was one seen within 24 hours of death, but we have extended that to anytime where the same emotional connection seems to be at play. It is our belief that it is not the time frame but rather the connections which are the important factors.

Name: Across The Lake
Location: Killegar, Ireland
Date: February 1926
Source: *The Catalogue of Ghost Sightings* by Brian Innes

Miss Anna Godley lived on an estate at Killegar and had recently broken her leg and was travelling for a while in a trap. She decided to visit one of her farm labourers, Robert Bowes, who had been ill for some time. She rode with her steward, Robert Gallagher, and a Miss Goldsmith to Bowes's cottage and spoke to him through his window. When they left they passed the shore of a lake and the steward asked Miss Godley if she had seen the man on the lake. She looked and saw a man with a long white beard crossing to the other side of the lake, apparently working a punt, but no boat was actually visible. All three witnesses saw the figure who looked 'exactly like Robert Bowes'.

They left after they saw the figure disappear among the reeds on the far side of the lake. Just after reaching home, the local doctor arrived to tell her that Bowes had died just minutes ago.

Name: The Airman
Location: Calcutta, India, and England
Date: 19 March 1917
Source: *Apparitions* by G.N.M. Tyrrell

On the morning of 19 March 1917, Royal Flying Corps airman Eldred Bowyer-Bower was shot down over France and died. In Calcutta, his half-sister Mrs Spearman was in a hotel 'either sewing or talking to my baby'. She saw the apparition of Eldred with his 'dear, mischievous look' and held out her hand to greet him, but he disappeared. She was so convinced he was real she searched for him but then became frightened that he might be dead. In England at the same time, his full sister Mrs Chater was told by her three-year-old daughter that her uncle was downstairs. Both these apparitions were apparently seen long before news of the airman's death had reached the percipients.

Name: By The Tomb
Location: Hinxton Churchyard, Cambridgeshire, eastern England
Date: 8 May 1885
Source: *Phantasms of the Living* by Gurney, Myers and Podmore
    (abridged by Mrs H. Sidgwick)

Alfred Bard reported the sighting of an apparition he had seen one night returning from work. He was a gardener employed in Sawston and on Friday 8 May 1885 was walking home through Hinxton churchyard as he often did. He saw, standing beside a square stone vault in which a Mr de Fréville was buried, Mrs de Fréville leaning on the rails 'dressed much as I had usually seen her, in a coal-scuttle bonnet, black jacket with crepe, and black dress'. Bard knew Mrs de Fréville well, having once been employed by her. He noticed that her face was whiter than usual. He assumed that she was doing something in the vault and that possibly she was accompanied by someone who was assisting her. Momentarily his attention was taken away and when he looked back she was gone. 'She could not possibly have got out of the churchyard, as in order to reach any of the exits she must have passed me.' He assumed she had gone into the vault but, when he inspected it, found it was locked and there was no key in the lock. Mrs Bard remembered her husband telling her that night what he had seen earlier that day.

Bard later discovered that Mrs de Fréville had been found dead that afternoon. The Reverend C.T. Forster, the vicar of Hinxton, confirmed, 'I must add that I am absolutely certain that news of Mrs de Fréville's death did not reach Hinxton until the next morning, 9 May.'

Name: 'Everything Is All Right'
Location: South Africa
Date: Not given
Source: Matthew Titmus (witness) / authors' own files

Matthew, who pointed out to us that he was the seventh child of a seventh child, which is reputed to give enhanced psychic powers, described to us a crisis apparition he experienced after moving abroad.

'I had recently emigrated to South Africa and left my family back in England. In the early hours one morning, my grandmother "visited" me as I slept. She came and stood beside my bed wearing a silky white gown and looked down at me. Strangely, she looked as young as she had on her wedding day, like a photograph I have of her from 1939. She said "Everything is all right," and told me not to worry as she had come to say goodbye.'

It would be easy to dismiss Matthew's report as a dream, since he was asleep at the time. But had he picked up a real telepathic message from his grandmother? The events the next morning suggest possibly so. 'Quite disturbed by this "vision", I woke up and described it to my wife. That evening I phoned my mother in Luton, England. Not wanting to upset her, I just asked if everything was all right there. I was told my gran was very ill.' Later he found out that she died that same day.

Name: First In A Dream
Location: Leamington Spa, Warwickshire, central England
Date: 21 November 1885
Source: *Phantasms of the Living* by Gurney, Myers and Podmore
   (abridged by Mrs H. Sidgwick)

Mr M dreamed one night that his sister-in-law Maggie had been taken seriously ill. The following evening, when he was in his dining room, he saw the apparition of his sister-in-law dressed in white, 'with the most heavenly expression on her face'. She looked at him, walked around the room and then disappeared through a door leading to the garden. M followed her but could see no-one beyond the door.

His sister-in-law had in fact been taken ill at the theatre, worsened and died in the late afternoon of the day when M had had his dream. M's mother speculated why Maggie should have appeared to her son, and considered that it might have been because a telegram informing the family of her death had actually been delayed and Maggie might have wanted to ensure that they knew the news.

Name: Goodbye
Location: Lingwood, Norwich, eastern England
Date: Early 1900s
Source: Strange Phenomena Investigations (SPI) / Malcolm
  Robinson

The event related in this account was to have a profound effect on Mrs Fox, the witness, and resulted in her strong interest in the paranormal. One night she saw the apparition of a young man appear at the foot of her bed. It did not frighten her, though she found it somewhat baffling. She was not, however, baffled by the identity of the apparition; she knew precisely who it was. Some years before, she had looked after him and cared for his needs. He was regarded as 'slightly backward'. She had not seen him for over four years. The apparition smiled at Mrs Fox and after a few seconds faded away. The following day Mrs Fox was confronted by this young man's mother, who came into her office and told her that her son had passed away in the night. Mrs Fox became certain that this young man had made his last appearance to her, no doubt as a token of his respect and love for the care and attention she had given him.

This is of course a classic crisis or death-bed apparition and it is warming to know that Mrs Fox gained comfort as a result.

Name: Grandfather
Location: St Paul's Cray, near Bromley, Kent, southern England
Date: 1982
Source: Mr D. Park of Orpington (witness)/ authors' own files

This account was related to us by the witness, recalling a time when possible ghostly events happened in a house when his grandparents had recently died. Three people all seem to have experienced a sense of presence which either suggests some factor in the house, in other words a genuine ghost or spirit return, or that their closeness as a family encouraged them to share their inner feelings, mixed with beliefs about the house.

The final comment by Mr Park indicates his awareness that bereavement brings about changes in the way we view the world around us, but this change still begs the all-important question for ghost research: does it mean that the mind creates fantasies we call ghosts, or does it open the mind up to what is really there but which we find difficult to perceive until we are touched by profound emotion?

'I was brought up by my now-deceased grandmother while my mother was out at work. My gran's house was built in the early 1950s on what used to be an apple orchard. I noticed odd happenings in the house and she told me that it had been built on part of a site where a monastery used to be a few hundred years previously.

'These "happenings" seemed to start after my granddad died in 1982. My grandmother told me that the night after he had died, she felt his presence lying next to her in the bed. Also, I went into my bedroom at the front of the house and I thought I heard him call my name. I was only 13 years old at the time of his death, which might account somewhat for the grief felt at the time, more than if I were older, say?

'Things then seemed to go quiet and the "atmosphere" of the house seemed to return to normal. But about four, maybe five, years later, my gran and I noticed a change again. One night, when I couldn't sleep, I noticed a chill in the rooms upstairs. I heard what sounded like a person walking slowly up the stairs; then "it" seemed to walk onto the landing, turn and walk into my gran's bedroom. The floorboards creaked quite a lot, which made it seem more obvious to both her and myself. Over time this seemed to happen with more regularity. My brother, who is 10 years younger than me and was three when Granddad died, also told me that he noticed a very odd atmosphere about the house.

'My mother told me some events from that time also. While my grandfather was ill, there was a time when pictures would spontaneously fall off the walls, and on one occasion a mirror in the kitchen was found broken though no cause could be determined. Ornaments and pictures in the living room would move sideways, and so on. All of this stopped when my granddad died.'

Name: 'In Such Sympathy'

Location: Southern England
Date: 24 March 1883
Source: *Phantasms of the Living* by Gurney, Myers and Podmore
   (abridged by Mrs H. Sidgwick)

In *Phantasms of the Living* one N.J.S. narrated a personal account of an apparition just a few weeks after it had happened. He and his colleague F.L. were employed together in an office for about eight years and became very close colleagues. F.L. became ill on 19 March and was under medical care for a few days.

On the evening of 24 March N.J.S. had a headache and remarked to his wife that he was feeling rather warm. He leaned back on his couch and 'the next minute saw his friend F.L., standing before him, dressed in his usual manner'. Apparently, this apparition 'looked with a fixed regard' at N.J.S. and then passed away.

N.J.S. knew that he had seen 'a spirit' and turned to his wife to ask the precise time, which was twelve minutes to nine. He explained to his wife that the reason he wanted to know the time was that he had just seen F.L. and knew he was dead. The following day A.L., F.L.'s brother, arrived at the house around three in the afternoon and immediately said to N.J.S., 'I suppose you know what I have come to tell you?' N.J.S. told A.L. that he knew his brother was dead. A.L. had in fact already formed the opinion that he would know, knowing of their closeness and assuming that he would have had some sense of the passing. Although the precise moment of death cannot be determined, he was known to be alive at twenty-five minutes to nine and his sister found him dead at nine o'clock.

Name: 'I Saw Her Distinctly Pass You'

Location: Southport, Merseyside, north west England
Date: 18 December 1873
Source: *Phantasms of the Living* by Gurney, Myers and Podmore
   (abridged by Mrs H. Sidgwick)

On 18 December 1873 the Reverend Robert Bee and his wife were visiting her parents in Southport. During the evening he felt disturbed and commented, 'A deep melancholy was oppressing me.' He walked out of the drawing room and onto the landing at exactly ten minutes to eight and was standing there when he suddenly saw a lady 'dressed as if she were going on a business errand' walk out from an adjoining bedroom and pass close by him. He could not distinctly see her features but saw the form go down the narrow winding stairs at almost the exact moment that his wife came up them. He was convinced that there was no way that his wife could not have seen the figure and asked who she was. His wife was adamant that she had seen no-one. He told his wife, 'I am certain that I saw and spoke to a lady, just before you came upstairs, and I saw her distinctly pass you.'

The following morning the Reverend Bee received a telegram telling him that his mother had died the night before. His brother told him that Julia, his sister, had been with her at the end, which had been, 'as nearly as I can recollect, ten minutes to eight o'clock'.

It appears that despite the fact that Reverend Bee did not recognise the shadowy form that passed him, he had seen the apparition of his mother at her moment of death.

There is something in this story which gives evidence to the fact that the apparition appeared to the person rather than the place. Reverend Bee was at the time at his in-laws' house and not in his own house, where perhaps his mother had spent some time. On the other hand, she did not appear to notice him nor did she attempt to communicate with him but actually passed him without comment and, what's more, manifested coming from a room in which she presumably had no particular purpose. Perhaps there is evidence here that the apparition was constructed not by the dying mother but by Reverend Bee himself, maybe as a way of 'receiving' a telepathic message from his mother that he was unable to comprehend. Perhaps he had to 'make her' come from a room in order that her appearance should be 'logical'.

It does seem to have been a sighting personal to Reverend Bee, as his wife did not see the apparition despite the fact that they passed on a narrow staircase where she could hardly have missed her in normal circumstances.

Name: The Return Of William Farrar
Location: Cambridgeshire, eastern England
Date: 1992
Source: Lionel and Patricia Fanthorpe

Lionel and Patricia offered us this personal account of the death of a friend. Lionel said: 'I met Billy Farrar at Gamlingay Village College, Cambridgeshire, way back in the 1960s. I was then the further education tutor and Bill was head of the science department. I left Gamlingay to go into the timber business and Bill went on to become warden of the college. We always kept in touch and even wrote a textbook together. I had the highest possible admiration for him: as a first-class human being, as a fine scientist and mathematician, and as an outstandingly good driver. Bill was one of nature's great wheelmen. He could make a car talk, or sit up and beg. He'd have established a top reputation in Grand Prix circles if he'd chosen driving as a career.

'After he retired, Bill became terminally ill and asked me to conduct his funeral at a little church just outside Cambridge in the village where he then lived. We had been like brothers over many years and it was a heart-breaking occasion. I drove over from Cardiff to Cambridge the night before the service and stayed at the vicarage with Father Ian, the parish priest. Around midnight, we were eating biscuits and cheese and sipping a glass or two of wine together as we prepared Bill's service. We were sitting on Ian's couch when I was suddenly aware that Bill was very definitely in the room with us. This was an extremely rare experience for me. Despite nearly half a century as an investigator of anomalous phenomena, I hardly ever see or hear anything paranormal myself. I normally need a psychic friend with me. On this occasion, however, I knew that Bill was standing behind us with his arms on our shoulders. He looked very fit and well – as he had been in his prime – and his strong, broad, happy face was wreathed in smiles. His words came to my mind – they were not audible, yet it was clearly Bill's voice, which I recognised instantly. It wasn't just the voice, it was his characteristic phrasing and buoyant humour: "It's really good of you two pals to go to all this trouble for me, after a hard day's work!" I told Ian that I was certain Bill was there with us, and I passed on his cheery comment.

'Then came Bill's second message. *"All shall be well, and all shall be well, and all manner of thing shall be well!"* I told Ian that Bill was giving me that quotation from Lady Juliana of Norwich (1342-1416), a truly remarkable Christian mystic, who had had a vision of Heaven and returned to tell her fellow nuns about the experience. Her euphoric description of the joys of Heaven were summed up in those ecstatic words. Ian looked very surprised. "When Bill was dying," he told me, "I was in the hospital with him, clasping his hand as he slipped away. The last thing I said to him was: 'Bill, hold on to this – *all shall be well, and all shall be well, and all manner of thing shall be well.*' Now you're telling me that he's just given that message back to us!" We sat looking at each other in profound, thoughtful silence for several minutes.

The following day, as I was driving back from Cambridge to Cardiff along the motorway, I was overtaking a large lorry with a trailer. The driver didn't see me and pulled out to avoid a deer suddenly from the inside lane into my central lane. His front bumper caught my nearside rear and spun my car right across the road in front of his lorry. He pushed me sideways up the road for several metres before he realised that there was a car stuck on his front bumper! Then he braked, which made a space between us. The car was still spinning merrily anti-clockwise because of the initial impact, so I hit him head on, bounced off and went over the hard shoulder and a grass verge, coming to rest with the car's nose in a hedge. The car was a write-off, but I didn't have a single scratch or bruise. Neither was there any trace of whiplash injury. During the strangely unreal seconds that the car had been more or less helplessly out of control, I'd been trying various things with clutch, brakes and accelerator in turn. I'd just buried the only man I knew who could have emerged from that horrendous road mess alive and intact by pure driving skill – Billy Farrar. I stood beside the remains of my car and looked skywards, thanking God for a miraculous escape. I couldn't help adding: "Was that your first job as a guardian angel, Bill?" I felt sure that it was!'

Name: The Strange Case Of Mrs Dower
Location: Newfoundland, Canada
Date: 1873
Source: Dale Gilbert Jarvis, researcher and folklorist

The Island of Newfoundland off the east coast of Canada has a tradition of what are known locally as death tokens. A death token describes when a person becomes aware, through some paranormal means, that someone close to them has either recently died or that their death is about to occur. The victim may appear visually or the loss may be communicated in some other way, such as through the stopping of a clock or some unexplainable event. Tokens have also taken the form of animal figures, strange noises, moving lights and voices calling as if from a great distance.

The belief that the spirit of a loved one would appear at the moment of their death was not uncommon throughout Newfoundland's history, and exists to the present day. Sometimes, they say, in special circumstances, powerful emotions even had the power to blur the line between life and death altogether. An example of this can be found in the strange tale of Mrs Dower of Conche, a fishing community on the eastern shore of the Great Northern Peninsula of Newfoundland. The tale was first recorded in written form by Joseph Smallwood, the journalist turned politician who became the first premier of Newfoundland after confederation with Canada in 1949.

On 10 March 1873, skipper John Dower left Conche with his son on board his ship *Eleanor* to pursue the lucrative seal fishing industry. Mrs Dower, who loved her husband very much, became ill a week after he had left and within a matter of hours died, much to the shock of the community. During the second night of the wake for poor Mrs Dower, the *Eleanor* slipped back into port, its flag at half-mast. No sooner had the ship entered the port than a truly miraculous event occurred.

Much to the terror of the mourners keeping vigil beside her, the dead woman emitted a great sigh and suddenly sat straight up in her coffin. The corpse then spoke, saying, 'I am tired, I have been far. I have been with John.'

While this may sound unbelievable, apparently she had. When skipper John Dower reached his house, he told the assembled crowd that the ghost of his wife had appeared to him while on the ice. Convinced that he had seen a token of her death, he put his flag at half-mast and returned home with his son to attend the funeral. The spirit of his wife, it seems, had followed his ship out to the ice while her body remained at home, such was her love and anxiety for his safety.

The good captain, it is said, never went to the ice again.

Name: Mrs Veal

Location: Canterbury, Kent, southern England
Date: September 1705
Source: *True Relation of the Apparition of One Mrs Veal* by Daniel Defoe

When Daniel Defoe wrote his account of this crisis apparition seen by Mrs Bargrave, he made a point that writers and researchers of the paranormal have been making in the centuries since. Why should we doubt Mrs Bargrave's 'authority and sincerity' because she is making an extraordinary claim, when we would not doubt her in 'normal' circumstances?

At noon on 8 September 1705, Mrs Bargrave opened her door to see an old friend standing there, Mrs Veal. They had fallen out of touch some time before. Mrs Bargrave said during their conversation,

'I thought you were like the rest of the world, and prosperity had made you forget yourself and me.' At the door they almost kissed but Mrs Veal waved the touch away, claiming to be not quite well. Mrs Veal told her old friend that she was about to embark on a journey and 'I had so great a Mind to see you before I took my Journey.'

The two went into Mrs Bargrave's parlour and talked. Mrs Veal asked if she looked well; Mrs Bargrave thought she looked well enough.

The meeting ended, in Defoe's description: 'As they were admiring Friendship, Mrs Veal said, Dear Mrs Bargrave, I shall love you for ever ... and walk'd from Mrs Bargrave in her view, till a turning interrupted the sight of her, which was three quarter after One in the Afternoon.' It transpired that Mrs Veal had died at noon on 7 September, precisely 24 hours before she appeared to her old friend.

Name: Prince Victor Duleep Singh
Location: Berlin, Germany
Date: 21 October 1893
Source: Various

On 21 October 1893 Prince Victor Duleep Singh was staying in Berlin with Lord Caernarfon. When he went to bed that night, he looked across the room at a framed picture hanging on the wall and saw the face of his father looking at him. Interested that the picture should resemble his father, he got out of bed and walked across to it but then saw that it was in fact the picture of a girl holding a flower. The Prince told Lord Caernarfon of his experiences the following morning and later that day received a telegram telling him that his father had died of a stroke the previous night. The Prince had seen his father's face looking at him when his father was lying unconscious after having suffered a stroke, just a few hours before he died.

Name: Robinson Kelsey
Location: Redhill, Surrey, southern England
Date: 21 October 1881
Source: *Phantasms of the Living* by Gurney, Myers and Podmore
   (abridged by Mrs H. Sidgwick)

George Marchant was awake at two o'clock on the morning of 21 October 1881 and looking at a lamp on his wash stand when he saw someone come into his room, which he assumed was by mistake. As Mr Marchant described: 'It soon occurred to me it [the apparition] represented Robinson Kelsey, by his dress and wearing his hair long behind. When I raised myself up in bed and called out, it instantly disappeared.'

Marchant was so convinced that this represented the death of his friend that he searched the local papers over the following days to see if his obituary was included. A mutual colleague subsequently informed him that Robinson Kelsey had indeed died, and at the moment he had been seen by Marchant in his room.

Kelsey had suffered a horseriding accident and had died at Lingfield in Surrey, some miles from where Mr Marchant had been in his home at Redhill. Marchant confirmed that he had not been thinking about Kelsey, nor had he spoken to him for around 20 years and had only seen him once since, some three or four years prior, in a train station. Marchant also confirmed that he had spoken about Kelsey's death days before it was confirmed as a result of seeing the apparition, and three people confirmed that he had indeed spoken about this prior to acquiring the knowledge through normal channels.

Marchant made the point that he had never had other such visions and believes that the figure was visible for over a minute, commenting, 'My recollection of him was as clear as if I had his photo before me.'

Name: Smoke
Location: Lincoln, eastern England
Date: 1970s
Source: Heather Woods (witness) / authors' own files

Heather described the death of her husband, and his subsequent contact with his cousin: 'I met my husband, got engaged and married in 12 weeks; he was lovely. We had a son and a daughter and life was good; he was in work and things were okay. One day we were planning what birds we were going to send to a race – we were pigeon racers – and I looked over at my husband and he seemed to just slowly disappear. He was still there, but I could see through him. I just said to him, "We're not going to grow old together, sweetheart." And he said, "Oh, don't be daft, I'm going to live to be a hundred. I'll outlive everybody." But he realised I was serious; I said, "I want you to promise me that if you die before me, you'll let me know you're okay." He pooh-poohed it, saying, 'Look, you know I believe when you're dead, you're dead and that's it." But he could see in my eyes that it meant a lot to me, so I got him to promise.

'My husband was dead a year later. An hour before he died my sister screamed out; I thought a mouse had run across the floor because she went: "Aaagh, did you see that?" I asked what she had seen. She said that she had seen this grey, dark wisp of smoke – it was quite vivid – seem to come from my husband's chest, slowly move up to the top of his chest and on upwards. The bed was in an alcove downstairs and this wisp of "smoke" followed the curvature of the arch and then just drifted through the ceiling. I said, "I believe that to have been my husband's soul." He was in a coma, the physical body was relaxed, there was no tension and it was a natural death, so the soul was moving on into the transitional stage.

'My husband died an hour later, at ten to three in the morning. I didn't ring anybody to tell them he was dead until nine o'clock, but at a quarter past five that same morning, a couple of hours after my husband had died, his cousin was "visited" by him. This cousin and he had grown up together and shared a lot together. She had become very restless, so she got up, lit a cigarette and had a cup of tea. She went downstairs and became aware that my husband was in the kitchen with her. Like my husband, she didn't believe in anything paranormal. But now she was aware that my husband was in the kitchen with her. She knew that he was very ill, but she was not aware he had died. And she said she saw, in the corner of the kitchen, a little wisp three or four inches, like white-grey smoke, in the corner, and a voice was saying, "It's me, don't be frightened. It's me, don't be frightened. Can you give Heather a message for me?" And she replied, "I can't do that, it would frighten her surely?" But he said, "No, no, no, she understands. It's something I promised her. Will you tell her not to worry, I'm all right and it's lovely here. Just promise me you'll tell her not to worry." And she said with that he just seemed to disappear. She had sensed him in the kitchen with her and that feeling went away as well. She wasn't frightened, she said it was a lovely feeling.'

Name: Through Adult Eyes
Location: Whitstable, Kent, southern England
Date: 1971
Source: James Richardson (witness) / authors' own files

James Richardson first contacted us when he was nearing 70 and living in Australia, telling us of various experiences with the paranormal over the previous 40 or so years.

One such event happened a few days after his stepfather died of emphysema in October 1971. 'I was sitting with my mother in her sitting room, positioned opposite her. She was in deep grief. I saw my stepfather walk past me, between my mother and me, and through the wall into next door. He was just looking straight ahead. He had been crippled and bowed for some months with this illness. When he walked past me he was upright and looked younger.'

James also experienced apparitions when his mother died. 'My mother and my grandparents had always seemed to me to be very self-assured, self-possessed people; they were simple country people, well-travelled. When my mother died in hospital I was sitting with her and as she died I saw my grandmother and grandfather appear. As I saw them approaching my mother, I realised they looked very timid and overawed; they were seeing her as an experienced, mature woman. I had been used to thinking of them as the senior, wise heads of the family. Now I saw them in a totally different way to the way I would have expected them to be. This made the experience very real for me.'

Perhaps James was seeing them through his own adult eyes, and not through the awed eyes of a child as he had last seen them in life. We asked if he thought the experiences could have been in his own mind, or outside of him.

'The two experiences were outside me, and appeared solid. My grandparents were off the ground in one corner of the room and clearly focusing on my mother and not me, looking down at her with a sort of awe and uncertainty. My stepfather just walked past me very fast, through the closed door, through the wall of a terraced house and into the next house.'

What we found interesting was that on neither occasion did it seem that the apparitions were 'for him'. Neither his stepfather nor his grandparents were apparently focused on him; in the stepfather's case on no one at all and in his grandparents' case on his dying mother. The possibility that he saw his grandparents through adult eyes rather than as he had last remembered them implies something genuinely outside of him. Either James was seeing a genuine external apparition or he may have been seeing a telepathic projection from someone else. In other words, could his mother have generated the image of his stepfather to comfort her, and James saw the image? Could his mother have generated her parents' image to comfort her, and again James saw them? That would have interesting implications for the mechanisms of the paranormal.

Name: Through The Glass Door
Location: Heaton, Newcastle Upon Tyne, north-east England
Date: April 1995
Source: Gloria Dixon, researcher

Patricia, whose account of a possible malignant presence in a hotel in Cheltenham is recalled in an earlier chapter, The Wicked And The Cruel, also experienced the apparition of her late husband. She related her experiences to Gloria Dixon, a well-known researcher of the paranormal.

'Within the week after my husband Ron was buried, I was in the bathroom in the morning getting dressed and putting my make-up on. We have a radio in the bathroom. There was music playing and suddenly this voice shouted out "Pat!" and it was exactly like my husband calling my name. I thought I must be imagining it and it must be on the radio. But I felt quite perturbed about it so I turned and walked out of the bathroom door and went out onto the landing to the room that he used to be in a lot. It was a sort of office where he did lots of things after he was retired, and I looked up and looked around thinking, "Well, that sounds just like Ron's voice." And again it came in a loud voice, "Pat!", calling out as though, you know, you've got to hear me; this was the way it felt to me. I knew then that it was definitely Ron's voice, calling me from wherever or whatever place he was in.'

Gloria asked Patricia if she had been thinking about Ron at the time.

'No I can't say that I was, particularly, at that moment.'

Gloria asked if the second time she heard the voice it still seemed to be coming from the radio.

'No, because I was out of the room and nowhere near the radio. I was in another room.'

Gloria enquired what did Patricia feel about the experience?

'I was most definitely convinced. There is no-one who could make me think otherwise. That was definitely Ron's voice both times.'

Could she have imagined it; she had, after all, just been bereaved? Patricia was adamant that it was not her imagination. 'It was exactly the kind of call he would give when he called me . . . it was clear, very clear.'

Patricia confirmed that it was the first and only time she heard Ron's voice. However, it was not the last 'contact' with her late husband. As she described: 'Two to three months after this incident, I was sitting in my dining room watching a television programme and I started to drift off. I came to and I doubt I had been asleep more than ten minutes or so at the most. I looked back at the programme, then happened to look across at the dining room door, which has four lots of glass in it. I don't know why I did this, but it was as though something was compelling me to look across at the door. When I looked across through the glass, I saw my husband standing in the hall . . . most definitely saw him very clearly in the jacket he most often wore, which was like a blue-grey Harris tweed jacket. I looked in amazement, actually, asking myself, "Am I imagining this?" and I looked again and then it became stronger . . . the picture of him became stronger, the apparition or whatever you want to call it was clearly there, defined. His face, hair – he had sort of wavy grey hair and everything . . . just standing in the hall with his head turned towards the glass dining room door. Now, I don't know why I didn't get up and go towards the door, but I think it was because I was held spellbound looking at him. I would say in a fraction of another minute it had gone. That was it. It seemed to fade . . . faded away and I have never seen him again.

'I believed absolutely, and still do, that Ron was there, trying to show himself to me. He was very clear to me. I don't know why I didn't get up and go towards the door, but I think I was so amazed to see him, I wanted to see that picture and hold it and look at him, and not make an effort to get up. But I don't know why I didn't make an effort to get up. Seeing him did not frighten me, I was spellbound by this image of him. He was there exactly as he was in life . . . he was just standing there all dressed in his normal gear, standing there with his head turned toward the glass dining room door.'

Gloria enquired whether Patricia had considered the apparition could have been a hypnagogic image – a hallucination caused by the state of moving from sleep to wakefulness – but Patricia was certain she was fully awake. 'I think maybe he was showing me that he was still somewhere around.'

Many people recently bereaved report seeing their loved ones in the short period after their loss, and some of these sightings might be wishful thinking. Gloria is well aware of this and considered the possibility here, but she summarised: 'I have a problem feeling that this is the case here. Both these experiences only happened once. They did not occur again, so these incidents were not repeated. Patricia is adamant that she saw and heard Ron, her deceased husband, and in both cases felt that her senses were indeed correct and that Ron was trying in some way to communicate with her. It is, of course, thought-provoking as to what these experiences mean and whether psychological explanations can account for some of these reports.'

Ghosts Associated With Transport

Ghosts associated with all forms of transport have been reported through the ages, from the horse-drawn carriage – likely as not reported with headless horses! – to the return of bombers from World War II and even double-decker buses in a London street. How long can it be before we have an authoritative ghost account relating to space exploration?

Name: The American Airmen
Location: Ridgewell American Airbase, Essex, southern England
Date: Second World War to the present
Source: *Stories of Ghosts and Hauntings Along the Essex and Suffolk Border*
  by Wesley H. Downes

The 381st Bomb Group USAAF were based at Ridgewell airbase in Essex, from where they made their strikes into Germany during the Second World War. Virtually all of the raids were undertaken in daylight, the planes taking off around 6.30am. It is said that local residents did not bother using alarm clocks to wake up, as the noise of the engines being warmed up was sufficient and equally regular. The base would 'come alive' with the sounds of ground vehicles on the move, the shouting of aircraft personnel and, in winter, the bright base illuminations.

The airfield is now decommissioned with very little remaining 'apart from rusting Nissen huts', as Wesley H. Downes puts it. But in the years since the war, 'local residents still claim they see ghostly lights across the derelict airfield and hear the shouts of the airmen, the revving Jeep engines, and the sounds of returning aircraft tyres screeching on the tarmac. Some people claim to hear the occasional crash of a badly shot-up plane that has made it back to base, but was unable to get its undercarriage down.'

Name: An Awful Death
Location: USS *Constellation*, Baltimore, USA
Date: 1799
Source: Various

The first United States Navy ship to carry the name *Constellation* – in honour of the constellation of stars on the American flag – was launched in Baltimore on 7 September 1797. The frigate carried 36 guns, and combined the firepower of a standard frigate with the speed of a Baltimore Clipper. Capable of cruising at 14 knots, she gained the nickname the 'Yankee Racehorse'. *Constellation* was captained by Thomas Truxton and under his command had several bloody and hard-fought engagements. She fought in the so-called 'Quasi War' with France, winning the first ship versus ship victory of the US Navy's history.

One event from Truxton's days in command is behind the current ghost seen to this day. In 1799 seaman Neil Harvey was found asleep on watch and as punishment, and no doubt as an example to others, tied across one of the frigate's formidable guns and blown to pieces. But Harvey's ghost does not haunt his original *Constellation*; the eventual whereabouts of that ship are a mystery. In 1853 another ship was built and named *Constellation* to carry on the honour of the name. Over the next century this ship also had a long war service and was eventually decommissioned in 1955, being brought to rest as a tourist attraction in Baltimore. It was restored, but in a way that resembled the design of the original 1797 ship.

It is this restored ship that Harvey's ghost is said to haunt. His apparition has been seen to wander the orlop deck, below the main deck.

Name: The *Discovery*
Location: Discovery Point, Dundee, Scotland
Date: Since 1901
Source: Various

The *Discovery* was built by the Dundee Shipbuilders' Company for the Royal Geographical Society. Her keel was laid in March 1900 and she was launched on 21 March 1901. That August she sailed from Cowes under the command of Robert Falcon Scott for an expedition south into the Antarctic. She crossed the Antarctic Circle on 3 January 1902. Just over a month later she reached her winter quarters at Ross

Island, McMurdo Sound. *Discovery* became locked in the ice and remained so for two years. During that time a great deal of scientific research was undertaken, and an attempt made on foot to reach the South Pole which, although it failed, achieved a new record for reaching into the southern latitudes. The ship is now a tourist attraction restored by the Maritime Trust and maintained by the Dundee Heritage Trust.

On that expedition, seaman Charles Bonner died when he fell to his death from the crow's nest. It is believed that his ghost haunts the ship still – strange sounds have been heard above the officer's wardroom, just below the spot where Bonner fell to his death.

Name: Electrifying
Location: Aldgate East Underground Station, London, England
Date: Not given
Source: *Ghost Encounters* by Cassandra Eason

There are several ghost reports attributed to the London Underground system. One thought to be benign has been reported at Aldgate East on the Hammersmith and City and District lines. Footsteps and whistling have been heard on an older section of track there, walking towards a place where a door to the control room used to be. One engineer in the control room reported seeing an old woman appear and stroke the hair of a worker using high voltage equipment. Minutes later this man touched a live wire receiving a shock of 22,000 volts. But he lived; perhaps protected by the ghostly intruder.

Name: *Great Eastern*
Location: Transatlantic
Date: 1859-89
Source: Various

Isambard Kingdom Brunel's iron-hulled liner the *Great Eastern* was by far the largest ship of her day. However, throughout her entire life she was plagued by misfortune said to be the result of an extraordinary haunting.

During the construction five men were killed (not necessarily an extraordinary number for that scale of operation) and one riveter disappeared. The rumour spread that the riveter had accidentally been sealed up in the ship's double hull during construction.

Throughout her time the ship's captain complained he was 'rudely awakened by constant hammering', which soon became attributed to the ghost of the trapped riveter. The *Great Eastern* was a financial disaster and never paid her way. Even on the ship's first voyage in 1859 a boiler burst, killing five crew members. In 1889 the ship's life was over and she was taken to a scrapyard. It is said that workers cutting into the hull found inside a human skeleton.

Name: One That Got Away?
Location: The Trawler Pickering
Date: 1987
Source: Beverley Durham of Fishing News (18 December 1987)

When senior British officials of the Department of Health and Social Security asked why the crew of a Bridlington trawler, the *Pickering*, were on the dole and not out at sea fishing, they hardly expected the answer they got. The ship, said skipper Derek Gates and his crew, was haunted by a poltergeist.

Over time they had reported that something had interfered with the ship's steering sending the trawler in circles; that radar would malfunction, often at around one-thirty in the morning; and that lighting would go on and off for no reason. The ship would be freezing cold even with the heating up full, and the engines malfunctioned. A previous skipper, Michael Laws, said that one of his crew had seen an apparition, a figure in a flat cap, on the deck late one night. Laws himself had felt someone getting in and out of the bunk above his at night, when no-one was there.

'Ghost busting' vicar Tom Willis was called in. He discovered that when the boat had been registered in Ireland, then as the *Family Crest*, a man had been lost overboard. Could it be his apparition that was seen on deck?

Willis took to sea with the crew in order to perform a service of exorcism, with the permission of the owners. He sprinkled holy water around the ship, called on the restless spirit to depart and then led prayers on the deck with the whole crew.

Skipper Gates said of the following day: 'We sensed a totally different atmosphere on the trawler. It was warm and friendly and since then we have not had problems.' He confirmed that later fishing trips had been successful.

Name: The Queen Mary
Location: Long Beach, California, USA
Date: 1942 to the present day
Source: Various

The *Queen Mary* was commissioned in 1936 and sailed the Atlantic over a thousand times before becoming a dry-docked attraction at Long Beach in California in 1967. She served as a passenger liner and as a troop ship during the Second World War. In October 1942 she was zigzagging to avoid enemy submarines when she accidentally struck an escorting cruiser, HMS *Curaçao*, killing more than 300 sailors. After the liner had been set up as a tourist attraction in Long Beach, a carpenter, John Smith, reported hearing voices and the sounds of water below decks in the bow, the part of the ship that had impacted with the *Curaçao*. Smith had not been aware of the accident when he first reported the noises. In 1988 the ship was investigated by para-psychologist William G. Roll, who left a sound-activated tape recorder overnight in the bow area, and picked up voices and 'a noise suggestive of running water'.

The ship is alleged to have many ghosts, including that of 18-year-old John Pedder, whose apparition has appeared near an escalator and engine room on 'D' deck; he was crushed to death by a watertight door during a drill.

The swimming pools in first class and tourist class are also said to be haunted by two women who drowned in the 1930s and 1960s respectively, and there are reports of poltergeist activity in the kitchen, allegedly the ghost of a cook who had served on the ship during the war. It is said that his cooking was so bad that the troops rioted and pushed him into his own oven, where he died.

Name: The Vanishing Lights
Location: Irchester, Northamtonshire, central England
Date: 1992
Source: Kettering *Evening Telegraph*, 22 February 1994

In 1992 S.E. Dexter was walking along Firndish Road in Irchester at around 9.45 one summer evening. Dexter's mother and their pet dog were there also. A car drove past them, seemingly very slowly. As it did so, the couple noticed that 'it just seemed to disappear into thin air'. Confused, they ran back to their own car to follow the one they had seen, but could find nothing. But it was not the end of the sighting. As Dexter reported, 'I drove to the end of the road and looked back, as I could see two headlights behind us. I turned right at the end of the junction and looked back to see if they were behind me. There were no lights, no car.' Dexter also commented that they never again took the dog there after six o'clock, summer or winter.

Name: Vicky The Vicious Virgin
Location: Peak District, central England
Date: 1997
Source: Various

On 18 May 1945 Captain 'Sonny' Clifford and the Canadian crew of the Lancaster bomber known as 'Vicky the Vicious Virgin' were on a routine training flight. The plane and its crew had had a daring career during the war that had just ended, including targeting Hitler's hideaway at Berchtesgaden. The plane got lost over the northern moors of the English Peak District between Sheffield and Manchester, and crashed in cloud on the notorious 'Dark Peak', killing the crew of six.

It is thought to have been the 'Vicious Virgin' that was seen still flying 37 years later when, in October 1982, David and Helen Shaw were parked near the Ladybower Reservoir and Mr Shaw saw a plane in the air. 'I was just turning away from the reservoir when, out of the corner of my eye, I caught sight of something flying over the water towards me,' he said. By the time the plane was just 400 yards away, illuminated by bright moonlight, they could see quite clearly that it was a Lancaster bomber.

Fifteen years later, in March 1997, Mariafrance Tattersfield and a companion were on the moors at around ten o'clock in the evening. They saw a plane flying very low, almost at ground level, as did a nearby farmer who was so alarmed at its low altitude that he instinctively ducked. Shortly after that a gamekeeper and his wife heard the impact and explosion of a plane crash and saw an orange flash light up the sky. The emergency services were called out and spent over 15 hours hunting for the crash, using two helicopters, over 140 mountain rescue personnel, 100 police officers and tracker dogs. Nothing was ever found and there were no reports of an aircraft missing.

The fact that a lot of reports of ghost aircraft come from this area is perhaps not too surprising. It is believed that there have been at least 55 'real' crashes there, several in wartime. Any number of their ghosts could be returning.

Phantom Hitchhikers

The phantom hitchhiker has many characteristics which combine ghost reports with urban legend. The stories often involve a 'friend of a friend', or are too conveniently wrapped up in a way many ghost stories are not. But there are cases which seem realistically the account of a true interaction with a ghost. And it is a phenomenon that is found all around the world, with remarkable consistency.

Name: The Edwardian Lady
Location: Willingdon, near Eastbourne, Sussex, southern England
Date: Possibly 1920s onwards
Source: Various

Willingdon is now part of the conurbation of Eastbourne on the London Road, A22, towards Polegate. There have been reports that the road is haunted by a woman dressed in the coat and veil of an Edwardian motorist. It is said that she appears to stop motorists and to warn them of danger, but then disappears when approached.

As with most phantom hitchhiker stories there are assorted legends to explain the origin of the sightings. One story is that she was the victim of a crash in which she and two male companions were killed. Another local story is that she was a golfer killed in a car crash in the 1920s.

Name: Highway 666
Location: Colorado to New Mexico, USA
Date: To the present day
Source: Various

If Route 66 is the most famous road in America, immortalised by the TV series of decades ago, then 666 is arguably one of the country's most haunted highways. There is little doubt that some of the association is because of its number; the so-called 'Number of the Beast' which has given the road the nicknames 'Satan's Speedway' and 'The Devil's Dragstrip'. Highway 666's most frequently seen ghost is a thin girl with pale skin walking barefoot along the road in a white nightgown. Those who have stopped to assist her usually watch as the ghost fades away in front of them. No identity has ever been suggested for the girl.

Name: The Hunchback
Location: Chatsworth Avenue, Fleetwood, Lancashire, north-west England
Date: March 1964
Source: West Lancashire *Evening Gazette* (14 March 1964)

Two workmates, Cyril Stirzaker and Stanley Ball, both independently saw an apparition in the same area at around the same time. Both worked at Fleetwood Docks and left home at around 1.30am, Mr Stirzaker in his car and Mr Ball on his moped. Mr Stirzaker was just going to his car in Derwent Avenue when he saw a 6ft stooping black shadow near him. 'I thought it was just the shadow of a lamp,' he said, 'but when I reversed my car the figure loomed up behind me.' The figure approached the car from the side window and followed Mr Stirzaker as he drove away. 'Scared to death' (his words), he drove pretty hard with his foot on the accelerator and later commented, 'I've never got to work faster in all my life.'

It turned out that Mr Ball from nearby Chatsworth Avenue had also seen an apparition. Having just left his home, he saw what he described as 'a 6ft black shadow just up the road. It was leaning over – just like a giant hunchback.' Thinking it was someone up very early in the morning, he went over to investigate and saw the shadow set off into the middle of the road. Mr Ball then decided it must be someone riding a bicycle, but watched the figure in the middle of the road as it disappeared into thin air.

Mr Stirzaker said: 'At first I thought somebody was playing a practical joke on me, but I am convinced now that it's something that can't be explained away. It's unnerving.'

Name: Impact!

Location: Cirencester to Cricklade Road, South Cerney, Gloucestershire, south-west England
Date: 1968
Source: Bristol *Evening Post* (13 January 1968)

Arthur Gibbs had been driving along the road that runs from Cirencester to Cricklade and was just near South Cerney when he thought he struck a person. He was so concerned, although he could see no-one, that he stopped the car, got out and searched the area. He could not find any sign of a person nor any sign of injuries, such as blood. That there had been an impact, however, seemed certain; there was a dent in the door and the wing mirror was twisted. He called the police, who attended but also found no sign of anyone injured. Subsequent investigation found no-one who claimed to have been struck by the car.

Name: A Smiling Blonde

Location: White Hill, Wye, Kent, southern England
Date: January 2000
Source: *Kentish Gazette* [20 January 2000]

North-east of Ashford in Kent is the small community of Wye. There have been several reports of a ghostly woman in white seen in the area called White Hill. However, for one motorist the apparition took on a slightly more sinister note when he encountered a phantom hitchhiker not unlike a more famous counterpart from Bluebell Hill near Chatham, also in Kent.

Fifty-three-year-old Keith Scales was rounding a bend on White Hill early in the morning on his way to work when he saw what appeared to be a woman standing in the middle of the road. The woman made no attempt to get out of the path of his car and he hit her. 'She just looked at me and smiled as I hit her,' he said. 'She just bounced over my bonnet and disappeared.' Mr Scales, 'shaking like a leaf', stopped the car, got out and searched the area but could find no sign of the woman. When he arrived at work he phoned the police, who searched the area and the woods and found no trace of the woman, nor any sign of blood or injury. He described the woman as blonde, aged between 30 and 35, and wearing a long brown coat. She was smiling at him just before the collision.

Mr Scales is adamant that he hit her. He felt the thump on the front of the car and even displayed a broken wing mirror as evidence of the encounter. He commented: 'I used to think ghosts were just a fantasy, but I don't anymore.'

Name: A Tramp? A Drunk? An Alien?
Location: Warminster, Wiltshire, southern England
Date: 7 October 1965
Source: *The Warminster Triangle* by Ken Rogers

Annabelle Randall and her fiancé John Ploughman were driving home late one night on 7 October 1965. At 11.35 they approached Skew Railway Bridge near Haytesbury on the Salisbury Road. It being a notorious accident spot, they drove carefully. However, Annabelle had to swerve the car violently to avoid hitting a figure sprawled over the top of the bridge, with its legs and feet protruding well into the road. She said, 'If I had been travelling at speed, I would definitely have run over his feet at least.' She thought it was a tramp; John considered it may have been a drunken soldier. But John was not sure they had missed the figure and they pulled the car up just along the road and went back to inspect any damage. No trace of any figure or any bloodstains could be found, the body had simply vanished. John searched under the bridge, in the fields and on the side of a hill, and checked the railway embankment. He said, 'How did the man manage to disappear so suddenly? He was nowhere near that bridge when I went back and that was barely seconds after Annabelle stopped the car. My search lasted for about 12 minutes.'

After having dropped her fiancé off, however, Annabelle returned along the same route at 1.25am and, nearing the bridge, saw a circular bright light in the same location. The light flew off at a tangent into the sky. Then, straight in front of her, Annabelle saw two people standing in the middle of the road and again she had to swerve to avoid hitting them. 'They wore dark balaclavas on their heads. These clung tight and showed only a small portion of their faces. I could see only their noses, in fact, and the merest suspicion of eyes, wide-spaced and deep sunk.' She fled the area, understandably.

Warminster was then about to become the British centre of UFO phenomena and many of the figures sighted in the area were reported as alien entities. But apart from the bright light and the association with UFOs at Warminster, much of John and Annabelle's experience parallels that of phantom hitchhikers all over the world.

Name: A Young Boy On The Highway
Location: Highway 20, Oklahoma, USA
Date: Since 1936
Source: Pursuit, vol 18 no 2 (article by Harry Lebelson)

In the winter of 1965 Mae Doria was driving on Highway 20 in Oklahoma, about 20 miles to the east of Claremore, when she saw a young boy of around 11 or 12 hitchhiking along the road. She stopped to give him a lift and they talked as they drove to Pryor. The boy asked to get out of the car there. Doria looked around but could see only a few trees and no houses. She asked the boy where he lived. He said, 'Over there.' Doria turned to follow the line he was indicating, saw nothing and turned again to question the boy. 'He had disappeared,' she said, 'the seat next to me was bare, he had vanished!' The boy had disappeared from a moving car.

Shocked, Doria stopped the car, jumped out and ran around searching for the boy; there was no sign of him. Two years later she discovered that others had known of the ghostly boy and that there were stories of him having been picked up in the same area since 1936.

Timeslips

Glimpses into the past? Time travel? Psychometry? All are theories claimed for the strange phenomenon reported from all around the world of people apparently experiencing a different time to their own. Some modern aspects of physics are now admitting the possibility of time travel in theory; are these reports the experiences of those for whom it is no longer only theory?

Name: A Choking Odour
Location: Nebraska Wesleyan University, Lincoln, Nebraska, USA
Date: 3 October 1963
Source: *The Catalogue of Ghost Sightings* **by Brian Innes**

Just before nine o'clock in the morning of 3 October 1963, secretary Coleen Butterbaugh was taking a message to a Professor Martin. She pushed her way through groups of students in the hallway and as she headed for the Professor's rooms particularly noticed the sound of a marimba (a type of xylophone) being played. As she entered the first of his suite of rooms she was hit by an almost choking odour and felt immediately someone was in the room with her.

Suddenly she became aware that there were no sounds in the hall where the noisy students had been just moments before. Everything was quiet. 'Something drew my eyes to a cabinet along the wall in the next room. I looked up and there she was. She had her back to me, reaching up into one of the shelves of the cabinet with her right hand and standing perfectly still. She never moved. She was not transparent and yet I knew she wasn't real. While I was looking at her she just faded away – not parts of her body one at a time, but her whole body all at once.' Mrs Butterbaugh described the figure as a tall woman with black hair, wearing a blouse and ankle-length skirt. She also had the feeling there was a man sitting at the desk, though she could see nothing. She described looking out of the window:

'There were a few scattered trees . . . the rest was open fields: the new Willard Sorority House and also Maddison Street were not there . . . It was then, when I looked out of the window, that I got frightened and left the room.' When she got back in the hall she heard the familiar sounds of the throngs of students again and the marimba still playing.

It seemed that for a moment Coleen had stepped back through time and was seeing her surroundings as they had been many years before. She later told one of the Deans, 'I realised that these people were not of my time but were back in their time.' Looking through the year books of the university she located a photograph of a Miss Clarisa Mills who had lectured in music and piano, who had started work at the college in 1912 and who had collapsed and died there in 1936, at about nine o'clock in the morning – the time that Coleen had entered the offices – after struggling through a bitter wind to reach her office across the hall. Miss Mills had dealt with singing, and it turned out the cabinet at which the apparition had been seen contained choral arrangements, some dating back to before Miss Mills's death.

Name: The City On The Hill
Location: Sparta, Greece
Date: 23 May 1912
Source: *A Study of History* by Arnold Toynbee

Toynbee was a British historian whose 12-volume series *A Study of History* influenced many people in their attitude towards culture, religion and international affairs. He served as Professor of Modern Greek and Byzantine History at the University of London from 1919 to 1924.

He wrote of his own visionary experience which could well have been a timeslip. He described sitting on a hillside overlooking Sparta in the twilight, tired after a day's hiking. He looked at the city in front of him and wondered whether there had been a city there before the one he could see. Then, he wrote, speaking of himself in the third person, 'The gazer saw staring him in the face, on the crown of the bluff that overhung the farther bank of the Eurotas just opposite the all-but-coincidence sites of Sparta the First and Sparta the Second, a monument that signalled to him the location of the pre-Hellenic counterpart of the Frankish and Ottoman citadel over whose battlements he was looking out.'

Toynbee greatly valued this vision of ancient Sparta. There is an indication that he believes he may never have produced *The Study of History* if he had not had the experience, that he might never have been inspired 'if this synoptic view had not unfolded itself physically before his eyes from the summit of Mistra on 23 May 1912 in an experience that had been personal to the spectator.'

Name: The Cottage
Location: Loch Mallardoch, Scotland
Date: May 1987
Source: Modern Mysteries of the World by Janet and Colin Bord

Two members of Lochaber Mountain Rescue, Donald Watt and George Bruce, were climbing in the mountains near Loch Mallardoch in May 1987 when they saw a granite-built cottage on the shore of the loch below them. It appeared to be in very good condition.

Bruce explained: 'We decided to head for it. It caught us completely by surprise. We headed on down towards the cottage, discussing it. We kept it in our sights for some time and then lost view of it. We assumed that we would see it again when we got over the crest of a hillock, but when we joined the path along the shore there was no cottage to be seen.' They searched the whole lake shore, right round the hut they were staying in, but could not find the cottage. They discovered later that there had been a lodge on the lochside in the 1950s but it was now underwater after the area had been dammed and flooded. Bruce said: 'Thank goodness Donald was there to back me up . . . I have an open mind but this defies all explanation as far as I'm concerned.'

Name: Down In The Valley
Location: Olympia, Greece
Date: March 15-16 1954
Source: Colin Sandhurst (witness) / authors' own files

What is nice about including this account is that the author was inspired to write to us after reading *The Encyclopedia of Ghosts and Spirits*. He contacted us when he was 82 years old; his story relates to over 40 years earlier.

Colin Sandhurst was on a touring holiday in Greece with a companion, Reginald Renwick. He described: 'I decided to spend a few days in Olympia. I cannot say why this strong desire came to me, but I knew I had to visit Olympia. Reginald was not happy about my intention but I could not change my mind, I had to go. The following day Reginald left with me by train for Olympia, less than a village in those days. After spending a few days in the games area I asked the owner of the cottage-sized hotel if there were other places to see. He suggested we go up the mountains overlooking the games area. From there on a clear day one can see the sea in the distance. The following day Reginald and I went up the mountain, not that difficult a climb.

'On arrival at the top, it was a remarkable sight. No boulders or rocks, trees or dwellings, just very flat grassland as far as one could see. We crossed to the opposite side from the spot we arrived at. On our left we passed many very old, rusty farm implements and an empty cattleshed with no-one around. A few metres further on we arrived at the edge of the mountain. From here it went down very steeply to the valley below, but the bottom of the valley we could not see on account of a mist covering the valley like a white cloth. We were looking down on this mist when suddenly it parted in a straight line as if cut by a knife. One half passed away to the right and the other half to the left. There was no wind to blow it away. This was remarkable – I had never seen anything like this before.

'We could now see the valley below – we were very high up from its bottom. A building looking as if it was made of wood stood in the centre of a large circle of light sand or soil. Both Reginald and I heard voices as if children were chanting. We thought it was coming from the wood building, which looked a bit like a church or school. On the outside of this large sandy area there were houses and rows of flat-top mud huts with roads between each row. In several places smoke was going up in perfect spirals from these mud huts – no wind to break it up. We watched this for five minutes or so. There was no movement whatsoever in the valley. No-one was walking about. It was about ten o'clock that morning.

'I do not know what made me turn around with my back to the valley below. Reginald turned also. We were confronted by a young man and a horse, both standing very close to us. The young man could have been about 20 or so, wearing a long-sleeved white shirt, a dark waistcoat and a large wide-brimmed hat made of brown leather. The young man lifted his hand up to his mouth with something like a cigarette between his fingers. He did say something very softly but it was not in English. I did not understand what he said. I looked to Reginald and said, "He wants to light his cigarette; give him your matches!"

'I turned at that moment to look at the horse standing so quiet and close to me. It was rather a short animal and could have been a pony. I could not see its entire head which was at the back of me. Its colour was light grey with brown patches and a rug was over its back. I could not see anything else on the animal. There was no "horsey" smell one would normally get from being so close. I looked back at the young man. His hand was now away from his face. It was not a cigarette he was holding between his fingers, it was a piece of brown paper carefully folded up, the size of a cigarette. I did not notice if he had Reginald's matches and I didn't ask Reginald if he had given the young man his matches.

'Later I wondered, "How was it they approached us and we could hear not a sound?" Something seemed to tell me to move away, so I said to Reginald, "We must go back to the hotel."

'We both left the man and horse and walked away about 20 metres. I turned to see if the man and horse were still there. They were not to be seen – both had vanished. If they had moved away to the right I would have seen them as it was flat and open grassland. If they had gone to the left I would have found them as I again walked round the empty cattleshed. The young man and horse had vanished. Reginald said he must have gone down the mountainside, but, as I told Reginald, that would have been impossible as no man or horse could have walked down such a steep gradient.

'On arrival back at the hotel I asked the owner the name of the village we had seen in the valley. He was surprised about my question, saying there was no village in the valley. I spoke to Reginald about this, so the following morning he left the hotel about 9.30 and arrived back about 4.30 that afternoon. He had been round the mountain to the spot we had seen from the top the day before. He said there were no houses, mud huts, roads, schools or churches of any kind. Nothing of what we had seen from the top.

'To this day I realise I ought to have gone back up the mountain myself to see if what we had seen was really there, but Reginald said there wasn't anything there and I believed him. I guess what Reginald and I had seen in Olympia must have been timeslips. The wood-built structure was of a different period in time, as were the rows of mud-built dwellings.'

Name: The Emperor?
Location: St Albans, Hertfordshire, southern England
Date: Not given
Source: Various

The city of St Albans stands on the site of Roman Verulamium, one of the most important locations for the Roman army of occupation in that part of England. Mrs Rawlings, from Barnet, north London, was visiting the Roman ruins displayed at the Verulamium arena, part of a major local exhibition which includes a museum, when she saw, entering the arena, a procession of Romans. The procession marched in rank and file with military precision. Standard bearers carried what seemed to be the unit insignia; in particular, carved eagles. Following them was an individual dressed in white and wearing a laurel crown. He is presumed to have been a high-ranking official, perhaps even one of the emperors known to have visited the area. This person moved to a chair in the centre of a platform area and two standard bearers positioned themselves on either side. As Mrs Rawlings watched, the whole scene disappeared and she was again looking at the modern-day ruins of Verulamium.

Name: In The Porter's Room
Location: Irlam train station (now closed), Manchester, northern England
Date: C. 1970s
Source: Leo De'V'ill (witness) / authors' own files

Leo, a clairvoyant with a long history of paranormal experience, gave us this account of a fascinating encounter that could well represent a timeslip.

'On a rainy Thursday night, just after 11pm, I arrived at the train station having just had a row with a girlfriend. I had missed the last train. The platform was open, which meant that the rain was pouring in on me. Within a few minutes of me being there an old man with a flat cap, collarless shirt, black waistcoat, black trousers and working boots came up to me and told me that I'd missed the last train. He invited me into his porter's room. In there was an old-fashioned round, coke-type fire/boiler with a chimney going up to the ceiling. I had tea and sandwiches with the man. The room was decorated with timetables and train posters; there was a desk in one corner. We sat together and watched the rain all night.

'At about 5.30am he locked up and I watched him ride off on his bike after saying good night. By this time the rain had stopped. Some minutes later two railway staff approached me and asked me what I was doing on the platform. I replied that I had missed the last train the night before and I was waiting for the 6am train. They looked at my dry clothes and didn't quite believe me. Then I told them the story of the old man and showed them the door where I went in. At this they looked at me rather strangely, then got the key and opened the door. Inside was the boiler – broken and with about 10 inches of dust on its shelving. There was rope on the floor with other railway rubbish scattered round. The men said there was no way that I could have been in there during the night. I bought my ticket, scratched my head and went home. "Had I stepped back in time?" I asked myself.'

Name: Nechtansmere
Location: Letham, Scotland
Date: 1950
Source: Various

In 685 the Battle of Nechtansmere, between the Picts and Northumbrians, had been a crucial engagement ending with the death of Ecgfrith, the King of Northumbria.

On 2 January 1950 Miss E.F. Smith was driving in the area when her car skidded off the road. It was around two o'clock in the morning and she began walking home. As she neared the site of the ancient battle, she could see figures in a field, walking around carrying flaming torches. She could see that the figures were dressed in rough tights and tunics and were carrying swords. It is thought possible that she saw a timeslip of the post-battle search for the dead.

Name: Phantom Flames
Location: South-west of Tain, Highlands, Scotland
Date: 1960s
Source: Haunted Scotland by Norman Adams

When Susanna Stone was driving a friend from Tain to Easter Ross she saw, near Rosskeen Free Church, a house on fire less than half a mile away. She could see the flames pouring out of the windows. They drove towards the house to see if they could help and immediately lost sight of the blaze, assuming their view was obscured by bushes and fences. However, as they rounded the bend there was no sign of the blaze.

After dropping her passenger off, Mrs Stone returned to the scene and could see no sign of a fire. When she checked with the Fire Brigade they confirmed that they had had only a minor fire to deal with the previous night, but not in the same location. Nor could she see a house, though some years later she investigated the area and found beneath the grass traces of stonework and an old driveway that suggested there must have once been a building on the site. She was also able to locate another couple who had had an experience of seeing the burning phantom house.

Mrs Stone said, 35 years after the incident but with the memory still clear in her mind, 'It was only afterwards I realised there had been no noise and no smoke. I saw no people or firemen and I remembered I had never seen a house there before.'

Name: The Phantom Hotel
Location: Mount Lowe, California, USA
Date: June 1974
Source: Fate, December 1987

Bo Linus Orsjo was hiking around Mount Lowe in California in June 1974 when he saw a 'large green building' which he thought was possibly a hotel. It looked as if it was closed, perhaps just 'for the season', but he did see a servant sweeping up on a big staircase in the building.

It appears that Orsjo had had a vision of a hotel that was there in the 1930s. At that time an 'Alpine Village' resort had been built but had never succeeded due to storms and fires. The hotel, which Orsjo recognised from a photograph, had burned down in 1937. Orsjo retraced his trip two years later but found only a campsite, picnic-style tables and ruins.

Name: The Regency Theatre
Location: Toynbee Hall, Commercial Street, east London, England
Date: Mid 20th century
Source: Vera Conway (witness) / authors' own files

Vera Conway had had several paranormal experiences in her life, and she told us a story of what seems to have been a timeslip when she attended a piano class many years ago in Toynbee Hall. 'I went there in order to practise piano at evening classes. I had never been there before and I could not find my class. So I went downstairs again to the entrance and I enquired where my class was. I was told to go upstairs to the first floor and it (my class) was at the end of the corridor. So I went up. I suppose I was about 10 minutes early. I went to the first floor and I could hear a violin coming from one side and from another room somebody singing. I walked to the end of the corridor and there was a ladies' and a gents' (toilet) room, and in between the two was a door. Not knowing whether that was my class or not, I opened the door and what I saw was so amazing. I moved in and I closed the door behind me. I held my hands behind my back holding the door behind me.

'I found that I was in a theatre. There were no electric lights, there were lanterns with a yellow glow. It could have been something like the Regency period. Perhaps 17th or 18th century. The curtains on stage closed as I came in. Coming up towards me was a man wearing breeches and powdered hair. The audience was moving, there were sounds, everybody was talking and two women came past me wearing very old-fashioned, sort of tight-waisted dresses. They were talking to one another and I remember thinking, "I wonder if I should ask them where my class is?" and I thought, "I dare not. This is not right." But I often wonder what would have happened if I had.'

Vera later confirmed that when she returned to the Hall she found the toilets in the location she had earlier seen them, but there was no door in between them. She also confirmed that she had been wearing her ordinary dress throughout the incident; she had not appeared 'in costume'. It seemed that she was observing an earlier time, but was not actually a part of it. Since she was in 'modern' dress but attracted no attention from the two women who walked towards her, it seems that she was probably not visible to them.

Name: A Vision Of The Future?
Location: Drem airfield, Scotland
Date: 1934
Source: Various

In 1934 Air Marshal Sir Victor Goddard was flying over Scotland on a misty and rainy day, looking below for a landmark. Suddenly, below him – and bathed in sunlight – he saw Drem airfield, which should have been disused. But as he looked he could see yellow aircraft tended by technicians dressed in blue overalls.

The airfield became operational a few years later, as a flight training station. In 1938 Goddard had reason to remember his earlier sighting when he saw that – for the first time – the airfield was host to yellow-painted aircraft, and that the ground crew were dressed in new blue uniforms.

Name: The Wild West
Location: Birdcage Theatre, Tombstone, Arizona, USA
Date: 1880s onwards
Source: Various

Probably the most famous town in the American Wild West from the cowboy era is Tombstone, Arizona. Famous for such characters as Wyatt Earp, Doc Holiday, Johnny Ringo, Jessie James, Wild Bill Hickock and The Clanton Gangs, and the Gunfight at the OK Corral, the history of Tombstone is virtually a microcosm of the history of the pioneering days of opening up the western United States. Many ghosts, many of them gunfighters, are attributed to the town and the area around Boothill Cemetery.

However, one of the more thrilling for those who experience it is the alleged timeslip phenomenon in the Birdcage Theatre in Tombstone, now a National Historic site. Several people entering the Birdcage Theatre have found themselves momentarily seeing the building as it must have been around the 1880s. According to W. Haden Blackman in The Field Guide to North American Hauntings, 'they hear, see and even smell the Birdcage Theatre as it was . . . glimpse the prostitutes swinging in their cages and hear these women calling out to prospective clients . . . sometimes they witness a gunfight . . .'

Tombstone is one of the 'cowboy' tourist attractions and no doubt many of the ghostly stories from there are promoted to attract tourists; but on the other hand, if there is any validity in the belief that emotion helps to imprint ghostly imagery then it would be remarkable if something had not been imprinted in such an extraordinary town.

Poltergeists

The responses to the books we have written on ghosts and spirits, or to appearances we make on television and radio, always contain a number of poltergeist reports. It seems that the incidents of such claims are increasing, to the point where they are now among the most often reported hauntings. It is interesting that in April 2000 the Catholic Church announced that it was amending its rituals for exorcism due to the increasing number of reports it was receiving, which it believed was partly due to media attention on the subject. The Catholic Church was considering incidents of possession rather than poltergeistery, but claims of both such phenomena are increasing.

Poltergeists are known as 'noisy ghosts'. They may be spirit entities, or alternatively many believe they are a form of energy 'transmitted' from the witnesses themselves, perhaps an exteriorisation of their stresses. They generally manifest by a variety of sounds, from scratchings to bangings, and the apparently spontaneous movement of objects. Most cases contain 'special effects', i.e. rarer manifestations such as spontaneous fires, pools of water, and the spontaneous appearance of objects (apports). In one case in this encyclopedia, one poltergeist 'specialised' in turning glass into sand!

Hollywood may well have contributed to the current fascination for poltergeists, possession and hauntings with a rash of movies that have dramatised such claims. But it has not been without cost. In the 1970s one of the most famous of such movies was made, The Exorcist, loosely based on the experiences of an American boy. The film was released on video in 1999. William Peter Blatty, author of the film and book, confirmed that during filming the sets had to be blessed twice by a Jesuit priest, Father Tom Birmingham, to stop haunting-type phenomena happening. Two people, including Blatty himself, watched a telephone receiver levitate, one actor died, and a carpenter received mutilating injuries. 'I certainly believe that something unknowable was operating on us at the time,' he said.

Name: The 1820 Tavern

Location: Strathaven, Scotland
Date: 1980s
Source: Judith Ja'afar and David Hill (witnesses) / authors' own files

The following account was given to us by the proprietor of the tavern, through one of our most valued colleagues, Judith Ja'afar, the proprietor's sister, who herself also experienced some events in the tavern.

'My wife and I arrived back from Africa and took on a public house in the old Lanarkshire town of Strathaven. Over the years it had had many names, and in fact the building dated from the early 17th century at least, perhaps earlier, and had been variously a tavern, a barber shop, a brothel, a coach inn and so on.

'We decided to call it the 1820 Tavern after the aborted radical rising in Scotland in 1820 and in honour of James 'Purlie' Wilson of Strathaven, who was hanged at Glasgow Cross for his part in it.

'In the hubbub of moving into the pub and redecorating it, we noticed nothing unusual except perhaps a cloying dampness about the place, which we put down to a stream which ran directly under the lounge bar, and the unusual feature of a large room above the main bar which was completely bricked off. Little, odd things started to happen soon after we opened for business and most I didn't register initially, as we were very busy. But I remember the first strange incident to really register as extraordinary with us.

'We heard a sort of "plopping" sound from the lounge bar one morning before we opened for business and found a decorative plate had jumped off the wall bracket it was displayed on and somehow made its way about 12 or 14 feet into the middle of the floor. We put this down to perhaps vibrations of passing heavy traffic along the narrow street outside. As an explanation it doesn't seem any likelier now in retrospect than it did at the time, however.

'On another occasion a kettle was heard coming to the boil in the small kitchen. A usual enough occurrence, perhaps, except nobody seemed to have switched it on and it wasn't plugged in. This kitchen was a problem. For a start we never seemed to be able to get the floor dry. Little things starting happening all the time. Pots and pans would leave their shelves and hit my wife when she was in the kitchen. This was never with any apparent force or velocity and it was always possible to imagine they had merely fallen. Often, for no apparent reason, the kitchen door would suddenly swing open.

'Many of the customers were very blasé about all this. Quite regularly what sounded like footsteps could be heard coming from the bricked-up room immediately above the main bar. The large pendant light fixture in the middle of the ceiling would bounce in time with the "footsteps" above. "Just the ghost," the customers would observe and get on with their pints.

'The happenings became steadily more bizarre. Barmaids alone behind the bar were nipped in the back of the neck. One night when Sheila, who had already suffered being nipped, was filling in a quiet night by cleaning the gantry, a whole shelf of bottles of spirits fell onto the floor. There were 13 or 14 bottles and none of them broken, which was remarkable. What was even more remarkable when we thought about it later was that they should by rights have fallen onto the bottom shelf, which protruded about 18 inches out below the shelf the bottles had come from. And they had all been behind the optic holders, which meant they had to have gone up first then arched out to have fallen onto the floor while avoiding the bottom shelf or counter.

'Things started going haywire in the beer cellar shortly after this. One night a member of staff noticed beer running down the short flight of steps to the cellar. When we got into the cellar we found one of the barrels of light ale spraying its contents right up to the ceiling. Somehow the screw on the top of the grundy had loosened and the liquid under pressure was gushing out. This, of course, can't happen. The screw fixing is about eight inches long and it takes considerable pressure and a lot of turns to loosen it. If it isn't firmly enough down some beer would seep out and you would tighten it. But no way could it unscrew itself to such an extent that we were in danger of losing a whole keg. With much trouble – and getting completely drenched in beer in the process – I turned the screw back down and halted the gushing. I must have screwed it down several inches. Then I went home and changed my clothes. Exactly the same impossible thing happened a couple of nights later. In fact, we lost the most part of an 80-pint keg in the two instances.

'The next surprise in the cellar happened shortly afterwards on a very busy Friday night. I had just poured some friends four pints of lager. The place was mobbed and a full staff were serving continuously. A few minutes later one of my friends struggled his way to the counter again and asked for four more pints. "Make it lager this time", he added. I replied that I had given them lager last time. "No, it's four heavy we've got," he said, "but we've drunk them anyway. No problem." I went to the lager font and started pouring. What looked like heavy beer instead of lager came out. Had anybody just changed a keg of lager, I enquired of my staff? Perhaps they had put the wrong keg on. None of the staff had changed a keg, however. I went through to the cellar and checked. All the kegs were correctly fixed up. I went back and tried again. The lager font was still pouring heavy ale. I decided that the keg that was pouring the heavy must have been wrongly labelled and went through and disconnected it, putting another keg similarly marked "Tennent's Lager" on. I couldn't see how this peculiar thing could have happened. Nobody had changed the keg. It must have been pouring lager for several days. The pub was so busy, however, I put the matter out of my mind. Until on the Sunday, that is, when the replacement keg ran out. I put on the keg that had been pouring heavy back on and it poured lager. I have never been able to even stab at an explanation for that.'

'Then our full-time barmaid got a really hard slap on the bottom one morning before we opened. There was nobody near her at the time. She turned round quickly expecting to see someone known to be an inveterate bottom-pincher, but he was 20 feet away sitting with me in the lounge bar. Her face drained and she went flying past us into the kitchen. Both of us and my wife, who was making tea in the kitchen at the time, had heard the slap very distinctly.

'Many other small things happened over the short period we were in the tavern but it all seemed to be mainly irritating mischief. The only other incident of note I can remember was shortly before we left the place. Late on a Sunday night we were sitting down in the lounge bar drinking tea and counting the takings from the till. The kitchen door opposite us, as was its wont, suddenly swung open. My wife looked at me and then seemed to be watching something else. I went to say "What is it?" She put her finger to her lips and pointed up to the bar. All I could see was my barmaid cleaning up the beer trays.

'When the barmaid had left, my wife told me that a shadowy figure of a woman had come out of the kitchen, up the steps into the bar area, along behind the bar, past the barmaid and had seemed to go out through the cellar door.'

Although David and his wife Avril did not live on the premises, they left the pub eventually, partly because it was not doing too well but also because the incessant poltergeist activity was beginning to wear them down. We contacted the present occupants of the building, which now trades under a different name, but they had not experienced anything and were unaware of any reputation for hauntings or history of strangeness. Perhaps the pub is at peace at last.

Name: The Amityville Horror
Location: Amityville, Long Island, USA
Date: 1975
Source: Various

Several reputedly haunted locations around the world have achieved a certain amount of notoriety, mainly due to media attention. When that attention extends to major films and film series the notoriety becomes widespread; this is certainly so in the case of the so-called Amityville Horror, which became a major film starring James Brolin and Margot Kidder.

The story would seem to begin on 13 November 1974 when 24-year-old Ronald De Feo ran into a bar claiming that someone had broken into his house and slaughtered six members of his family. Police discovered both his parents, two sisters and two brothers all shot dead in their beds. Police prosecuted De Foe for the crimes; he was sentenced to six consecutive life terms.

The Dutch Colonial-style house that had been built in 1928 was put up for sale and, given its recent tragic history, was sold quite cheaply and even then only after a year's delay. On 18 December 1975 the Lutz family moved in. They stayed only a month and fled in terror, their story becoming the basis of the book and film.

The hauntings apparently started with an overpowering stench permeating through the house, which always felt cold. Black slime coated bathroom fittings and could not be cleaned, and a second-floor bedroom was the target of a massive swarm of flies. On one occasion the front door was almost ripped off its hinges. It appeared that a 4ft-high ceramic lion statue was moving unaided, to the fright of the occupants. Once, the Lutzes saw cloven hoof tracks in the snow leading to the garage door, which had also been ripped off its frame.

Cathy Lutz, wife of George and mother of their three children, became terrorised when she felt invisible arms grabbing her. This later manifested as painful red weals on her body. George heard the sound of what he believed to be at least 50 musicians and a marching band yet none were seen. On several occasions members of the family saw a towering hooded figure in white and a demonic creature with horns. One night the couple's five-year-old daughter saw, apparently looking in the window, 'the flaming red eyes of some evil, feral, pig-like creature'. On 14 January 1976 the Lutzes left, never to return.

That is the story of the Amityville Horror but other researchers have denied that the hauntings were so extreme or ever happened at all. Dr Stephen Kaplan, director of the Parapsychology Institute of America, commented: 'We found no evidence to support any claim of a haunted house. What we did find is a couple who had purchased a house that they economically could not afford. It is our professional opinion that the story of the haunting is mostly fiction.' Several of the people quoted in the book written about the hauntings denied that they were present in the house, including a police sergeant said to have found a secret room; he denied ever investigating it. And a priest said to have blessed the building denied ever entering it.

It appears that some of the notoriety of the house was actually promoted by Ronald De Feo's defence attorney, William Webber, who was possibly trying to establish that De Feo had been driven to kill by a haunting voice that had spoken to him in the house. In a press release of 27 July 1979, Webber commented, 'We created this horror story over many bottles of wine that George was drinking. We were really playing with each other.' Webber asserted that he created the idea and the Lutzes took the publicity for themselves; he sued them for a share of the profits from the book and film, and the Lutzes countersued. Judge Jack Weinstein, who presided over Webber's suit against the Lutzes, commented: 'The evidence shows fairly clearly that the Lutzes during this entire period were considering and acting with the thought of having a book published.'

Since then, later occupants of the house have reported little or no haunting phenomena. The next occupants, Jim and Barbara Cromarty, experienced nothing. Psychics invited there have reported that although they believe the building to be haunted, probably by the spirits of the murdered De Feo family, they do not detect anything significantly malign.

Truth or fiction? A lot of fiction for sure; some truth . . . possibly.

Name: Apparitions And Poltergeistery
Location: Blaenrhondda, Mid-Glamorgan, south Wales
Date: Early 1990s
Source: Kathryn Baker (witness) / authors' own files

Kathryn told us of a prolonged series of poltergeist activity that has affected her and her family: 'The occurrences started when I used to live at Blaenrhondda and although I have moved several times since then, I am still affected by things, though not as badly as at first.

'The house in Blaenrhondda was a council owned semi-detached property built near the site of an old farm and over old pit works. The house had three bedrooms, a bathroom, toilet, front room, living room, kitchen, a small hallway, a coal shed and an outhouse. At the time I had three small children: Nicola, Alex and Luke. The first event I remember happened when I was in the house with Alex and Luke one afternoon. I heard what sounded like a person walking backwards and forwards in the room above me, which was Nicola's room. I asked a neighbour to watch my boys while I checked upstairs. But there was no-one there.

'On another occasion I was with my mother one summer; we were fitting a carpet in my bedroom and went into my daughter's room to measure it so that we could get a carpet for that room. On opening the door there was a sweet, sickly smell almost like something rotting. The windows were open. It was so strong that neither of us could enter the room and I was physically sick. After about ten minutes the smell was completely gone. This has happened several times since.

'One time, my children and I were watching TV in the living room when the back kitchen door started to rattle violently. There was no wind and the windows were shut. We went to a friend's house for a while to get over it. On another occasion I was in the kitchen when "someone" passed the door and went into the living room. There was no-one there and the only person it could have been, my daughter, was far too short to have been the figure I saw.

'So many things have happened. Once when a friend called round she went upstairs to use the toilet and told me that Alex must be banging and crashing his bedroom door; but Alex was at my mother's house at the time and the only people in the house were downstairs. One afternoon my daughter told me that there was "someone" standing by her bedroom door waving to her. In the kitchen one time a cup exploded in my face, cutting it. Another time a Pyrex casserole dish shattered on the floor just after I left the kitchen. I have watched the attic cover raise three or four feet and then slam back though there was no wind to account for it.

'Nicola was once trapped in her room because the door was stuck. This often happened and it never bothered the children – they knew the way to "free" it – but this time she was screaming frantically. When we got to her she said that someone dressed in black and red had been on her bed.

'The children were disturbed in their bedrooms and sometimes came to sleep with me. Alex came in one night telling me he felt afraid, then Nicola came in claiming that there was a scratching noise coming from Alex's room. Nicola also heard voices of children

asking her, "Come and play with us, Nicola, you know who we are."
She said she felt afraid to answer and then the voices got deep, low,
and were nasty, still pressing her to come and play with them.'

The family were virtually forced out of the house, living with
Kathryn's mother. 'Even away from the house things happen. At my
mother's house we have all seen a figure at the top of the stairs, doors
have slammed, crockery has rattled strangely. I did phone the council
about another house on the estate. I had not filled in a transfer form
but I thought it was worth a try. However, I was told that I would
have to wait a substantial time and was at the bottom of the list. I
must point out that I like the area, and my home. If everything was
okay I would go back, but there's no way the children will return.'

Name: Attack
Location: Iceland
Date: 1907
Source: Can We Explain the Poltergeist? by A. R. G. Owen
   (also Ghosts and Poltergeists by Father Herbert Thurston)

This case was written up by the Icelandic Psychical Research Society
and is a well-respected case due to the quality of the witnesses.
Present during certain manifestations were Mr Kvaran, president of
the society, Mr Thorlaksson of the Ministries of Industry and
Commerce, professor of Theology the Reverend Haraldur Nielsson
and others, all of whom testified that the record given to the
Research Society was correct. In his commentary on the case, Father
Herbert Thurston makes the point that, 'it is exceedingly difficult to
believe that they can all have been hallucinated'.

The subject of the poltergeist activity was a young boy called
Indridi Indridason, who is described as having mediumistic powers
and living in some terror of an entity called 'Jon', whom he believed
to be the soul of a recent suicide.

One vivid attack is described when a Mr Oddgeirsson shared
Indridason's bedroom and Mr Kvaran was in the neighbouring
room. During the night Indridason claimed he was being dragged
out of bed and was in some terror. He cried out to Mr Oddgeirsson,
who grabbed his hand and pulled him but could not hold him back.
Indridason was lifted above the end of the bed and was pulled down
onto the floor, sustaining injuries to his back. A pair of boots flew
across the room and broke the lamp and Indridason was dragged
across the floor, in spite of trying to grab everything he could and in
spite of both Mr Kvaran and Mr Oddgeirsson now pulling at his legs.

Two nights later Mr Thorlaksson and Mr Oddgeirsson were sleeping in Indridason's bedroom when crockery was thrown about and smashed and again Indridason was being dragged out of bed. Both Thorlaksson and Oddgeirsson leapt onto the young boy and only with the greatest difficulty prevented him from being dragged out of bed. While all this was going on, a table behind them lifted up and came down onto Mr Oddgeirsson's back. This inspired the people to leave the house and Indridason was left alone in his bedroom to get dressed. Soon they heard him shouting for help and Mr Thorlaksson entered the room to find the boy 'balancing in the air with his feet towards the window'. Thorlaksson grabbed hold of the boy and pulled him down to the bed and held him there, but then felt that both the boy and himself were being lifted up and he called for help. Mr Oddgeirsson entered the bedroom, narrowly missed being hurt by a chair which flew across the room at him and added his weight to the boy's knees. Mr Thorlaksson now pressed down on the boy's chest. During this activity candlesticks flew in from another room and a bolster flew out of its place from the bed.

A.R.G. Owen points out that this poltergeist was of short duration, though the details of its ending are not recorded.

Name: The Birth Of Spiritualism
Location: Hydesville, New York, USA
Date: 1848
Source: Various

The significance of the case that arose in 1848 in Hydesville was not in the actual manifestations that occurred but rather in the effect it had on religion. It was to represent the birth of Spiritualism.

Maggie and Katie Fox and their parents John and Margaret were a family of Methodists. They had moved in December 1847 to a temporary home in Hydesville. In the following March they were disturbed by thumping noises in the night which Margaret believed were the product of a haunting by a ghost. Frightened, the children insisted on sleeping in their parents' bedroom. (The knocking sounds were apparently first heard by a former occupant of the house, Michael Weekman.)

The Foxes soon discovered that the knocking noises could be responsive, and would 'reply' to them when they made noises. On Friday 31 March the first real attempt to communicate was recorded by Mrs Fox: 'It commenced as usual. I knew it from all the other noises I had ever heard before. The children, who slept in the other bed in the room, heard the rappings and tried to make similar sounds by snapping their fingers. My youngest child said: "Mr Splitfoot, do as I do," clapping her hands. The sounds instantly followed her with the same number of raps. When she stopped, the sounds ceased for a short time. Then Margaret said, in sport, "Now, do just as I do: count one, two, three, four," striking one hand against the other at the same time. The raps came as before . . . I then thought I could put a test that no one in the place could answer. I asked the noise to rap my different children's ages, successively. Instantly each one of my children's ages was given correctly, pausing between them sufficiently long to individualise them, until the seventh, at which a longer pause was made and then three more emphatic raps were given, corresponding to the age of the little one that died . . . I then asked: "Is this a human being that answers my questions?" There was no rap. "Is it a spirit? If it is, make two raps." The sounds were given as soon as the request was made.'

Over time the ghost identified itself as a murdered pedlar, Charles Rosa (or Rosma), who claimed that his throat had been slashed by a former occupant of the house five years earlier. He also claimed that his earthly remains had been buried under the cellar floorboards. (Later, in 1904, a skeleton was found in the cellar and a tin box, allegedly a pedlar's box, found nearby by school children, following the collapse of the cellar wall.)

Neighbours witnessed the rapping communication and the story became big news locally. Hundreds of people would turn up at the house to hear the sounds. This was happening at a time when channelling messages from the dead through mesmerism was a popular pastime. The claims of the Fox sisters allowed various strands of belief to be woven into Spiritualism.

The children, who seemed to be the focus of the sounds, were investigated – for example, they were made to stand on pillows while the sounds were being heard – but through the tests the noises continued.

Circumstances forced the children to be split up; Kate moved in with her sister Leah in Rochester and Maggie stayed with her brother David. The noises continued at both new addresses and Kate continued to communicate with the entity. The family Kate was living with found that the haunting in their home was becoming aggressive: some people had pins stabbed at them while they prayed.

The family moved to Rochester, leaving Hydesville. One day a message was received from the spirit: 'Dear friends, you must proclaim this truth to the world. This is the dawning of a new era . . .' The result was the launch of Spiritualism and an immediate polarised fight between sections of the press who demanded that their readers believe or disbelieve according to their editorials. The Fox sisters became a 'road show', taking their seances to various cities. The craze caught on: by 1850 there were 100 mediums in the Rochester area alone, and the movement was spreading as far afield as Europe.

Many investigators who examined the Fox sisters with a view to proving them fraudulent ended up believing them sincere. William Crookes stated of Katie: 'For several months I enjoyed almost unlimited opportunity of testing the various phenomena occurring in the presence of this lady, and I especially examined the phenomena of these sounds . . . it seems only necessary for her to place her hand on any substance for loud thuds to be heard in it, like a triple pulsation, sometimes loud enough to be heard several rooms off. I have heard these sounds proceeding from the floor, walls, etc, when the medium's hands and feet were held, when she was standing on a chair, when she was suspended in her swing from the ceiling, when she was enclosed in a wire cage, and when she had fallen fainting on a sofa. I have tested them in every way that I could devise, until there has been no escape from the conviction that they were true objective occurrences not produced by trickery or mechanical means.' Other researchers have disagreed, and the case is still today hotly debated.

Name: Damodar
Location: Poona, India
Date: 1930s
Source: *Ghosts and Poltergeists* by Herbert Thurston S.J. / *The Spectator* 31 March 1934

In the early 1930s a haunting arose involving Damodar Bapat, an eight-year-old Brahmin boy adopted after the death of his parents. Furniture and objects were seen to move and apports of coins were discovered. It was thought that Damodar might be faking some of the activity, though it was not believed he could have faked all of it. Toys were found under his mosquito net in such quantity that Damodar became afraid to use the net. Despite this he still suffered several of his toys being 'thrown' at him. The toys had been inside a closed wooden toy box and to prevent them being 'used' a heavy dictionary was placed on the box, but still the toys from within the box were thrown at Damodar and Miss Kohn, who slept in the same room and looked after him. Miss Kohn had her own pillow moved, 'gently lifted from its place at the head of my bed . . . and placed by an invisible hand at the foot of my bed.'

Perhaps the most extraordinary aspect of the case was the levitation. A medical man, Mr Jenkins, visited the family and witnessed this as he recorded in his diary: 'When I entered, I asked all those present to leave the room. I placed the lad (stark naked) on a small bed, felt his pulse and told him to lie down quietly. I then closed the door and windows and sat down on a chair in the corner of the room. I looked at my watch; it was exactly 1.30pm. I put a sheet over him. In about 15 minutes I saw the bedclothes pulled off the bed on which the lad was lying, the bed pulled into the middle of the room, and the lad actually lifted off the bed and deposited gently on the floor. The lad could feel the arm of the unseen person at work.'

Name: The Devil's Action
Location: Southern India
Date: 3–19 March 1920
Source: *Ghosts and Poltergeists* **by Father Herbert Thurston**

The account of a poltergeist attributed to the Devil in southern India in 1920 was related by A. S. Thangapragasam Pillay, Deputy Tahsildar and Sub-Magistrate in the town of Nidamangalam.

The first manifestation on 3 March 1920 was the apparent spontaneous combustion of clothes upstairs in the house. Women in the house were alerted that something was wrong by the crying of a child in a cradle upstairs and the fire was extinguished. Just half an hour later the wet clothes and the chair on which they had been placed were again burning. The following morning silk hanging up to dry caught fire along with a curtain in the 'cooking apartment'. Mr Pillay, who was at his office at the time, was called back to the house and, suspicious that it was an act of the Devil, 'suspended pictures of the Sacred Heart, Blessed Virgin and other saints' in the house. These pictures were themselves soon the object of destruction by fire.

The following day Mr Pillay stood a crucifix on the mantelpiece and sat nearby; within seconds the crucifix was missing. It was located in the fire, burning. A replacement crucifix of silver was placed upstairs. Shortly afterwards it was missing and shortly after that a neighbour came to the house to say that something had fallen on his roof. It was the crucifix.

The following day Mr Pillay and others heard the door to the 'cooking room' slam with force and heard it bolted inside, though no-one was in the room at the time. Mr Pillay ordered his servant to climb over the wall and into the room and when he did so he found the door bolted from the inside. Chalk crosses had been rubbed out with cow dung, not the first time that such crosses had been removed in the house. As Mr Pillay relates, 'How the Devil was able to get cow dung and rub all these several crosses within five minutes and how the door bolted inside are matters requiring deep consideration.' Often during mealtimes the food and utensils were thrown around, causing great disturbance.

During a move to another house recommended by a Hindu priest, 'diabolical acts resumed', causing Mr Pillay further concern. On 8 March writings were found on the walls of the lavatory, including 'My name is Rajamadan. I will not leave you' (Rajamadan is a chief mischief-maker in Hindu lore). After further outbreaks of fire, and indeed a time when Mr Pillay was attacked by burning wood resulting in a fire breaking out in his hall, he seemed to get the idea that Hindu gods were trying to convert him to Hinduism from his chosen Catholicism. 'Oh Devil, you think it is easy to convert me to Hinduism by your threatening writings. Beware, I am the child of God . . . I am ready to die a martyr for the sake of my Saviour, Lord Jesus Christ.'

The poltergeist then caused apparitions. On 11 March Mr Pillay saw 'a shadow high as a human being, covered with black blankets, but no human being visible'. On another occasion Mr Pillay saw the apparition of a female figure. The end of the invasion revealed some very interesting facets. On 19 March the day started with some activity; an iron frying pan falling suddenly next to Mr Pillay's head and the combustion of cloth. Then, 'to our great joy and surprise', writings in the bathroom indicated that the Devil had left, that it would never appear again and that – and this is the interesting facet – it was now going to go and trouble the person 'who instigated it to trouble us', the implication being that this poltergeist had been sent by someone almost as a curse or hex on the family.

This is one of few poltergeists – the Bell Witch is perhaps another famous case – which has announced its own forthcoming departure.

Name: Disturbances In The Dining Room
Location: Beverly Hills, California, USA
Date: 1964
Source: *Saturday Evening Post* of 2 July 1966, article by Joe Hyams

Joe Hyams and his actress wife Elke Sommer moved into a house in Beverly Hills in 1964. Throughout their time there they appeared to have suffered various forms of haunting phenomena, much to their surprise as neither was particularly given to a belief in the paranormal. On 6 July 1964 a German journalist, Edith Dahlfeld, visiting the house, saw the apparition of a man in the hall but no-one could be found to account for the figure. Two weeks later Elke Sommer's mother awoke to find an apparition at the foot of the bed, staring at her.

Around this time the couple also heard strange noises repeated frequently: the sound of dining-room chairs scraped across the floor. Hyams used recording 'bugs' to see if the sounds could be recorded and also marked the locations of the chairs with chalk marks on the floor. That night, when he heard the sounds of the chairs scraping, he checked the room and found that the chairs were undisturbed and still in their exact same place but the tapes had recorded the sound of the chairs being moved.

Over the course of a year or so, various house guests, some terrified, reported seeing the apparition of a man in a white shirt and black tie. Psychics were called into the house, several of whom, without being told what they were investigating, identified a spirit in the house with the same description as had been given by many of the guests: a heavy-set European. In March 1967 Hyams and Sommer were awakened by loud banging on their bedroom door and the sound of laughter from downstairs. They saw smoke and escaped from the house, discovering that the dining room was ablaze. Subsequent arson investigators could not attribute a cause to the fire. It was enough for the couple, who put the house up for sale.

Name: Electrical Poltergeist
Location: Rosenheim, Germany
Date: 1966
Source: Various

When electrical problems beset a lawyer's office in Rosenheim in 1966, it started a train of investigation by police and reporters. Lights were 'blowing', bulbs were flying out of their sockets or exploding, the telephones apparently making calls of their own. Between 7.42 and 7.57am on 20 October 1967 alone, 46 calls were registered to the 'speaking clock'; one every 20 seconds. Over five weeks the clock was phoned up to 600 times. The problems could not be traced by engineers to an explainable fault.

Parapsychologist professor Hans Bender was called in to investigate and he concluded that the focus of this poltergeist was a

The ghostly face in the back row belongs to a man who died three days before this photograph of HMS Daedalus' Maintenance Group was taken in Lincolnshire (*J. Roberts*)

The world's most famous ghosts – a Roman army – were seen marching through the cellar (below) of the Treasurer's House in York (*John and Anne Spencer/Paranormal Picture Library*)

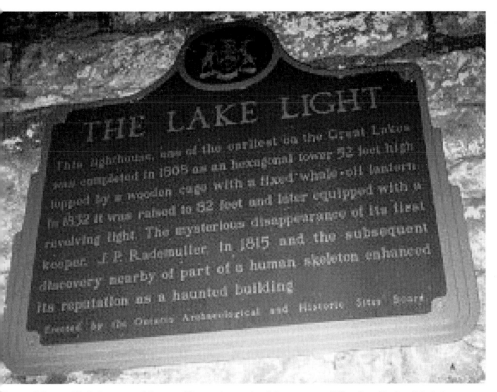

One of few official recognitions of hauntings; in this case at Gibraltar Point Lighthouse in Canada (*Toronto Ghosts and Hauntings Research Association / Matthew Didier*)

Portsmouth House: leading Canadian researcher H. Michael Ball used to live in this haunted house in Oregon, USA. 'This house has it all,' he said (*H. Michael Ball*)

Footsteps, screams and doors opening by themselves were all manifestations of the hauntings in this Princeton Street house in Portland, Oregon, USA (*H. Michael Ball*)

At West Norwwod Cemetery in London the photographer came 'face to face with a little child in Victorian clothes, with a flower in her hand, as if she was putting it on her own grave' (*P. Lee*)

The tortured ghost of Lady Blanche de Warren is said to haunt the battlements of Kent's Rochester Castle (*John and Anne Spencer/Paranormal Picture Library*)

The apparitional double of Pope Alexander VI was seen in the Vatican while the Pope was known to be elsewhere; a few days later he was dead (*John and Anne Spencer/Paranormal Picture Library*)

Was the ill-fated and highly controversial Millennium Dome in London dogged by the ghost of a former occupant of the site? (*Jennifer Spencer/Paranormal Picture Library*)

One recurrent appearance in alleged 'ghost photographs' are spiral beams of light such as in the photograph above. But this image was created 'to order' – proof of at least one ghostly mystery solved (*John and Anne Spencer/Paranormal Picture Library*)

The image on the left, reproduced faithfully with the help of the witness, shows how one woman saw the ghost of her husband in her home at Heaton, Newcastle Upon Tyne (*Gloria Dixon*)

This photograph, taken during a casual stop-over near Portchester Castle in Hampshire, revealed a ghostly face when developed, just to the left of the subject's eyes (*Anthony and Samantha Woods*)

The ghost of eccentric Lucy Kingston is said to haunt the restored Kingston House in Adelaide, Australia (*Kingston House Development Committee Inc*)

Electronic surveillance cameras repeatedly filmed a ghostly figure in the North Portland Library, Oregon, USA (*H. Michael Ball*)

His Majesty's Theatre, Aberdeen, is haunted by the ghost of stagehand John (Jake) Murray, who was accidentally decapitated there in 1942 (*His Majesty's Theatre*)

This grandfather's ghost was perceived on several occasions by his grandson and others in his house in Kent after his death in 1982 (*D. Park*)

19-year-old girl, Annemarie Schneider. Light fittings were seen to swing spontaneously as she walked beneath them, and the events happened after she arrived at work in the morning. The offices were 'quiet' over the Christmas break, but the poltergeistery resumed on 9 January after she returned to work.

When the activity reached a crescendo several people saw objects moving and chairs apparently levitating into the air, and people received electric shocks. During police surveillance of the premises, they watched as a heavy oak cabinet moved; it took two strong policemen to replace it.

Annemarie was tense, possibly realising that she was the focus of the events. 'I never had influence over anything. I was very hurt indeed,' she said. Bender commented: 'Annemarie seemed to instigate psycho-kinesis in response to emotional problems.' Terry White in *The Sceptical Occultist* points out: 'She reacted to the disturbances around her with hysteria and muscular spasms which temporarily paralysed one of her arms.'

Annemarie was dismissed from her job, and it seems that she later left other jobs when poltergeistery happened at those other premises also.

Name: From Within Or From Without?
Location: Southend-on-Sea, Essex, southern England
Date: 1998
Source: Mike Barnet (witness) / authors' own files

Mike told us his story in October 1998. There are parts of his account that could be unconnected to him but other parts sound typical of exteriorisation of inner turmoil. Does that mean that Mike has experienced two types of phenomena, or is it a clue that even seemingly spontaneous, unconnected events are more likely seen, or even generated, by those with inner emotions running high?

As Mike explained: 'This series of events started happening following a bust-up with my girlfriend. At first it was nothing much; a couple of times I saw the figure of a man standing in the doorway of my lounge, a big, powerful-looking man. Upon blinking, the figure would be gone. On the third occasion I had been asleep on the couch in the lounge and, upon waking, there he was, only this time I kept a good eye on him. I probably looked at him for about ten seconds then I must have moved or blinked and, again, he was gone. Also I have heard several 'odd' noises, such as footsteps, shuffling and doors closing. I have seen a ball of yellow-orange light over the top of the table in my dining room while I was on the phone. I carried on the conversation while trying to move around to see if it was a reflection, but I don't think it was.

'The most recent event, and as far as I'm concerned the one that can't be explained, happened when I was suing a guy for some work he did for me. I was reading a letter that I was writing to him and getting rather angry to say the least, though I wasn't speaking out loud. But as I was reading I was imagining punching him all over the place (which a few years ago would probably have been the case, but not now). I looked up from the letter to see a wooden spoon slide about three inches across the top of a cup in a pile of washing-up waiting to be done and then fall on the floor. It was as if it slid across the cup until it got off balance and then "flicked" off; it didn't fall directly to the floor. I got up, went over and picked it up, and tried to re-enact the action I had just seen. I couldn't make it happen like that again.

'I have had several other incidents happen at different addresses. One happened when I was with another ex-girlfriend; she freaked.'

Name: Gef
Location: Dalby, Isle of Man, UK
Date: 1931
Source: Various

In 1931, in an isolated house near Dalby on the Isle of Man, the Irving family became the subject of poltergeist-like activity they attributed to a creature they called 'Gef'. In September they heard a 'tapping' sound in the attic, a common start to poltergeist activity. Over the next few days the noises increased somewhat and included 'animal sounds'. James Irving, the head of the family, believed that the house had been invaded by an animal.

But in November the poltergeist-like noises had worsened, and then a voice was heard. Later, writing to Harry Price, the famous investigator who researched the case, Irving said: 'Its first sounds were those of an animal nature and it used to keep us awake at night . . . It occurred to me that if it could make these weird noises, why not others?' At first Irving encouraged it to repeat bird and animal sounds. As the voice developed, it could repeat nursery rhymes. Irving said: 'The voice is quite two octaves above any human voice . . . but lately it can and does come down to the range of the human voice . . .' The voice was confirmed by a local reporter in the

Daily Dispatch: 'The mysterious man-weasel has . . . spoken to me today . . . Leaves me in a state of considerable perplexity. Had I heard a weasel speak? I do not know, but I do know that I've heard today a voice which I should never have imagined could issue from a human voice.'

The family seemed to consider that Gef was physically real and the case became known as that of the talking mongoose. Few people who have had poltergeist activity have failed to consider the possibility that an intelligent, if mischievous, spirit might be behind the experience; that a spirit in the form of a mongoose should be considered is perhaps less strange than it at first seems.

The poltergeist seemed to focus on James and Margaret's 11-year-old daughter Voirrey. She first became the victim of stone-throwing. She moved into the same bedroom as her parents, but the banging sounds in the walls continued. The voice said: 'I'll follow her, wherever you move her.' Crockery, furniture and stones were thrown around the house.

Gef moved into the strangest realm of all: 'he' exhibited a detailed knowledge of what was going on in the world around him. He would tell the family the correct time, local gossip that turned out to be correct – or at least was indeed being gossiped about in the town – and answered arithmetic questions correctly. Gef moved on to some bizarre claims, calling out: 'I can split the atom', 'I am the Holy Ghost' and other strange claims. Readers of *The Encyclopedia of Ghosts and Spirits* will find these claims comparable to the claims of the poltergeist that was known as the Bell Witch.

A reporter from the *Daily Dispatch* examined the possibility that Gef might be a sub-personality of Voirrey. He tried to watch her lips whenever Gef spoke, but somehow failed to be able to see them. Either Gef or Voirrey was being secretive.

On one occasion, Gef explained himself: 'I did it for devilment.' If only all poltergeists were so honest.

Name: The Ghosthouse
Location: Speke, Liverpool, north-west England
Date: 1995 to 1996
Source: Researchers Anthony Eccles / John L. Hall / Elaine Hannah / Mark Glover / Gary Theys of the Merseyside Anomalies Research Association (MARA)

The details below are abridged from a report published by MARA, and available from them (details at the back of the book).

The house, known locally as the 'Ghosthouse', is a large, renovated council house. The family, who have lived there for seven years, have three girls, one boy and a number of dogs. There is a possible history of hauntings to the house as several families apparently 'could not abide the property and so moved out'. Neighbours confirmed that the house had been empty for sometime and was gutted by a fire in the upstairs rooms while being renovated by the council.

Initial poltergeist-like activity had been 'low level', more mischievous in nature, but it worsened after a medium had been called in. The medium's assessment was that the ghost of a young girl was the cause; in life she had, the medium believed, been locked in a cupboard in an upstairs room.

Dogs in the house had reacted to 'invisible presences' in the entrance to the hall. One dog had been seen cowering with its tail between its legs, barking at something that could not be seen. The dog had refused to come out of the kitchen.

From the kitchen, the mother of the family had, one night, watched as a pair of disembodied legs moved slowly up the stairs. Only the lower parts of the legs were visible, the 'flesh' having a pinky appearance. In the front room downstairs the sound of crying from no known source had been noted. One of the neighbours next door had apparently heard the crying of a small girl from the same area of the house.

The top floor was also an area of high activity. On the landing, cold spots had been felt, particularly near the airing cupboard and door to the room. The airing cupboard was thought to be the location where the girl had been locked up, according to the medium. An apparition had been witnessed in the doorway to the top-floor front room by one of the children playing there. The family had experienced various noises such as banging, knocking and creaking floorboards, a sand-filled punch bag mysteriously swinging and numerous smells, and the mother of the family had watched the handle to a door turn and the door being pushed open with no-one behind it. The dogs did not feel comfortable on the top floor.

The MARA team undertook an overnight vigil in the house on 22 March 1996 to determine if there was paranormal activity happening, to record and try to analyse it, and to devise a way of eradicating it so that the family could lead a more relaxed life. During the vigil the team noticed slight cold areas and swinging movements in a sand-filled punch bag, as had been reported by the family at other times. Some noises were heard: bumping sounds and a cough from a room known to be empty. Knocking sounds were heard in rooms where no-one was present.

The team rationally examined other possibilities for the low level of phenomena experienced during their presence. Electrical disturbances (lights downstairs going on spontaneously) could have been faulty wiring, though there had been no earlier reports of such from the house. Could any activity have been due to vibration from the nearby Ford factory? The team reasoned logically that had that been so, more obvious effects should also have been observed, such as vibrating windows in the frames, but were not. The punch bag was far too heavy to be moved by draughts even if any had been present, and no-one was near the bag at the times of movement.

The overall conclusions of the vigil were: 'It is difficult to offer any solid conclusions about the events that took place in an alleged haunted house . . . The knocks were in places under direct observation, such as the children's playroom, which was wide open for all to see and was empty; the banging there was very similar to someone using a knuckle to rap on a cupboard door, it is distinctive. Some of the other knocks were not hollow-sounding and occurred on walls that were not part of neighbouring houses. If these were hoaxed they would have been discovered. Those knocks that had taken place downstairs while the team was present remain inconclusive, whereas the knocks and thumps heard upstairs are convincingly paranormal . . .

'Between husband and wife . . . maybe their emotions were feeding the phenomenon, maybe they were the catalyst of unbalanced mental tension in the home, we cannot comment further on this. However, the principal witness, J.G., and her children may have been demonstrating possible RSPK [Recurrent Spontaneous Psycho-Kinesis] and/or providing sufficient energy for poltergeist phenomena to take place.

'The investigation into this house may have shown a low level presence of paranormal activity but nothing more . . . all of the activity tended to focus on the top floor of the house where a punch bag and children's playroom is located.

'MARA was there predominantly for the interests of the family concerned, the case has received no publicity at all and the witnesses remain out of the media's attention, as they specifically requested anonymity.'

Name: Haunted Bomb Shelter
Location: Enbrook Manor, Folkestone, Kent, southern England
Date: November 1917–December 1918
Source: *The Poltergeist* by William G. Roll

Over the turn of the year 1917 to 1918, R.P. Jacques was building a
bomb shelter which became a target of poltergeist attack, with
stones falling inside the shelter. Jacques was alone in the 'dugout'
inspecting the work. He left the shelter, closed the door and
immediately heard a stone hitting the inside of the door, followed
by three others. There was nobody present in the shelter. Between
eight to 11 stones then followed and Jacques went back inside,
found the stones by the door and confirmed there was nobody
within. Jacques believed that a young boy who was helping to build
the shelter was the focus of this poltergeist, though he was not
present at that time, being at dinner.

   On another occasion the builder, Rolfe, took a 6lb hammer out of
the shelter and then returned to the shelter without the hammer. Just
a minute later he heard a thud on the earth, turned round and saw
the hammer at his feet again. He commented, 'It seemed to hit the
ground very lightly and, despite its weight, made hardly any noise.'
Rolfe asked the boy, his assistant, to take it out again, which he did,
and it quickly fell back beside him again 'just as a bird would settle
down'. A third time Rolfe asked the assistant to take it away and the
assistant took it further, beside the stable, 'but hardly had he told me
when it was back at my feet again.'

Name: A Horrible White Face
Location: Newcastle, New South Wales, Australia
Date: 1970
Source: Sydney *Morning Herald*, 25 February 1970

When Michael and Dianne Cooke and their baby daughter moved
into rented accommodation in 1970, they hardly expected to be
sharing it with a ghost. But it turned out to be a very frightening
encounter. For two weeks during February they suffered several
haunting manifestations, including finding the beds ruffled, toys
apparently 'played with' when their infant was nowhere near them
and a rattling door. On one occasion they saw their child jerked
upright as if pulled by invisible hands.

They discovered that they were not the only tenants of the property that had suffered such intrusion. One previous occupant was woken up by an invisible hand apparently shaking his shoulder. Another woke to find a figure standing over him, looking at him.

The Cookes moved out after a most frightening incident when they saw a ghostly face. As Michael Cooke described: 'I saw a horrible white face looking out of one of the windows . . . the eyes were white with green in the middle. I was so scared the tears just ran out of my eyes. That was the end. I was thinking of buying the house, but I'll never live there again.'

Name: A Jinn In Transylvania
Location: Transylvania, Romania
Date: 1913/1914
Source: Hereward Carrington (The Story of the Poltergeist by Carrington and Fodor)

In 1914 the prominent poltergeist researcher Hereward Carrington received a letter from the Hon. Everard Fielding who had investigated the case of a Hungarian lawyer suffering the attentions of a poltergeist. 'A friendly, sportive hobgoblin, late a Romanian, and now the most desirable imp that anyone could wish for.'

The poltergeist activity started when the lawyer, facing financial ruin, contemplated suicide. 'He suddenly found money in his pocket which he knew wasn't there before.' The lawyer even wondered if he had stolen it in despair, without being able to recall doing so, but then watched as more money began to drop on the table. As he walked out of his house stones fell beside him and over a period many things were thrown at him, including bromide tablets when he couldn't sleep, bottles of schnapps on cold nights, cigarettes which appeared out of the air when he had run out of them, and even, apparently, cigars bearing the Emperor's monogram.

Clearly, this seems to have been a 'responsive' poltergeist in much the same way as in the Cardiff case three-quarters of a century later (outlined later in this chapter), responding to the needs and wishes of the witness. As in Cardiff, there were also dramatic appearances. 'As things materially eased then, the character of the phenomena changed and now the things are mostly ancient and useless tag-rags and bobtails ranging from bottle tops to an elderly pump, about 50lb in weight and 4ft long, slabs of marble, 5ft poles, pieces of wood, heavy iron screws, pincers, knives, wire lampshades, toy animals – all hurtled into the room at unexpected moments.'

Fielding himself saw many of the manifestations. When he and the Hungarian lawyer were alone in a room a 5ft pole fell at the other end of it. 'On another occasion, I being the first to enter the room, a 4ft pole jumped out at me from the corner which I was facing at a distance of three feet – the lawyer at the time just entering the door.' When Fielding was alone in the room, a glass fell at his feet.

The poltergeist manifested rapping noises and caused the dinner table to 'jump' at mealtimes. An attempt using a ouija board to communicate with the 'jinn' produced a romantic story from a spirit claiming to have once been a German Baron called Schindtreffer who lived in Mindelheim, Bavaria, in the 1700s. Central to the communication was a detailed description of where valuable jewellery and papers were buried in Brittany, France, but subsequent searching did not locate them.

Fielding followed up his earlier analysis by commenting that he believed many, if not all, of the phenomena could be attributed to the lawyer's wife and he suspected some fraud on her part, having found that an apparent apport had in fact been purchased by her. The wife did not remember purchasing the object, but under regression hypnosis she recalled being in a park and her deceased sister 'coming to her' and insisting on her going and buying the object.

Fielding's conclusion was: 'All this looks very much like double personality action, and therefore in the realm of subconscious and not conscious fraud, in a trance condition.'

The husband was concerned about the possibility of double personality in case his wife should commit crimes while in trance. The majority of the manifestations appeared to be paranormal, possibly 'generated' by RSPK from the wife. The couple unsuccessfully attempted to find the buried treasure in Brittany, then found that the poltergeist had ceased on their return to Transylvania.

Name: Karin
Location: Southern Sweden
Date: 1904–05
Source: *Can We Explain the Poltergeist?* by A.R.G. Owen

Karin, her husband and a maidservant moved into a country villa in southern Sweden on 18 April 1904. It had a long reputation in the neighbourhood for 'weird lights and strange noises'.

Between 9 May and 4 July Karin, her husband and the servant heard knocking noises which seemed to occur wherever Karin was. The disturbances had a regular pattern. When Karin had gone to bed but was still awake, three loud knocks were heard near her bed. Karin and her husband attempted to experiment with the knocks, asking for particular patterns in particular parts of the room, but the results were sketchy. The blows gradually became more irregular and variable and there is some suggestion that they believed it was another form of communication from a spirit calling himself Piscator. Karin also had 'a vague feeling of an invisible being in the room, particularly marked before and during the course of the rappings'.

The family moved into town until 12 September but on their return to the villa they again heard mild knocking noises. After 12 September the rappings were preceded by Karin's having anxious feelings.

On 5 November researchers Hjalmar Wijk and Dr Paul Bjerre began experiments using hypnotic trance to communicate with the poltergeist by asking for particular patterns at particular times which was often successful. As Owen comments, 'Karin herself appeared to be genuinely unaware that instructions had been given.' Broadly speaking, Piscator was spoken of in the third person, which Wijk noted 'as a feature distinguishing Karin's hypnosis from the medium-istic trance in which it is the control who speaks'. Bjerre tried a psychological approach to cure the poltergeist phenomena and this appears to have worked, the phenomena becoming feebler and recommencing only briefly in January 1905 when Karin and her husband were living in town.

Name: Kitchen Disarray
Location: Münchhof, Austria
Date: October 1818
Source: *Ghosts and Poltergeists* by Father Herbert Thurston

H.J. Aschauer, who later went on to become a Professor of Mathematics, was eye-witness to a frenzied poltergeist. His report was also corroborated by a police report, the poltergeist having drawn the attention of the police to the home of the witness. The house in Münchhof was occupied by Aschauer's son-in-law, Mr Obergemeiner.

At first the poltergeist was a classic stone-throwing 'spook'. This happened only in the afternoons and evenings and Obergemeiner believed they must be schoolboy pranks. Several ground-floor windows were broken by flying stones. Despite his vigilance, Obergemeiner could not locate the schoolboys he believed responsible. In the next few days the stone throwing was augmented by strange rapping noises in the front and back doors of the building and his family were becoming distressed.

Obergemeiner put together a posse of around 30 or so local people and created a cordon around the house, gradually closing in on the house and allowing no-one to pass between them. While this was going on, he and another man, Koppbauer, kept all the members of the house in one room while they searched the entire building from top to bottom. As all these precautions were being carried out, stones continued to strike the kitchen windows. Koppbauer, looking out of one of the windows to identify where the stones were coming from, suddenly saw the very window he was looking out of broken by a stone, which he was convinced had to have come from inside the room but could not have done, as Obergemeiner and the others assured him they had not been involved.

The manifestations increased. From stones, the poltergeist went on to throwing spoons, dishes, kitchen utensils and fire irons. As in many poltergeist cases, people were hit by these extremely heavy objects and yet somehow were unhurt. As Father Thurston reports, 'Many of the moving objects upon contact with a living person or with a resisting surface fell dead as if a hand had arrested them in their flight.' Almost everything breakable in the kitchen was shattered and when several people tried to remove crockery to the hall to get it out of the line of fire, they claimed it was snatched from their grasp and then shattered. Candlesticks were thrown and the stopper three times flew out of a decanter, despite each time being replaced.

Aschauer attended the house and became witness to events in the following days. He, together with Obergemeiner's wife and Koppbauer, were talking when a big iron spoon suddenly left the shelf it was on and flew towards Koppbauer's head. It struck him but 'the stricken man declared he felt only a light touch and the spoon dropped perpendicularly at his feet'. Other objects – a soup tureen, a bucket, colander and saucepan – were flung around or appeared to levitate over the course of Aschauer's time there.

Name: Legal Intervention

Location: Bradford Road, Brighouse, West Yorkshire, northern England
Date: 1970s to the present
Source: Mary Hartley (witness) / authors' own files

Mary Hartley wrote to us to tell us of her experiences of haunting in her place of work: 'I have worked here for nearly 23 years. It is a solicitor's office which is comprised of two offices and a kitchen downstairs, two offices on the first floor and two toilets and a staff room on the top floor.

'On the day I started to work here, every time I went into the kitchen I felt as though someone was looking over my shoulder. This lasted for a good few months, then I suppose it either stopped or I got used to it, but I don't notice it anymore.

'In 1988 I was in the staff room with another member of staff when we heard footsteps coming up the stairs followed by a loud thud – so loud that it shook the floor – and then a dragging sound. We went out into the corridor but there was no-one there; in fact, there was no-one else in the building. I decided that it must have been the shop next door having a delivery, until it was pointed out to me that it was Tuesday and the shop next door is closed on Tuesday.

'Another time, the telephone rang and, as I went to answer it, it was answered from the back office upstairs. When Mr Cornwell, the boss, came downstairs, I told him he had left the phone off the hook in the back office. He said he hadn't been in the back office and certainly didn't answer the phone. He went back upstairs, into the back office, and found the phone was off the hook and laying at the side of the telephone. It couldn't have fallen off and landed in that position. A few days later it happened again.'

Miss Hartley gave us a long list of 43 events that she had noted in the office in just over five and a half years. There were several times when the front door, known to be locked, was found unlocked; several items disappeared and turned up after a time; window blinds would swing for no obvious cause, even after they had just been steadied; and electrical equipment seemed to malfunction irrationally. There were sightings of apparitions, voices on the telephone when no-one was touching it, a sense of being followed when no-one was there, and a voice heard by June, another member of staff, in the kitchen, asking 'Do you want this?' when there was no-one else in the room.

Miss Hartley continued: 'We invited a clairvoyant to visit the premises and she told us that we have two permanent spirits. One is male; she told us he is trying to protect us and the building. She described him as wearing a brown suit and smoking a pipe. She thought he may have died of a heart attack as he had blue lips. This apparently matches the description of a man who owned the building a long time ago. The other spirit is a woman; her hair is in a bun, she wears a tweed skirt, twin set and pearls. The clairvoyant thought this spirit is also trying to help us, though she doesn't know how to.

'The clairvoyant also told us there were other spirits who came and went. She could feel the presence of a man whose description fitted exactly that of a man who used to work in the back office, and she said he wanted to say hello to Elsie. We later realised that Elsie was his wife. Since the death of Elsie we no longer feel him around and the door to the back office no longer bangs.'

Name: Losing Their Marbles?
Location: Warminster, Wiltshire, southern England
Date: 1964
Source: *The Warminster Triangle* by Ken Rogers

Ken Rogers was a dedicated researcher of the UFO phenomenon in the area of Warminster, the town which more or less put UFOs on the British map in the 1960s. With a background as a reporter, he worked diligently to try to make sense of the reports there. What emerged was that while the town and the media were concentrating on the things in the skies, there was much going on at ground level: ghosts, disembodied voices and poltergeists, to name but three.

One clear poltergeist case arose for Stan and Doreen Brookes at Crockerton. During the construction of an extension to their cottage in 1964, one evening the couple heard crashing sounds and ran out expecting to find the scaffolding collapsed, but found there was no visible reasons for the sounds.

After the extension was completed they heard further crashings and bangings but never found anything out of place or damaged. On one occasion when they heard a crash in the bedroom they found a broken glass ashtray which had apparently leapt from one side of the room to the other. Such unexplained noises are almost the signature of poltergeist activity.

The couple's pet labrador was terrified, apparently by some invisible presence. Their ten-year-old son disliked being in the house 'because of the bangings on the ceiling'. An electric clock would often gain or lose time.

But the answer was found literally beneath their feet. In 1970 Stan tore up tiles in order to lower the floor, and found beneath them six marble-like stones in the earth. Once they were removed all the strange phenomena they had suffered ceased.

The question that any poltergeist researcher asks – and has not yet had answered with certainty – is did the stones in some way cause the happenings which stopped when they were removed? If not, did the couple unwittingly create these events and then find in the stones a 'reason' to believe that something had changed, actually causing the events to cease.

Name: Lotion-Smearing
Location: Motlonyane village, Gauteng province, South Africa
Date: 31 January 2000
Source: Victor Khupiso writing in the *SunTimes*

An invisible 'creature' was blamed for attacking a family in Gauteng. The 'creature' exhibited the characteristics of a poltergeist, moving beds and breaking objects in the home. The father of the house, Masite Sejake, commented: 'When we sleep, blankets are removed from us and our bodies are smeared with lotions which are in the house.'

The attacks began on 8 January when their 12-year-old son, Tsamaiso, saw a *tokoloshe* (ghost) and, as the news report described, 'screamed that there was a short old man in the house'. During that night a wardrobe moved from the bedroom to the kitchen and other objects moved from the kitchen to the bedroom.

Over time the poltergeist has evolved along lines typical of that type of haunting. Strange writing has appeared on walls, stones have been thrown in the house and the creature has taken to swearing at the family. The family's mother, Mathulo, commented: 'It breaks my heart because my son seems to be the one who is most hated by the creature. It also writes in his schoolbooks and then destroys them – now he leaves his books at school. When I leave food for the children to eat in the morning before they go to school, I find the pots empty and even washed up. Now they go school with empty stomachs.'

The police have investigated but have had no more success in finding a 'culprit' than police the world over faced with such claims by frightened and angry families. Police Captain Patrick Asaneng said: 'I went with a prophet to the house to pray for the family but

nothing happened. The creature attacks them when they are alone.'
He added: 'Our hands are tied in this matter because no crime is
being committed.'

Name: The Old Man
Location: The Globe Public House, Littlehampton, West Sussex,
    southern England
Date: 1970s
Source: Elaine White (witness) / authors' own files

'When I was about three or four years old, my parents ran a pub in
Littlehampton, West Sussex, called The Globe. Also there were my two
brothers, who were about 14 or 15.

'Originally the pub had been three fishermen's cottages, and had
its very own "smugglers' run" to the local church. The side which
was our living quarters was once a cottage that apparently belonged
to one of the last surviving crewmembers of the Cutty Sark, which
gives an idea of the age of the property.

'From day one of moving in, there was an atmosphere we all
noticed, especially in our living area. It started off as being cold and
musty-smelling, no matter how much heating was on. It then
progressed to bangings, items moving, objects floating, sightings and
– for me the most frightening – an apparition. I saw this on several
occasions, either at the foot of my bed or by my window. He had a
very bushy beard and dressed in strange clothes. I eventually refused
to sleep in that room because of finding him staring at me. I slept in
my parents' room, where I never saw him.

'Among many happenings were things like heavy glass ashtrays
that would fly along the bar, doors banging and voices heard when
no-one was about. Things would go missing and be found in strange
places. Bottles would come from the back of the shelf and smash on
the floor. Packets of crisps would explode for no reason. Faces were
seen at the windows of empty rooms. My brother was bottling up in
the yard when he got the feeling of being watched. He looked up to
see a face at a window of a room which was locked and completely
empty.

'A friend of my brother's was staying overnight once and woke up
to see an alarm clock move from a bedside table and "walk" up the
wall to the pelmet above the window. Our pets, two cats and a dog,
virtually refused to enter some areas of the place; there were times
when they would bark, miaow or stand with their heckles up for no
apparent reason.

'During a party of mine, a little girl approached my mother and told her that "he wasn't happy". When asked "who" wasn't, she said, "The old man's not happy, we're making too much noise!"

'One night, while my parents were out and friends were baby-sitting, the babysitters heard doors banging, chairs being moved and voices. On going downstairs they found everything locked up and no-one about.

'We always had the impression that we were never meant any harm, just that we had in our midst a very mischievous spirit. This was all well over 20 years ago but I can still remember it quite vividly, as do the other members of my family.'

Name: Persistent Spook
Location: Jeffersonville, Indiana, USA
Date: 1991 to the present
Source: Bill and Teresa (witnesses) / authors' own files

Most poltergeists are short-lived, if somewhat spectacular. Current thinking suggests that the reason is that the people affected are going through change – adolescents are a typical case – and that when the process of change is ended, the poltergeist activity stops. But there are several cases where people not going through change experience poltergeists. As they have no process of change to end, so the poltergeist activity has no 'reason' to end. This usually happens to stable couples.

This case, submitted by Bill and Teresa, is just such a case. It is impossible to adequately summarise in a compilation such as this because of the repetitive, almost tedious, small activities which constantly 'nag' at the witnesses, but we have summarised here some of the sense of the poltergeist. At the time of writing, Bill and Teresa had counted well over 300 events in their homes.

'The first strange phenomenon we were aware of was greasy prints on a bathroom mirror in a Louisville, Kentucky, apartment we lived in in 1991-92. No-one else had been in the apartment. We were perplexed, but eventually we forgot about the prints. A year or so after we moved to our present home in Jeffersonville, I once again noticed the same greasy smudges on the bathroom mirror and window. Again we were puzzled. On our bedroom window we found greasy smudges that looked like a small child's handprint. No children had visited us.

'During the time that we were still able to ignore the grease smudges, we heard rapping sounds. We had just returned home on New Year's Eve 1995 in time to turn on the TV and watch the New Year celebrations in Times Square. A few minutes before midnight, while Bill was in the bathroom, I heard a knock at the TV room window. I didn't count the raps, but I would guess that there were three. Naturally, I looked towards the window, but there was nothing there. Bill entered the room and I told him about the knock. It knocked again and we looked together towards where the sound came from, but saw nothing. Our TV room is on the second floor and there are no trees nearby that could have made the sound. We had heard no knocks before, nor have there been any since. But wasn't knocking at 11:59 pm on New Year's Eve a good way to allow us to mark the time in our minds?

'One event that made us face the fact that something odd was going on happened in March 1996. A comb I knew I had in my shoebox of barber tools was missing and turned up next to the bathroom sink, in plain sight. I almost felt like "someone" was saying, "Gotcha!"

'On 15 July 1996 one of our strangest events happened. Soon after getting out of bed, Bill blew his nose and out came a live snail. At the time we still weren't accustomed to blaming things on the spook, so we were quite amazed and perplexed. Now we just consider it to be part of the phenomena.

'Over the next few months an assortment of odd things happened. Pain pills returned to the downstairs medicine chest two hours after we had both searched there for them. An over-the-counter medicine that we hadn't seen in years appeared in a prominent spot. Items were moved to places we knew we hadn't put them. Once, while I was home alone, I thought it would be creepy if the downstairs radio turned itself off while I was upstairs. A little later I went downstairs to discover that very thing had happened.

'The first of our "theme" events occurred in November 1996 when we found the lever on the bedroom closet lock slid to the locked position, and later found the front porch screen door locked. Two doors that we never lock were found locked on the same day.

'We got a list of new TV channels and Bill carefully set it aside so he could make a photocopy in case the original got lost. It went missing before he could copy it and he finally had to copy someone else's list so we could see what channels we had. A few days later he started to get into the car and our original list was hanging down from the sun visor, mocking him.

'For some time clothing was affected. Items would go missing and turn up in odd places. New items would suddenly turn up and

eventually we realised they were "gifts" from the spook. A handker-
chief we had lost turned up after I asked Bill what had happened to
it. A day or so after I mentioned it, he found it on top of his stack of
handkerchiefs, ripped and worn quite thin. Where had it been and
who wore it out?

'Gifts became a theme. A few days later one of my most intriguing
events happened. I was at home alone decorating the house for
Christmas and found a New Year horn from the year before. I placed
it next to our tiny tabletop tree, and the fleeting thought passed
through my mind that I wished I had another horn to go with the
first one. I knew we had two, but I had no idea where the other one
was. I left the room for a few minutes and returned to find the other
horn sitting on the sideboard. I said, "Thanks," placed the new horn
next to the tree and regretted not wishing for something more
valuable than a cardboard horn.

'During Christmas my daughter Michelle came home from college
just in time to see the beginning of a particularly busy time,
spook-wise. She planned to apply to law school while she was here
and had her applications mailed to our address. They arrived and she
put them in a safe place up in her room. Two days later she decided
to fill them out, but they were missing. She hunted frantically,
dreading having to contact the law school and admit that she was so
irresponsible that she had lost the application papers. I happened to
walk past my sewing table downstairs and the application papers
were on it. I gave them to Michelle and asked her if she had put them
there. She got that same perplexed look on her face that we had often
had and said, "Well . . . I guess I could have." But I had had enough
experience with the spook to know better.

'There have been several audio events in addition to the radio
coming on. Most of them have been for Bill's listening pleasure, but
while Michelle was visiting us she was awakened by one loud piano
chord being played downstairs. We don't have a piano.

'For about a month we found dimes in odd places. Sometimes
they seemed to fall out of thin air and make an audible plop as they
hit the floor. The final dime event was when Bill found one on his
chair. He took the coin to another room, thinking it was odd that it
wasn't the customary dime, and when he returned to his chair there
were two dimes on it.

'I liked our most recent event because it didn't leave me with any
doubts; I know this was a genuine spook gift. Six years ago we went
to Egypt and I wrote down some useful Arabic words that I had
found in a book by a man who travelled in Egypt. Knowing we were
shortly to return to Egypt, once again I read the book, making a

mental note of the page that had the Arabic words on it. I intended to write them down again to take with us. A day or so later I needed some blank paper to make labels for fabric I had bought, and I glanced at my sewing table and saw a little note pad. When I opened it I found my six-year-old list of Arabic words. I know I have cleaned my sewing table off in the past six years.

'I already mentioned the "gotcha" aspect of some events. Another feature is the attempt to create doubt; often there is an "escape hatch" for us to use. It usually takes a lot of ridiculous stretching to use the escape hatch to explain away the event, and we have long since stopped trying.

Sometimes events occur after a guest or workman has been here briefly. We are certain the visitor didn't rearrange our possessions, turn on lights or fans or leave items in the pantry, but the fact that another person was in our house casts doubt on the likelihood of it having been done by the spook.

'Our house is 129 years old and two self-proclaimed psychics told us (independently of each other) that long ago a man killed his wife and little girl in our basement. Both psychics hated being downstairs and they think the bodies are buried under the concrete basement floor or in the walls. Despite that grisly tale, Bill and I don't feel that we are being visited by dead people. Poltergeist stories tend to have many similarities, and I don't think all dead people would have the same sense of humour. We have no clue as to why this entity came into our lives, but we don't think it has anything to do with our house. The greasy prints started before we moved here, and the spook has gone on several trips with us. The house isn't haunted; we are, and we think Bill is the main focus.

'The frequency of our poltergeist activities has sharply declined, but the spook is still with us and probably always will be. We have come to enjoy the strange happenings and miss him when he neglects us for a while.'

Name: Pete
Location: Cardiff, south Wales
Date: 1988-89 to the late 1990s
Source: Journal of the Society for Psychical Research (SPR) /
    researcher David Fontana / authors' own files

Some time around 1988 or 1989 a poltergeist infested an engineering workshop in Cardiff and became something of a local celebrity.

David Fontana investigated the case in June 1989 for the SPR, by which time 15 events had already been catalogued. Four adults were involved: the couple who owned the shop, John and Pat; Gerry, a relative who worked for them, and her husband Fred. The poltergeist was quickly given a name: Pete.

Objects such as coins, stones and bits of engineering equipment seemed to apport into the shop. Carburettor floats were often found with their needle-ends embedded in the polystyrene ceiling. Soon the poltergeist became responsive; for example, when John and Pat said they should write down an account of what was happening, a pen and a piece of paper appeared. One of the most spectacular responses came when John said to Pat: 'All we need now are some planks of wood.' Planks of wood immediately flew into the workshop. John was adamant that they were too heavy to have been lifted, aimed and thrown in the short moment between his comment and their arrival.

As Fontana arrived for the first time, a stone 'pinged' on some machinery. Fontana is certain that no-one could have seen him coming or would have known when he was going to arrive. He commented: 'Though minor in itself, the apparent incident of the stone hitting the machinery at the exact moment I arrived appeared to have some significance.' Fontana was present during several incidents.

One feature that became locally famous was that stones thrown into a particular corner would be 'returned'. To test this, John would mark the stones; sometimes the ones returned were the marked ones, sometimes not. Fontana also experimented, stating: 'I found that I was able to reproduce this phenomenon myself, and did so on a number of separate occasions. There was no question of my own stone bouncing back and being mistaken for that "thrown" by "Pete".'

On one occasion a local man brought a bag of stones in because he had heard about 'Pete' in the local media and asked if he could 'play' with the poltergeist, throwing the stones into the corner and getting them back. John agreed, and the man amused, and perplexed, himself doing just that.

Customers and sales people visiting encountered 'Pete'. One woman became somewhat alarmed sitting in a chair by the counter as a ring of coins fell in a circle all around her.

One Monday morning, when opening up the premises, the staff found the engine of a petrol lawnmower was running despite the fact that it took three separate operations to start it. It was very loud and could not have been left on accidentally when the shop was closed on the Friday; had it been, it would have run out of petrol long before the Monday.

Fontana examined the case very thoroughly. In subsequent visits, looking for fraud, he dismissed such a suggestion on the grounds of lack of both motive and opportunity.

Perhaps 'Pete' decided it was time to make himself more clearly known. Fred saw the apparition of a small boy sitting on shelves near the ceiling, and again saw a small figure in short trousers and a peaked cap waving as if to say goodbye.

It seems that 'Pete' might well have left the shop around then. The shop was closed down and indeed demolished (we visited the original site, which was just a pile of rubble), as the business moved to another location.

But the activity had not ceased; it seemed to have been transferred to Fred and Gerry's home. Apports of coins and other objects were being found there. Fred might well have been irritated by these events, but he was also open about feeling somewhat special that 'Pete' had chosen him.

Name: The Portsmouth House
Location: 7100 Block of N. Portsmouth Ave, Portland, Oregon,
   USA
Date: 1988 onwards
Source: H. Michael Ball / The Ghosts of North Portland website

The main value of this report is that it comes first hand from local researcher H. Michael Ball who, apart from his familiarity with local hauntings, is especially familiar with what was once his own home. In his words: 'This house has it all. I know, I used to live there at one time. My daughters are still there and unexplained phenomena still occurs, although not with the same frequency and force. There was a "natural" death in the house – a woman died in her sleep in 1987 (the year before we moved in). Her husband was very hurried about selling and moving out. We got a very good deal for such a nice house, but we didn't plan on all the phenomena which would soon occur.

'Shortly after moving in, my youngest daughter was alone on the main floor while I was out back chatting with a neighbour. My daughter was looking for a missing shoe. She said out loud, "Now where is that shoe?" Just as she said that, the shoe came tumbling down the stairs, landing at her feet. There was no-one upstairs; no humans or animals. She was quite scared and had me come into the house to explain what had happened.

'My daughters have seen a transparent silver form upstairs. This has been seen many times. It doesn't last long and it does not take on a clear form. The smell of rotting fish has frequented the upstairs and basement areas. Electronic equipment runs by itself. Objects move position – my oldest daughter used to place tape around her knick-knacks. No-one would touch them and, when checked, they had moved position.

'One of the strangest occurrences I have personally experienced is when it would rain inside the house. Drops of water would hit us on the arms, shoulders and head. This happened on the main floor, usually in the kitchen. I wish it *was* a leaky faucet or roof but no, there was no apparent source. The drops were odourless and tasteless, which made us believe it was probably water.

'Voices have also been heard. Soft, quiet voices asking simple questions such as, "Oh, really?" or "Are you sure?".'

Name: Revenge From The Grave?
Location: Ooty (now Udagamandalam), southern India
Date: 1897
Source: *Can We Explain the Poltergeist?* by A.R.G. Owen

The *Madras Times* of 7 May 1897 described the account of two girls, Gracie and Floralina, who had suffered extraordinary after-effects of a childish prank. In April the two girls had been fooling around in a cemetery and had danced on the grave of a recent suicide. Whether the spirit of the suicide sought revenge for their disrespect or whether their own guilt projected a bizarre effect in them, both girls acted as if possessed: 'Their eyes were wild; they tore their clothes, went into frenzies and were held down with difficulty.'

From 20 April Floralina became the victim of a stone-throwing poltergeist in her home. Drinking glasses were smashed, 'almost reduced to powder' by large stones thrown with great force from within the house. One witness, who had attended the house with another friend and a policeman, commented, 'What astonished us most was the breaking of the glasses, which could not have been accomplished by stones thrown from outside.' Over a period of several days stones damaged the glasses in the house, grazed Floralina's head and bombarded the windows of the house from outside. Mr James Kelly, superintendent of St Bartholomew's Hospital, forwarded a letter to the Madras Times stating, 'I was an eye witness of the phenomena, and although I looked for the cause with much care, I could find none.'

Name: Sandman?
Location: Yorkhill Street, Partick, Glasgow, Scotland
Date: February 1974
Source: Strange Phenomena Investigations (SPI)/Malcolm
 Robinson

In our earlier book The Poltergeist Phenomenon, we demonstrated the astonishingly wide range of phenomena that poltergeists can manifest. But individual cases seem always to have their own surprises, and for every common occurrence, such as the movement of objects, stone throwing, strange noises and so on, there are 'one-off', extraordinary situations. Such was the case with the events that happened in a condemned tenement in Glasgow.

Kenneth J. Kelly provided this account 'The following is a true and accurate account of what I found in a room of my house early one morning in February 1974. I was awakened at 8am by my wife shaking me violently and saying, "We've been burgled!" I opened my eyes to a scene of mayhem. The whole room was a shambles. Every pane of glass in the window was shattered, the television was lying on the floor in the opposite corner from where it had been previously; the sideboard had been pushed over – it had wedged against the back of the heavy sofa, thus preventing it from fully toppling over, but all the contents were scattered over the floor; but most inexplicable was that almost every piece of glass had been changed to a very fine type of sand. Every cup, saucer, plate, bowl and tumbler, even my wife's collection of Italian glass ornaments which had stood on the high mantelpiece. There had been eight such pieces, all of heavy, multi-coloured glass, but in place of each stood a large mound of brightly coloured sand, the colours synonymous with those of each ornament. We also had a set of blue and white striped bowls but all we found were little mounds of blue and white striped sand.

'I checked the door and found it still locked, chained and bolted from the inside. It was this discovery which made me a bit apprehensive. The rest of the house was untouched and nothing was missing, if you accept that the mounds of sand were really the glass objects.

'We left the house and went to my parents and told them. My father suggested I take the dog over to my house and if there was "something" there, as he put it, the dog would probably sense it and react accordingly. The dog was a well-trained Alsatian guide dog (my parents both being totally blind). I went back to the house but when I tried to take the dog up to the entrance he became very agitated and would not enter. I tried to pull him but he began snarling and was very panicky. The dog would not enter the building, let alone the flat. I returned to tell my father and he said we should not go back to the house, and we didn't. I did go back a few days later to pick up our belongings and everything was as we had left it, except that the sand had been blown everywhere.

'I hope whoever reads this finds something useful in this description of what I have come to call "the aftermath of a visitation". I will simply reiterate that what I have written is what actually happened. Make of it what you will.'

Name: Scratching Fanny
Location: Cock Lane, London, England
Date: Mid 18th century
Source: Various

One of the most notorious poltergeist cases in history, which was highly publicised at the time, is the Cock Lane ghost. Cock Lane was a rundown street of tenements and moderately successful businesses in the 1750s.

William Kent and his wife Fanny took lodgings in Cock Lane. His landlord was Richard Parsons, who had an 11-year-old daughter, Elizabeth. Kent entrusted to Parsons a great secret: that Fanny was not in fact his wife, his true wife having died a year earlier in childbirth, but was actually his sister-in-law, who could not therefore legally become his wife. It says something about the bond between them that he was able to share such a secret with Parsons.

In 1759 Kent was away attending a wedding and Fanny, afraid of sleeping alone, asked Parsons if Elizabeth might spend the night with her to keep her company. That night their bedroom was filled with scratching, bumping and rapping noises.

Later, Kent and Parsons fell out over a business transaction. Kent had lent Parsons a considerable sum of money and then had to sue him to reclaim it. Parsons spitefully broadcast the news that the Kents were not married, and the couple had to move. Fanny, now pregnant, became certain that the noises in the bedroom were an omen of her death, and indeed she did die a few weeks later, of smallpox.

Back in Cock Lane, Elizabeth now 13, in 1761, was suffering poltergeist rappings and scratchings, more so than before. She changed bedrooms and slept with neighbours and still the poltergeist followed her. Parsons turned for help to Reverend John Moore, who began a series of seances which became notorious throughout London. The house was visited by Samuel Johnson, Oliver Goldsmith, Horace Wallpole and many others fascinated by the seances. Parsons came to believe that his daughter was being attacked by the ghost of Fanny Kent. According to communication with the spirit during the seances, Fanny had been murdered by her husband, using arsenic poisoning, and now wanted him to hang for the crime. Kent, a stockbroker, suddenly found himself sensationally accused in the Press and he was pointed out on the streets as a potential murderer. Eventually, he attended one of the seances and heard the spirit charge him with murder. Kent cried out, 'Thou art a lying spirit! Thou art not the ghost of my Fanny. She would never have said any such thing.'

It became important that Elizabeth be tested to rule out trickery. If the poltergeist activity was found to be genuine, Kent could be tried on murder charges; if faked, then Parsons was possibly guilty of a curious form of revenge. The tests were vigorous. Elizabeth was stretched across a hammock with her arms and legs under tight control and with her hands in plain view. Under these conditions the poltergeist activity did not occur and then, bizarrely, Elizabeth was told that unless she could produce the poltergeist manifestations her father would be imprisoned for fraud. She was then caught trying to fake the sounds – hardly surprising considering what she had been told was at stake. The result was that Parsons was convicted of conspiracy and condemned to the public pillory, where it was assumed he would be pelted with garbage by the public. The public, however, were not so convinced of his guilt and showered him instead with money. They had realised that the fact that Elizabeth had cheated to protect her father was no proof that she had always been faking.

Name: Stones And A Ghost
Location: Grenada, West Indies
Date: September 1934
Source: Ghosts and Poltergeists by Father Herbert Thurston

The story of this stone-throwing poltergeist associated with the apparition of a ghost was first recorded in the Grenadan newspaper

The West Indian of 23 September 1934. The house occupied by Mrs Excelia Mark, her two daughters and a grandchild, Ivy, was bombarded by stones for around two months. The stones, varying from between 2oz and 1lb in weight, were falling from the skies onto the house, as observed by police who had climbed onto the roof to investigate. One puzzling feature of the stones was that they did not bounce on impact.

Ivy was apparently the focus of the poltergeist. Mrs Mark commented, 'I noticed that whenever Ivy was present more stones would fall, but when she was not there everything was quiet. Besides stones, such things as salt, various powders, matches and letters were picked up on the roof of the house.'

Sometimes Ivy saw the apparition of a white man, dressed in white. She first saw him standing on the road 12 feet from the house but when she pointed him out to her grandmother, the elder lady could not see him. She commented that while stones were falling the man was there, though she never saw him throwing stones. She also pointed out that several times stones were falling inside the house even when the house was locked up. 'Every time the stones were falling, I used to see the man. I used to see the man inside the house sometimes; sometimes sitting on the bed.' At one point this apparition was in the company of two other figures, another man and a woman, both also dressed in white.

Over time furniture, tables, chairs and other objects were moved around in the house or pitched over, and on each occation Ivy said she could see the apparitions, though no-one else could. Detective Bernadine, who had investigated the case, added, 'I remember one morning I was inside the house and the doors and windows were all closed. I heard a sound on the galvanised roof and a stone fell in front of me without making or leaving any hole.'

What brought a lot of attention back to the case was that in the following year, the house was burnt to the ground. In *The West Indian's* report of 29 January, 'several of the witnesses spoke only of the fire and of the impossibility of explaining how it originated.'

There is the suggestion that the house was under attack by a curse. During the investigation a strange parcel of dirty 'odds and ends' was found on the roof, which Father Thurston believes was 'suggestive of Obeah practices'. It is known that one of the daughters of the house, Dolly, had just won a legal action for defamation after being referred to as 'Dracula' and was awarded damages.

Name: Stone Thrower
Location: Port Louis, Mauritius
Date: 1937
Source: The Forum publication, South Africa

In 1937 Cappy Ricks published his account of a stone-throwing poltergeist that affected his home in Port Louis for four days during September.

The first event was a stone that landed at the feet of his children's nanny (a Creole girl around 11 years old), frightening her. That day 40 other stones were to fall inside the house, and at least as many outside. The nanny left in a state of 'collapse', not returning that day.

The next day stones began bombarding the house from early morning to late evening, despite the fact that police had been called and were keeping the house under surveillance. By the Wednesday the stones were still coming, and getting more dangerous. One weighing 6lb hit Mr Ricks on the shoulder.

Understandably, the family were becoming concerned and they moved out to stay with Mr Ricks's mother. But the stone throwing followed them there, so they moved on again to a friend's house. Still the stone throwing followed them. They eventually moved into a hotel. Mr Ricks estimated that 300 stones attacked them on that day.

Returning to his own home, Mr Ricks was to experience even more frightening sights. He watched as a large stone levitated five feet in the air and moved towards the nanny. A stone also headed towards him. He avoided it but it smashed some glassware.

On the Thursday, Ricks and the nanny were present early and the stones began arriving immediately. Ricks left for his office having piled them up on his bed; 14 stones, up to 5lb in weight, an unripe melon and a quantity of reglisse seeds. He left a note for the police officer who was due to visit. But he had only just arrived at his office when he was telephoned with the news that 'much of his home had been wrecked'. Breakable items had been smashed, curtains had been pulled down and many items strewn about. He also got another call from the hotel asking him to get his family out at once.

Mr Ricks realised that these stonings were somehow connected to the nanny, even though they were affecting locations where she was not present. Her attachment to the family, he reasoned, must be a factor. In some way she was the focus. The nanny was dismissed and moved out; and the events stopped, never to recur.

Name: The Talking Chimney
Location: Saragossa, Spain
Date: 1934
Source: Nandor Fodor (*The Story of the Poltergeist* by Carrington and Fodor)

In the last months of 1934 an extraordinary story was being related in newspapers around the world, including several entries in that most staid of publications, *The Times* of London. On 24 November *The Times* reported from Madrid: 'A friendly ghost which speaks down the chimney of an economical cooker is a phenomenon sufficiently rare to cause some sensation even among the matter of fact inhabitants of Saragossa, who have set out to trace the mystery to its source. The "spirit" occupies a detached house, so it is difficult to imagine how a practical joker could be at work in a neighbouring building. [*Author's note: We should point out that it had eight flats within it, however.*] An architect and some workmen were called in. They searched the building from roof to cellar, but without finding a possible hiding place for the joker. Finally, the architect said: "Measure the chimney pipe." "You need not trouble, the diameter is just six inches," said the ghost politely. It was.'

The house in Callegascon de Gotor was the home of the Palazon family and their 16-year-old maid Maria Pascuela. The phenomenon was investigated by the Press, doctors and the police. The police were suspicious of the family and effectively evicted them from their own house while they staked out the premises, waiting for the ghost to speak. The result was, as reported in *The Times* of 27 November: 'Sitting solemnly through the night in front of the economical cooker and its mysterious flue, a police guard heard no voice. The report to the magistrate this morning being negative, that official has washed his hands of the affair, saying that he can find no grounds for charges against anybody. Medical circles are still interested, however, and the public is awaiting expectantly the return of the evicted family to their flat.'

The focus of attention was thought to be the maid. As reported by the London *Evening Standard* of 5 December: 'The whole trouble started one morning . . . when Maria, the maid . . . was lighting the fire in the kitchen range in order to get breakfast. She nearly fell over backwards when a voice came out of the chimney and greeted her effusively. Her mistress, who came to see what all the fuss was about, was also startled out of her wits.'

The maid was thought to be the centre of the disturbance and various suggestions were put forward that she was in effect an unconscious ventriloquist, although none of those using the term at the time explained to their readers what they thought that might be. It may well be that the maid, who was apparently at the point of puberty, was instilled with some of that extraordinary quality that perhaps aids poltergeists and other paranormal activity for short bursts of time. In this case, perhaps she did somehow project some inner turmoil in an unconscious voice. It is clear that others heard it too, so whether she did therefore possess some kind of ventriloquistic ability is still an open question.

But an open question was not what the civil governor of Saragossa wanted. He issued a statement on 30 November: 'I think that we will soon discover the joker and thus dispel the groundless anxiety which this incident has aroused.' In other words, the governor had decided to allay public fear by declaring the incidents to be fraud, although there was little ground for doing so and little investigation to support him. Nevertheless, on 4 December the governor announced that the 'ghost' of Saragossa had been located. 'The servant girl employed in the haunted flat,' he said, 'was an unconscious ventriloquist.' He added that 'this discovery disposed of the affair.'

Nandor Fodor, in his analysis, comments that, 'The last bow of the ghost was rather spectacular.' Apparently, 20 people were present, including doctors and police officials, and all heard the ghost. Furthermore, despite the governor's statement, they believed the voice had a supernatural origin. Fodor concluded that the records 'are sufficiently good to establish without any possibility of doubt, that Anno Domini 1934, in the City of Saragossa, a manifestation occurred which claimed to have its agency in another world of intelligence than our own, and which claim defied the efforts of the authorities to ascribe it to trickery or normal causation'.

Name: Threatened And Attacked
Location: St John's, Newfoundland, Canada
Date: 1998
Source: Dale Gilbert Jarvis, researcher and folklorist

In April 1998, Michelle, a young St John's woman, rented a room in one of the apartments in a large 19th-century house in the north half of Sutherland Place. By the second week of April, however, she had moved out and found shelter at a friend's house. She had fled her apartment, convinced that it was no longer a safe place.

During her very first night in her room in Sutherland Place, she had sat up in panic, sweating, for no apparent reason. Over the next few days, she experienced strange and unfocused feelings of unease while in the apartment. She was also overcome time and again by the sensation of an oppressive silence that engulfed her while there.

Once, while she was talking to a friend on the telephone, the couch she was sitting on began to rock back and forth. Her first assumption was that the movement of the couch was caused by activity in a nearby room. However, she found that she was entirely alone in the apartment. Even more unsettling, no other items in the room were moving, which ruled out shaking resulting from a movement of the floor.

The most frightening event occurred as Michelle was leaving the building one day. She was walking easily down the stairs but as she started down the last flight, she felt a weight in the small of her back, as if from the pressure of someone's hand. The invisible hand gave her a firm push which forced her violently down the last flight of steps, sending her crashing to the bottom.

After that, Michelle refused to return to the building alone and remained at her friend's house. Most of her personal belongings had been left behind. Apparently, she was not the first person to experience a haunting in the building. Just one month before she moved in, an earlier tenant had been terrified when she woke in the night to see the spectral figure of an old woman standing at the foot of her bed. The crone loomed over her, as if the woman had been standing watching her sleeping form. The ghost had long, black hair and was wearing long, flowing, black clothes.

Name: Very Powerful!
Location: Belle Monte Avenue, Lakeside Park, Kentucky, USA
Date: From summer 1979 to 1984
Source: Les Wilson and witnesses John and Mary Anna / authors' own files

Les has corresponded with us since late 1998 about a series of poltergeist events that happened to two friends of his. Les related the story to us and the witnesses have been through the transcript to check for accuracy.

'Our friends moved into Belle Monte during the summer of 1979. Shortly after they moved in, strange occurrences had them accusing one another of pranks. As the "pranks" progressed, it became apparent that much more was wrong.

'Mary Anna came home one day to find that every clock in the house had been set to a different time. Some were set ahead, some behind. They were all different. Shortly after this, their son Jerry discovered a message on the bathroom mirror: "Get out! MY HOUSE!" It was written in what appeared to be lipstick, but not of a shade that was in the house. Of course, the family jokingly accused one another, but they ultimately became concerned that someone was breaking into the house.

'The pranks continued; keys, jewellery and other items disappeared or moved. They heard strange noises and found furniture out of place. They still assumed that one of the family was playing an elaborate joke.

'Due to some family problems, two young girls, cousins, came to stay with John and Mary Anna. Almost immediately, they started losing toys and articles of clothing. After a short while they began to complain that a "dark man" was coming into the bedroom at night and standing over them. With all their difficulties and stress, Mary Anna was concerned about their stories. She thought they might need psychological help. That thought came to an end when Jerry, answering nature's call in the wee hours, walked out into the hall to see a tall, dark, shadowy figure standing before the cousins' bedroom door. Frozen to the spot, he stared in amazement as the figure dissolved into nothing. After a few weeks, the girls went home. Mary Anna went to the basement with a load of laundry and almost fainted from shock. There, in the middle of the basement floor, was a large pile of stuff: all the missing toys, clothing, and household items.

'My wife Beverly and I went to visit John and Mary Anna one evening. We had an uneventful night chatting about computers, cars, dogs and whatever. Suddenly there was a noise upstairs like furniture being dragged. Jerry muttered, "Not again," and started up the stairs. I was just a few steps behind him. The door to his room was open. He ran in with me just about six feet behind. The door suddenly slammed shut so hard that the frame made a loud cracking noise. Jerry screamed and it sounded like the room was being torn apart. I hit the door and it would not open. John and I worked together and finally got the door open enough to get in.

'Jerry was under the bedclothes and the mattress, which was flipped over, on the other side of the room. He was kicking and crying and trying to get up. The noise had come from the dresser. A huge dresser with a chest of drawers at each end and a low table across the middle had been moved. The dresser had been fastened to the wall. Two large mirrors were bolted to the table and to 1in x 2in strips that were toggle-bolted to the wall. The dresser had shifted about four feet to the right, blocking the doorway. It moved with such force that it sheared off the screw holding the doorknob in place and it cracked plaster and baseboard on the wall normally behind the door. The hardwood floor was gouged. The mirrors hung at an angle. The strips had split. The plaster wall was destroyed. This had all happened in a matter of seconds.

'We helped Jerry up and when he calmed down he said that he didn't see anything. As he had entered the room, he had felt someone grab his shoulders and push him on to the bed. He had rolled off the other side and suddenly the bedclothes and mattress were on top of him. He had heard the furniture crashing into the wall and heard us yelling, but was unable to see what was happening. John, Jerry and I had to work hard to push the heavy dresser back into position. The wall behind the dresser was a total loss. The plaster had gaping holes and the mesh behind it was ripped open as well. The strips on the wall had moved, shattering the plaster. When the toggle bolts encountered a stud in the wall, the strips just snapped.

'We went back downstairs. There was little or no discussion, it was more like stunned disbelief. Shortly afterwards, my wife took their white cat (named Ghost!) down to the basement. As she was walking across the floor, she heard heavy footsteps on the stairs. She turned and said, "Hi, John." But there was no-one there.

'John and Mary Anna had a minister come and bless the house, room by room. Unfortunately, this did not seem to help. A short time later, Mary Anna, unable to sleep, was resting on the couch. The old rocker in the corner began to rock. Mary Anna said she could "hear" a singsong chant: "It is time to rock. I must rock." As she watched, a smoky image began to materialise in the chair. She screamed and ran to get John. When they returned, there was nothing there.

'Now totally unable to sleep, she settled on the couch again. John returned to bed. The chair began to rock again. The chant returned. This time Mary Anna "shouted" mentally, "Stop this! This is our house. You get out!" The shadowy figure rose from the chair toward the ceiling. It then "receded", moving away "through" the wall, but remaining visible. It finally moved too far away to be seen. Shortly after this, the family sold the house and moved to another place they had inherited.'

We contacted the present owners, who told us that they were suffering from haunting phenomena; indeed, they had called in a priest and psychics to try to help them and were astonished when we told them of what we knew of the house from two decades ago. Our investigation will continue into this unfolding case.

Name: The Wild Beast
Location: Guarulhos, Northern San Marco, Brazil
Date: 1973 onwards
Source: Journal of the SPR vol. 56, no 820 / Investigator
  Hernani Guimaraes Andrade of the Brazilian Institute of
  Psychobiophysical Research

The poltergeist that invaded the home of Marcos, Noemia and their family in 1973 and stayed for three years – to some extent for 11 years – must be one of the most persistent in the history of the subject. The family moved homes and the poltergeist went with them; not surprising, as poltergeists are 'people centred', but it is rare for these activities to survive many changes in family circumstances.

The first attacks on the family came in April 1973 when they found long parallel cuts in furniture and mattresses. Although suspicion at first fell on a young boy in the house, three people later confirmed they had seen the cuts appear as if by an invisible agent. Pedro, Marcos's father, saw the apparition of an arm that seemed to belong to 'a wild beast . . . it was very strong and big; sharp-ended claws . . . black, shiny and curved'. Noemia later also saw a shadowy form. A neighbour called in to witness the cutting fainted when she saw the apparition of an enormous hand with dark brown fur and long fingers. Money disappeared and a slip of paper displaying a red cross appeared in the house.

These events seemed to come to an end in May, after a few violent days. But in April the following year, 1974, stone throwing began. Gravel and bricks dropped onto the house, falling directly downwards and not as if having been thrown. Cups and glasses in the house were smashed and other objects moved. Apports and disappearances continued. Money would both disappear and appear: 'The money was thrown on the floor or on some furniture, within everyone's sight, but it wasn't seen from where, nor how, it came.' Cuts in furniture continued as in the previous 'outbreak'. Bibles were cut with the shape of a cross.

The poltergeist moved on to acts of violence against people, which, despite the Hollywood image, is actually very rare. On 2 May 1974 Marcos woke to find his arm bleeding; other people, including visitors to the house, soon found themselves cut as well. Noemia saw more apparitions of the beast: 'something horrible with a face in fire and big teeth.' Pedro, an amateur exorcist with a flair for the dramatic, undertook a magical struggle with an invisible entity that he succeeding in killing with an imaginary sword. It may seem an unlikely cure for the poltergeist, but in fact the phenomena stopped for two months and the cuts never did happen again.

When incidents restarted, small, spontaneous fires broke out. In October 1974 the family sought help from the church and an evangelic exorcism was performed which stopped the phenomena again for a while.

In March 1975 it was back. Stonings continued, the victims including members of the family, guests and church missionaries who had come to help out. Objects were again being thrown about in the house. When the family were saying prayers in the kitchen, a glass left a basin and crashed near a witness's feet; later a Bible 'jumped' from a table and fell to the floor. Marcos watched a shoe levitate and hit the ceiling, leaving a mark. Apports began making appearances, including lit candles in the bedroom. The fires happened again, often centring on clothes in the wardrobe.

The family's youngest daughter, Ruth, saw the apparitions of beasts in her room. Noemia saw a 'shape' near the bedroom and Marcos was hit by a brick while praying in the same place. Twice people experienced trances which it was thought might be a sign of possession, but that, at least, did not develop. A further exorcism by the church virtually brought the events to an end in October 1976.

Over the next seven or so years there was still a 'low level' of activity in the house and around the family: money going missing, the movement of objects. The investigators drew a line at 21 April 1984, as being the 'official' end of the experiences for the family.

Doubles, Bi-Locations, Doppelgangers And Vardogers

From the authors' point of view, this section has a great deal of interest not only because it is a fascinating aspect of hauntings but because we have had personal experience of it – firstly when, many years ago, we discussed with researcher Maurice Grosse his own bi-location during his investigation of the Enfield Poltergeist (outlined in the previous volume), and secondly when John Spencer was reported by a team member as being present in a basement area of a haunted location when he was certainly known to be upstairs at the time. Ghosts of the living are the most frequently reported form of apparition and therefore a rich field for study into whatever mechanisms come into play during the production of such visions.

Name: The Doppelganger Car
Location: Kissimmee, Florida, USA
Date: 1944 or 1945
Source: A.F.C. St Clair (witness)

The following event happened when the witness was four or five years old. A.F.C. St Clair wrote: 'My mother and I were waiting by the side of the highway (Orange Blossom Trail) for my father and grandmother to drive us to Orlando. Back then there was very little traffic on the trail, as it was known. We watched as a black Ford approached from the south with the two of them inside. Neither person appeared to notice us waving at them. I saw their faces through the windshield. The two people looked like my father and grandmother – same clothing, etc. The car disappeared around the corner.

'We were both surprised that the car did not stop – my mother made some very unkind comments about my father and grand- mother. Several minutes later another black Ford appeared from the south. This time the car slowed down and stopped. It was my father and grandmother! We got into the car and asked them why they had driven past us the first time. Their response was: "We just got here." My father indicated that it must have been another couple that looked a lot like them. After a few minutes of arguing, my mother stopped talking about it.

'Twelve years later I asked my father if he remembered the incident. He still remembered the fuss my mother made when she got into the car. He indicated that this kind of situation had happened to him before, more than once, in Kissimmee during the 1940s. This kind of thing (being seen before arriving) appeared to run in the family.'

Name: From The Bedroom To The Garden
Location: Newbury Park, north-east London, England
Date: 1960s
Source: Fleur Conway (witness) / authors' own files

Fleur told us of a doppelganger experience that quite alarmed her: 'When the children were young and we had our first house in Newbury Park, I was in the playroom. We had converted the fourth bedroom into a playroom for the kids and I was painting, or something, at the table. I looked out of the window and what I saw really frightened me. Down in the garden I could actually see myself hanging washing out at the same time as I was here in the room. It was really quite creepy. I just couldn't understand. I did feel a bit weak and I thought, "This is creepy." I had to sit down.'

Name: Gone Fishing
Location: Templemore, County Tipperary, Republic of Ireland
Date: 20 February 1847
Soruce: *Human Personality and its Human Survival of Bodily Death* by
    Frederic W. H. Myers

Major William Bigge was walking from his quarters to the mess room when he saw Lieutenant Colonel Reed also walking towards the mess room door; he watched him go into the passage. Bigge noted that Reed was wearing a brown shooting jacket and tweed trousers and carrying a fishing rod and landing net. Bigge, following him into the mess hall, found Reed was not there. The only person in the room was Quartermaster Nolan. Bigge enquired after Reed but Nolan had not seen him.

Shortly afterwards, outside, Bigge again saw Reed walking into the barracks from the opposite direction accompanied by Ensign Willington and wearing exactly the same clothes Bigge had originally seen him in, and again carrying a fishing rod and landing net. Bigge asked Reed if he had gone into the mess room ten minutes earlier and Reed responded that he certainly hadn't, he had been out fishing for more than two hours and had not been near the mess room all morning.

Bigge commented, 'My eyesight being very good, and the Colonel's figure being somewhat remarkable, it is impossible that I could have mistaken any other person in the world for him. That I did see him I shall continue to believe until the last day of my existence.'

Name: Gordon Barrows
Location: Wyoming, USA
Date: 1946
Soruce: Time Life Books (*Phantom Encounters*)

After he was discharged from the United States Army, Gordon Barrows went to visit his parents in Wyoming and then attended college at the University of Wyoming in Laramie. During a bitter cold college break, Barrows returned home to pick up a Jeep and then drove back to Laramie. He was wrapped up in a Parka coat, mittens and thick boots and had been driving all day and into the night when he hit a blizzard.

As he was driving down into a canyon, he saw a man walking by the side of the road. He stopped and offered the man a lift. Barrows recognised immediately that the man looked just like him and was wearing a Tank Corps jacket identical to the one he himself had worn during wartime but was not wearing now. The man said to Barrows, 'You look sleepy. Want me to drive?' Barrows was tired and allowed the man to drive, falling asleep in the passenger seat. When Barrows awoke the engine was not running and the man was sitting motionless in the driver's seat; they were some 40 miles from the point where he had picked up the passenger. The passenger refused Barrows's offer of a ride into Laramie and when thanked for his assistance simply commented, 'You're welcome.' The figure walked back into the canyon.

Barrow recalled the whole thing almost in a dream-like way, in the sense that preposterous things happen in a dream which seem ordinary at the time and he felt this about the encounter. He knew, however, that something had happened. He realised that any figure walking in the canyon during that blizzard could not have survived for very long, and became convinced that it was a projection of himself.

Name: Guy de Maupassant
Location: Unknown
Date: 1885
Source: Various

Guy de Maupassant was a French author, held by many to be one of the greatest masters of the short story. He was trained in the art of literary fiction by a close family friend, the noted novelist Gustave Flaubert. Maupassant's first important work was the short story Boule de Suif (Ball of Fat) published in 1880 and considered a masterpiece. He wrote more than 200 short stories over the next 13 years. He was also the author of three collections of travel sketches and six novels.

In 1885 he was suffering from writer's block while working on his horror tale The Horla. As he was struggling, a figure entered the room, sat down opposite him and began to dictate passages of the book. De Maupassant was concerned – he could not understand how the individual had got into his rooms, nor could he understand why the figure knew so much about the book he was writing. Only then did he identify the individual: it was himself. The figure was his own double.

This is a useful case for examining the possible explanations for doubles. What can we make of this? Firstly, we can assume that de Maupassant, if interrupted where he expected not to be interrupted, must have looked up fairly quickly. Yet he apparently did not recognise the figure for some time, at least until he had listened to it dictating passages of text.

Perhaps de Maupassant was seeing a 'self' from another time that he didn't instantly recognise. Look at a few photographs of yourself from, say, ten years ago; confronted by a person looking like that you might not see it as yourself. It is hardly likely to be your first thought, in any case. Perhaps it was a 'self' from the future: after all, a future self would have been familiar with the text of the (by then finished) book. At least part of the explanation for doubles may be that the double is a projection from the sighter's own mind for a purpose. Perhaps those in stress can 'create' an image that helps them, from their own subconscious. This may be a complex way of talking to, or communicating with, oneself – perhaps the subconscious talking to the conscious. Why the brain might need to circumvent its 'normal' channels of communication is unclear, but there is evidence that it does in many situations.

Name: Henry Purdy
Location: Middlesex, southern England
Date: 1982
Source: Various

One night in 1982, Henry J. Purdy awoke to see his wife looking out of the window and into the garden below. He had seen her do this before and found nothing unusual in it; if she woke in the night she liked to gaze out 'to see what the weather outside was like'. However, as he shifted himself in bed, he could feel that his wife was still beside him. She was apparently sleeping peacefully. As he looked back towards the apparition by the window he noticed it slowly fade away. On later discussing it with his wife she had been quite unaware of anything out of the ordinary.

Name: Her Brother
Location: RAF Episkopi base, Cyprus
Date: 1967
Source: Gloria Dixon, researcher

Patricia, whose reports of a haunting and of the apparition of her late husband are recounted elsewhere in the book, also had a very different type of apparition. Gloria Dixon, who interviewed her, described: 'She saw her brother on one occasion during a night while she and her husband Ron were stationed with the RAF in Cyprus. She described her brother as standing at the bottom of the bed with a cigarette in his hand. This was certainly not the apparition of a deceased person, however; her brother was – and is – very much alive, and he had never been to Cyprus. She awoke Ron to observe this 'apparition', but he did not see it as by this time the image had gone.'

At face value, this could be regarded as a dream or hallucination, perhaps generated by hypnagogia (sleep state), but there is a factor weighing against this. Unprompted, her brother wrote to her after this event, asking her why her adult daughter was sleeping in the bed with her one night, and asking where Ron was. He was perfectly correct in this – there was a time in Cyprus when her adult daughter had been in the bed with her and it was a very unusual occurrence for them to be sleeping in the same bed. It was not the same night as the night when Patricia had seen her brother; on that night, her daughter was elsewhere and Ron was in the bed. But it is suggestive that somehow her brother did 'visit' and was perceived by her. Perhaps there was more than one 'visit', and each saw the other only on different occasions.

Name: John Cowper Powys
Location: New York, USA
Date: 1929
Source: Colin Wilson

The novelist John Cowper Powys had spent an evening at his colleague Theodore Dreiser's New York apartment. When Powys left, he told Drieser, 'You'll be seeing me later this evening.' Powys then left for his own home some 50 miles away. Drieser assumed Powys had been joking, since the distance was so great. However, just a few hours later Drieser saw Powys standing inside the door and said to him, 'John! Come on in and tell me how you did it.' As Drieser walked towards him Powys disappeared. Drieser immediately rang Powys's number at his home 50 miles away and Powys answered. Drieser explained what had just happened and Powys commented, 'I told you I'd see you later.' However, Powys never explained what he did or how he did it, and indeed may not have understood the mechanism himself.

Name: John Spencer
Location: North London Community Centre, England
Date: 1990s
Source: Authors' own files

Below we describe Maurice Grosse's experience of having been a 'double' at a poltergeist location. It was with some sense of surprise that when the authors were on site investigating a poltergeist at a

North London community centre, we found that the same thing apparently happened.

John Spencer was on the ground floor along with members of the team, while several other 'pairs' were stationed in the basement. During a ten-minute break for refreshment and changing locations, one of the downstairs team came up looking a little disappointed and said to John, 'It didn't make any difference, turning the light off.' John asked what he meant. According to this team member and his companion in the basement, John had been seen to walk into the room and comment that the lights were very bright, and had advised them to turn them down. John had then left the basement and they turned down the lighting. There had been no events to record during that part of the vigil, hence their comment to John that 'it hadn't made any difference'.

John had never left the ground floor area, nor left his own companion; it was a rigid rule of the vigil that team members should always remain in pairs. John had no recollection of anything untoward, was not aware of the 'interaction' and could not even recall thinking of that location or those collegues in any significant way during that part of the night.

Name: Maurice Grosse
Location: Enfield, north London, England
Date: 1970s
Source: Maurice Grosse

Maurice Grosse was the principal investigator of the Enfield poltergeist, one of the most active poltergeists ever recorded and described in The Encyclopedia of Ghosts and Spirits. In this instance he became part of the case, when he was himself the subject of a bi-location claim.

As he described it to us: 'I was upstairs in a bedroom with some of the family who were living there, including the girl who was the main subject of the investigation. I had been with her for well over an hour. Towards the end of that hour there was a knock on the front door, downstairs. I asked the mother to go downstairs and open the door, which she did.'

The caller was the mother's niece and she was upset that Maurice had ignored her, as she understood it. She had seen Maurice pull aside the curtain next to the door and look out. When the door wasn't opened the niece looked through the letter box to see Maurice plodding up the stairs. So she knocked again. But Maurice had been upstairs with the mother throughout that time.

There was no-one else in the house that could have been mistaken for Maurice, a fairly distinctive character with his 'trademark' handle-bar moustache, and no-one at all downstairs at the time. Maurice had no 'sense' of what had happened; he had been concentrating on the girl for whom he was concerned.

Name: Mrs Elgee
Location: Cairo, Egypt
Date: November 1864
Source: *Phantasms of the Living* by Gurney, Myers and Podmore
   (abridged by Mrs H. Sidgwick)

Mrs Elgee and a companion were travelling in November 1864 and, being held up in Cairo on their way to India, were forced to stay in a rather rundown hotel. Feeling a little nervous, they blocked the room doors with a settee and a chair and then retired to bed.

Mrs Elgee was awoken by a call and saw, in the bedroom, an old friend of hers who she knew to be in England. The intruder was also seen by her companion, who was now also awake. The intruder shook his head and then retreated away from them, and seemed to sink into the floor.

In the morning Mrs Elgee noticed that the settee and chair were undisturbed and she thought she might have been dreaming – until, that is, her companion told her what she had seen – exactly the same vision.

Mrs Elgee became convinced that her friend must have died and come to her to say goodbye, but in fact she discovered he was still very much alive. When she spoke to him about the incident, it seemed that at the time Mrs Elgee had seen his apparition he had been contemplating a job offer and wished Mrs Elgee had been there to advise him.

Name: Padre Pio
Location: Various European locations
Date: 1900s
Source: Various

Famous for exhibiting the marks of the stigmata for 50 years, Padre Pio, who died in 1968, was several times reported in bi-location.

In November 1917, after Italian General Luigi Cadorna had suffered defeat at the hands of the Germans in Slovenia, the General spent time alone in his tent, contemplating suicide. Suddenly he saw a monk beside him who said: 'Don't be so stupid!' The monk then vanished. Some years later the General was visiting Italy and met with Padre Pio, recognising him instantly as the monk he had seen in his tent. Padre Pio said to him: 'You had a lucky escape, my friend.' The padre is known to have been in his monastery at Foggia, Italy, at the time of the General's despair.

In 1942 the Archbishop of Montevideo, Uruguay, was woken up one night by a monk and told to go to the bedside of Monsignor Damiani, a devoted follower of Padre Pio. The archbishop discovered that the monsignor was already dead, but found by his side a note saying 'Padre Pio came'. Seven years later the archbishop met Padre Pio and recognised him as the monk who had awakened him.

When Padre Pio was asked if he knew about his bi-locating, he replied, 'Is there any doubt about it?'

Name: Passing Place?
Location: Near Wareham, Dorset, southern England
Date: February 1991
Source: *Daily Mail*, 30 April 1996

In 1991, Adrian Brown was a security supervisor and at around 11.15 one February evening was driving his firm's van on a regular patrol to a gravel extraction pit near Wareham. The company vans had very distinctive logos and there were only two such vans, one of which he knew was off the road. As he approached a roundabout he saw the lights of another vehicle approaching. As it got closer he realised it was a van exactly like his own. But his greatest shock was yet to come. As he told the story: 'As the van passed, three or four yards from me, I saw – clearly illuminated by the street lamps and headlights – myself. It was me. It was like looking in a mirror. I looked for five or six seconds as the van passed. The other "me" glanced across – the sort of cursory look you make as you pass another vehicle. There was no hint of recognition.'

Amazed and then perplexed, Brown drove on, taking a few minutes to come to terms with what he had seen. He became frightened and, as he said, 'I had goosebumps and the hair on the back of my neck stood on end.'

He was at pains to point out that it was not someone who looked like him, it was himself. He wondered whether he should have turned around and driven after the 'other' van, but he did not do so. For three or four days he felt fear, and had disturbing dreams until he came to terms with it. As he stated, 'I know it was not the product of an overactive imagination. While I was doing shift work I was always on the ball. The nature of the job demanded that I kept alert and wide awake. I was not tired and I had only just begun my shift which went on until early next morning.'

He was interviewed about the experience five years after it happened and said it no longer bothered him, yet he still had a very clear image, 'as if it happened yesterday'.

Name: Professor Thorstein Wereide
Location: Oslo, Norway
Date: 1950s
Source: Society for Psychical Research, Norway

In the 1950s Professor Thorstein Wereide, a professor at the University of Oslo and a member of the Norwegian Society for Psychical Research, set out the description of the vardoger, a kind of forerunner double.

Apart from cataloguing several cases, Wereide believed that he himself had a vardoger which would precede him. His wife would sometimes hear, and occasionally see, his apparition arriving home although he was only just about to leave the university. This would be a useful communication for his wife, who would then calculate when to expect him home.

Wereide discovered there were more claims of vardogers in Norway than anywhere else in the world and he believed this might be because the remote and sometimes impassable areas of country-side and mountains may have made ordinary communications difficult. He believed that 'nature seemed to have made use of "supernatural" means to compensate for this isolation.'

Name: Reverend W. Mountford
Location: England
Date: 1860
Source: Time Life Books (Phantom Encounters)

The Reverend W. Mountford of Boston was visiting friends in England when, through a window, he saw his host's brother and sister-in-law coming along the road in a horse-drawn open carriage. He called out to his host and both Mountford and his wife looked out of the window, making small talk about the couple due to arrive. However, they watched as the carriage drove straight past the house and disappeared, 'a thing they never did in their lives before.' Ten minutes later, Reverend Mountford, looking through the window, saw the pair coming down the road again, which was extraordinary since the configuration of roads would not have allowed the couple to have driven by the house the first time and then been approaching it from the original direction in so short a space of time. He asked them about it and they assured him that was the only time they had driven down the road, and indeed they had come straight from home.

Even more extraordinarily, the daughter of the couple in the carriage, who had been walking to the rendezvous, had also seen her parents pass her and ignore her when apparently they were only just leaving home.

Name: Sir Frederick Carne Rasch
Location: House of Commons
Date: 1905
Source: Time Life Books (*Phantom Encounters*)

In 1905 Sir Frederick Carne Rasch was unable to attend a debate at the House of Commons as he was unwell with flu. However, during the debate a colleague of his, Sir Gilbert Parker, saw Carne Rasch seated on one of the benches. Parker gestured to him saying, 'I hope you're feeling better.' Carne Rasch apparently did not acknowledge him and when Parker looked again, the figure had disappeared. The sighting of Carne Rasch on the benches was also confirmed by another MP, Sir Arthur Hayter.

When he was later told that he had been seen in the House of Commons, Carne Rasch was quite clear that he had not been there, but was equally unsurprised that he had been seen there as he was extremely concerned about the debate in question.

Some time afterwards Carne Rasch became annoyed to find that, the story having got round, his colleagues would poke and prod him to make sure he was actually there in the flesh!

Name: The Smoking Man?
Location: Not given
Date: 1967
Source: David Morgan (witness) / authors' own files

David contacted us with an account unique in our experience: 'One day in 1967, when I was a child, I remember sitting in our living room listening to my father talking about Christ. My father had come home early that day, as a mate of his had told him that I was not too well. Then, from the far side of the room, came a kind of pearl-grey type smoke. I was fascinated by it, even then as a child. Then it came across the room and went through my chest. My dad began to say the Lord's Prayer. But as I turned around there was a man behind me. He had a red tie, white shirt and a pin-stripe suit. He smiled but did not speak. I thought that he resembled me, but about 30 years older.'

Ghostly Balls Of Light

Strange lights, often seen in open areas such as moors and grave-yards, have a long history of association with spirits and are often known as 'ghost lights'. The tales of the North American Indians, of native Australians and Africans and of South American cultures all attribute souls of the dead to these lights. Perhaps they are a natural phenomenon – a luminous gas is a front-runner in speculation – and yet they play a strong part in belief. And belief, myth and sociology are not factors to be ignored in ghost research, however much the search continues for hard, scientific evidence as well.

Name: Bachelor's Grove Cemetery
Location: Midlothian, Illinois, USA
Date: To the present
Source: Various

Just outside Chicago is the Rubio Woods Forest Preserve at Midlothian. The now disused Bachelor's Grove Cemetery there is said by many to be the most haunted cemetery in North America. It is isolated, run down (there have been no internments since 1965), has been used for cult worship and animal sacrifices and is reputed to be where Chicago gangsters unofficially buried some of their victims.

Ironically, one ghost reported is thought to be the result of an accidental death near the cemetery when a farmer ploughing nearby land was dragged into the lagoon by a startled horse and both were drowned. There are reports of the spectres of both the farmer and the horse seen at night at the location.

Many of the reports are of indistinct shapes of blue light, which many believe are the ghosts of those buried at the cemetery. These lights have been seen flitting around the headstones. The cemetery has a White Lady ghost, nicknamed Mrs Rogers by the locals and thought to be a woman whose son died young and who roamed the cemetery in mourning after he was buried there. The reports state that her apparition is an amorphous white light rather than a clear figure. Other ghostly phenomena, which is widespread in the area, include a phantom farmhouse and phantom vehicles.

Name: Block Island Light
Location: Block Island, USA
Date: 1739
Source: Various

Block Island is situated just off the eastern end of New York's Long Island, surrounded by Long Island Sound, Block Island Sound and Rhode Island Sound. Since 1739 there have been sightings of a seaborne 'ghost light' visible off the coast. This is associated with local legends of seafaring disasters and is believed by many to be the apparition of a lost ship. It has mostly been observed from Settlers Rock Grove or the State Beach and at different times can vary in size, brilliance and position. In 1869 Benjamin Corydon, who had grown up in the area, claimed that he had seen this light on at least eight occasions and had seen the ship 'sails all set and ablaze'. The most recent sighting of the light was in 1969.

As with most ghost lights, it may be some form of natural phenomenon. Certainly the sea has various electrical and lumines-cent phenomena that can look quite strange in certain circumstances. However, some witnesses have claimed to have heard the sounds of crying and anguish when the light is seen.

Two ships have been proposed as candidates for the light, though one at least, the *Palatine*, is said to have sunk *after* the first confirmed sighting and is therefore attributed by legend only. It is uncertain whether the *Palatine*, by that name, ever existed, and it is more likely that the story relates to the ship known as the *Princess Augusta*. This was a Dutch ship that left Rotterdam in 1738 with 14 crew and 350 passengers, part of the exodus of the Palatine peoples, a religiously persecuted group from the German Rhineland. During the voyage 114 people perished through contaminated drinking water, includ-ing the captain. The first mate, who took control of the ship, proved incapable of bringing it through the storms off the New England coast. On 27 December the *Princess Augusta* grounded near Block Island and all but one aboard were rescued by local residents. One hysterical woman, Mary Vanderline, refused to leave the boat and died when it sank. It was in the following year, 1739, that the crew of the *Somerset* made the first report of the ghost light while they were sailing past Block Island. The captain reported that they 'followed the burning ship to its watery grave, but failed to find any survivors' – the implication being that they were following an illusion rather than a genuine ship.

Name: The Brown Mountain Lights
Location: Brown Mountain, North Carolina, USA
Date: Centuries or more . . .
Source: Howard Winters, historical interpreter for the Museum
  System of the State of Delaware.

The Brown Mountain Lights are a well-known case of ghost lights, and many believe they are among the most regularly seen in the world. The lights are described as red, blue, green or white balls which disappear when approached. There are several legends about their origin, one being that they are the spirits of Native American tribesmen killed in battle long ago.

Another ghostly legend associated with the lights is that in colonial times, prior to the American Civil War, a plantation owner, living near the mountain, went off hunting one day. When he failed to return at sundown, a trusted old retainer took up a lighted candle lantern and went looking for his master. He, too, failed to return. Local legend has it that the lights are the faithful servant still walking the hills searching for his lost master.

It has been suggested that the lights are ignited swamp gas, or the reflected lights of local towns, or train or car headlights. But surveyors and engineers, back in the 1950s and 60s, searched for mundane answers and found none. Similarities, true, but nothing else puts on a performance like this anywhere in the world almost every night. Police, military personnel and scores of seekers of official capacity have looked for the answer and come away empty-handed.

The Tennessee and Cherokee Indians considered them to be something mysterious and sacred. The lights were around in the time of George Washington, and he is said to have mused over them.

Howard Winters, who has been researching the lights for decades, told us of his encounters: 'I have had personal contact with the Brown Mountain Lights all my life. I first ran across them when I was in Gatlinburg, some 40 years ago. Some time after this, around 1961, when my new wife and I were again in Gatlinburg, wandering through the Smokies over a two-week period, we drove up to the area. I was fascinated as the lights began to show up at dusk, quite clearly visible back then because pollution had not yet filled all the hollows of the Smokies and other mountains. Their appearance coincided with dusk falling and they were roughly a half to three-quarters of a mile away from us, across the valley. Their colour was pale; yellows, blues, greens, pinks, oranges, all of a translucent colouring, as though there was some sort of light within them. I had studied all I could find on swamp gas, will-o'-the-wisp and other phosgene emissions, and it just didn't make sense.

'Over a period of about 45 minutes we sat there and watched as these large lighted objects would just appear, about five or 10 feet above the ground, and then ascend to a height of sometimes about 100 to 150 feet in the air, pause there for some minutes, descend again to the level of the mountain top as visible to us and then wink out. Immediately, others would appear, always different in colour, and continue the rising, resting and falling pattern, and again, each one starting at a different spot on the ridge. All this took place across the entire crest of the mountain.

'I was there 11 years later. When the sun began to set, the same activity began to occur, almost on schedule, and as my daughters and I watched, the same old panorama began. Though difficult to see, there again were the pale-coloured globes of light, somewhere around 50ft in diameter, possibly less, appearing from nowhere, rising 50 to 100 feet, pausing for a while then slowly dropping back to the ridge to stop and then wink out, just as before – not so clearly visible, due to the pollution, but still there and still performing as they've been doing since the days of the Cherokee Indians and probably before them. The girls were first fascinated and then a little bit frightened.

'Locally, around Cherokee and Gatlinburg and on to the east, people just accept them as something that has always been there and is a part of their surroundings. Papers, when times are slow, will run articles just for local colour and interest. People are forever fascinated by ghosts and the ghost light theory.'

Name: The Dancing Lights
Location: West Virginia, USA
Date: 1998
Source: Janet DeVoe (witness)

'My father had always told me about these "lights" that dance whenever someone dies. They start in the family graveyard, go up in the field and then back to the graveyard.

'On 23 March 1998 my father died. My sister flew into Virginia to make the drive with me to Heaters, West Virginia, a drive of about eight hours. We were going to the homestead which has been in the family for over 200 years and where my dad had been living. We started up the mountain around midnight and, lo and behold, as soon as we arrived at the top there were the lights. In the centre was a red light and a green light, and on each side of them were two white lights. They were dancing all around the field and were starting to go to the graveyard. We stayed up until around 2am and watched until the last one started going down. The next night my other two sisters arrived and again the lights were dancing. We were all crying because it was as if they were "welcoming" Dad.

'Thursday night was the night for the wake. We had told everyone in the family that the lights were dancing and after the wake the whole family went back to the farm to watch. This time it was two red lights in the centre and three white lights on each side. My uncle (Dad's brother) kept asking if one of the lights had left for the other field . . .well, they hadn't until that night. All of a sudden one of the red lights took off and shot across the sky and disappeared behind the next hill. We felt the second red light was Dad because he had red hair. I know it might sound silly but instead of being scared of these lights, it was comforting to think that it was Dad and he was being welcomed by our ancestors.'

Name: Light Fantastic
Location: Castle Hill, St Helens, Lancashire, north-west England
Date: 12 August 1999
Source: Peter Crawley of Ghost Quest

Castle Hill, in St Helens, was, 2,000 years ago, a Celtic burial ground for chiefs who died in battle. During excavation many of their bones were disturbed, which some local people believe could be the origin of the Hill's haunted reputation. Peter Crawley, founder and secretary of Ghost Quest and an active researcher for many years, was walking through Castle Hill on 12 August 1999, along with a colleague, Mike Birchall. Peter told us: 'All of a sudden we felt someone watching us. As soon as we got to Newton Lake, I heard a man breathe heavily behind us. Instinctively I turned round and took a picture. But when I had the film developed there was a ball of light on the print.'

Neither at the time, nor on the film was there any sight of the person who had been heard breathing. As Peter explained to us, the ball of light was not visible when the picture was taken: 'It was only when I had the film developed that it came out.'

Castle Hill also has a reputation for being haunted by a 'White Lady' ghost. Since the 1950s there have been reports of an unclear white figure seen in the woods on the Hill, or on the roads in the area – including across the carriageway of the M6 motorway which cuts through it. In the 1950s the figure was seen by a poacher. In the 1960s a cyclist saw the figure and described it as taller than an average human being. In the next decade the figure took on more of a 'phantom hitchhiker' role, actually moving out onto the road and in front of a motorcyclist. The rider said he thought he felt an arm touching him and he abandoned the bike, to return later with police. A motorist had to swerve to avoid the figure on another occasion. Three boys saw the apparition together near the nearby golf course.

Name: Silver Strike
Location: Silver Cliff, Colorado, USA
Date: 1880
Source: New York Times, 1967

The town of Silver Cliff grew up almost overnight after a silver outcrop was discovered in the West Mountain Valley. From early on, the graveyard at Silver Cliff was associated with ghost light phenomena. Several miners saw faint blue lights floating over the graves.

The New York Times of 1967 reported on the phenomena, picking up from an article in the West Mountain Tribune of 1956. The phenomena were investigated by Edward J. Linehan of National Geographic, who saw, 'dim, round spots of blue-white light'. He saw several such lights in the graveyard and they faded as he approached them, despite his chasing around the graveyard with a torch, trying to close in on one.

The lights were still seen after a power failure had cut off the electricity supply to the town and therefore were not the reflection of lights from there. The area was tested for radiation with a Geiger counter and proved negative.

Scientific analysis suggests that many of these ghost lights are escapes of methane deposits, luminous or ignited. Romantic interpretations suggest either that they are the souls of the dead, taken from Native American culture, or the ghosts of old miners still walking around with their lanterns.

Name: A Strange Area.

Location: Near the Humber Subway Bridge, Toronto, Canada
Date: Modern times
Source: Toronto Ghost and Hauntings Research Society /
  Matthew Didier

TGHRS receives a great many reports to its website from Canadians with stories to tell of local hauntings. Many become the subject of TGHRS investigations. The following is a report the society received about the area under and around the subway bridge at the Humber River.

The contributor had heard of sightings of balls of light in the trees in the area. One autumn, while fishing in the Humber, he saw balls of light and described how 'they followed me and my friend John through the trees (we were on the path). It took some calculated thinking and moving to figure out that what we saw was real.' They ran as fast as they could but the balls of light stayed right with them and remained perfectly level. 'The following week, John and I decided we'd drive down there to take another look, figuring the car was a great escape vehicle. We parked, shut the engine off and after about five minutes the car started rocking violently from side to side. A few weeks after our experience we heard of it happening again to a friend of a friend and his girlfriend.'

Another reader of the website submitted a first-hand account from the same place: 'As a teenager I liked to bike down at night and enjoy the river and the . . . ruins of the Old Mill, which had been destroyed by fire at the beginning of this century. Twice I have witnessed a figure near the surrounding security fence, first on the inside and then once when I watched it disappear into the ruins. I called out the first time I saw it, but when I actually watched the second time to see it walk through the fence, my curiosity was piqued.'

Ghostly Animals

In the World of Ghosts section of this book, we discuss the significance of animal ghosts. They may well reveal something very important about the conditions necessary to create a haunting, or at least an apparition. The core of the point made, as shown by any statistical sample of animal ghosts, is that the animals that produce ghosts seem for the most part to be domestic pets beloved by humans rather than wild animals. Why should that be? Are ghosts a uniquely human condition?

Name: Dying Dog
Location: On the road 50 miles from Los Angeles, USA
Date: 1970
Source: Jim Ferguson (witness) / authors' own files

The following story of an encounter with a dog is difficult to categorise. A ghost with a message? A dog possessed by another, dead, dog? Was it real at all? Was it some sort of animal version of a phantom hitchhiker? Read on ...

As Jim Ferguson described it to us: 'When staying in the States for a while around 1970, my aunt, cousin and I were driving from Los Angeles to Ontario, a town situated about 50 miles east of Los Angeles. My aunt was driving. The car was a green Buick station wagon; quite a large vehicle. This particular stretch of road went through the countryside with very easy bends, and at the time of the incident we were on a long, straight downgrade with a panoramic vista in front of us.

'Way in the distance I could see a dog come onto the opposite carriageway and start to head across the road. The dog was running but it was so far in the distance that I was confident it would complete its journey across the road safely. But then I began to notice that it was taking much longer than it should for the dog to get to where it was going. It came across the central barrier area, still running, into our carriageway. I called to my aunt, "Watch the dog. Watch the dog."

'At this point I just knew we were going to hit it, which seemed very unreal as the dog had initially been so far away. It had plenty of time to see us and my aunt equally had plenty of opportunity to see it. But she just did not see the dog and suddenly there was one hell of a bang and we hit the dog square on. My aunt realised she had hit something but had not seen it at all. She pulled up on the roadside. I said, "You ran over the dog," but she did not believe me, simply replying, "What dog?" We got out and the car grill was dented. A real impact. We looked back and we both saw the dog lying by the roadside. I thought how really odd the whole thing was, it did not make any sense. Surely we could have avoided the dog? Anyway, it was dead.

'I made a mental note of the time and date. It was a Tuesday in December, about 4.30pm. The incident left me feeling uneasy; this just was not right.

'Returning to England some months later, I was met by members of my family. During the journey home I could detect they were holding something back. Eventually they got around to telling me: "You're not going to see your dog. It died." When I told them the date and time, they were obviously shocked.'

Jim had connected, intuitively, his own dog in England with the road incident that he had known all along was somehow 'not right'.

'When I saw the dead dog by the roadside, I actually thought of my own dog in England. The situation was so unreal; a very strange experience, and that was partly why I made the mental note of the date and time it had happened. My mother had been with my dog at the time it had to be put down. This was quite a traumatic thing for her.

'I have said this incident happened to me at 4.30pm and when we worked out the time difference in England it was about the time that the vet had called to destroy my dog.'

Was the timing just a coincidence or had Jim's dog in England, away from his master, wanted to say goodbye in some way and to tell him that he was dying? If the dog hit on the road near Los Angeles was a real dog, and there seems no doubt of its physicality, then was it 'possessed' temporarily by Jim's dying dog?

Name: Faithful Horse
Location: Chelsea, London, England
Date: Not given
Source: *Ghosts of London* by J. A. Brooks

Dr John Phene was a local celebrity in Kensington and Chelsea – his name is commemorated in both a street and pub in the London borough. He developed the idea of planting rows of trees along the streets to enhance the neighbourhood, an idea that was endorsed by Queen Victoria and copied in many European cities. He lived in Glebe Place and was thought to have been devoted to his horse, as it had once saved his life. When the animal died, it was buried within sight of his house. (When Phene's house was subject to redevelopment the skeleton of a horse was discovered in the garden.) After Phene died there were reports of a man on horseback, thought to be Phene and his devoted animal, seen between Cheyne Walk and King's Road.

Name: Fluffy
Location: Chesterfield, Derbyshire, central England
Date: Mid 1990s
Source: Strange Phenomena Investigations (SPI)/Malcolm
  Robinson

Teacher Vivienne Brocklehurst found the dead body of her six-month-old kitten, Fluffy, beside the road. It was a distinctive cat with long white and tortoiseshell fur.

As Vivienne described: 'About a fortnight after Fluffy died, one of the children in my class showed me a nail which was protruding from her desk. I promised to fetch a hammer as soon as the bell rang for dinner time. This involved crossing the yard and going into another building. As I opened the heavy wooden door to go outside, I tripped up, looked down for a split second and saw my dead cat as clearly as in life. I was surrounded by children at the time but none of them saw the kitten.'

Name: Ginger
Location: Not given
Date: 1984
Source: B.C. Child (witness) / authors' own files

A short but warm story of a possible ghostly encounter with a loved pet was given to us by Mr Child: 'In 1984 I had an experience concerning a pet cat. I had a ginger and white cat and in October 1984 it died at the age of 12. I buried it in the back garden. One foggy November evening a month later, I stood in the garden and out from the fog, down the path, came the ginger and white cat right to my feet. Not only that, but from the direction of its resting place. After a few minutes the cat turned and walked back into the fog. I never saw it again.

'A spirit? It certainly wasn't my imagination. And in 1984 mine was the only cat that colour among my neighbours' homes.'

Name: Guy Gibson's Dog
Location: RAC Scampton, Lincolnshire, eastern England
Date: May 1943
Source: Various

Although it is sometimes difficult to classify ghost sightings, it is rare when the choice is between 'ghosts of the famous' and 'animal ghosts'. But this is one such case.

Anyone remembering the film The Dambusters, the story of the daring Second World War raid on the Ruhr Dams, will recall the poignant moment when the black labrador dog owned by the leader of the raid, Guy Penrose Gibson, was killed by a vehicle on the main road outside the camp just before Gibson left for the raid. Gibson kept the dog's death a secret from the rest of his team in case they would regard it as a bad omen. The dog was buried at Scampton. Gibson himself came back safely from the raid and was awarded a Victoria Cross for his leadership in the action, but he died the following year when his plane crashed in Holland, returning from a relatively minor target in Bavaria.

The labrador's ghost has been seen both during the day and the night, trotting around in the camp, the place where he was held in great affection not only by Gibson but by many of Gibson's colleagues.

Name: Laddie
Location: Hertfordshire, southern England
Date: 1950s
Source: Elizabeth (witness) / authors' own files

When Elizabeth was a young girl, the family had a golden cocker spaniel. The dog, Laddie, and Elizabeth were very close. Laddie would meet her after school and when she was returning home from her piano lessons. When Elizabeth was 11 years old and Laddie was seven, the dog became very ill and had to be put down.

Elizabeth continued her piano lessons and Laddie continued to meet her. Elizabeth related to us: 'I often saw a shadow of Laddie where Laddie would have been, and it trundled on home with me to the gates of our home. Then the shadow would disappear.' At the time Elizabeth did not tell anyone, but after every lesson she was met by Laddie and together they would walk home.

The nights were getting darker and about a month after Laddie's death, Elizabeth's father suggested: 'I'll come and meet you tonight, Elizabeth.'

'There's no need,' Elizabeth replied, 'Laddie will meet me like he always does.'

'So you have seen him, too,' her dad said. He had also seen the ghost of the family dog; the shadows were not just Elizabeth's imagination.

Name: Lurcher
Location: Near Kidderminster, Worcestershire, central England
Date: 1988
Source: Aaron Wood (witness) / authors' own files

Sometimes the difference between good luck, coincidence and the paranormal is hard to define. Aaron's story could be any of these; but had it not been for a black dog, he could well have died many years ago.

'When I was 18 years old, I was riding back from Worcester on my motorbike. I decided to use the back roads to Kidderminster as I had a faulty brake light on my bike. At around 3.30am, some seven miles away from home, the bike died on me. I realised I was out of petrol. I pushed the bike off the road into a field and put it up behind a rough stone wall. I sat down with my back against the wall. I intended to walk down the road for about five miles to the nearest garage, get some petrol and then take a taxi ride back to the bike. But I started to doze off to sleep.

'I was woken minutes later by the sound of something snarling and growling. I stood up and looked over the wall onto the road, and there I saw a big, old, black lurcher dog watching me. I was a little bit freaked because I had once been attacked by a dog when I was a kid, and this one looked mean. However, it didn't seem to be acting like it was going to attack me, so I walked out onto the road and headed off for the garage. The dog followed for about a mile.

'I got to the garage, borrowed a can, got my petrol, phoned a taxi from the phone box on the corner, and the taxi took me back to get the bike. When we rounded a bend in the road we could see the back end of a transit van hanging out of the wall and the driver was flagging us down. He turned out to be a bit shaken but unharmed. The cab driver radioed his firm to call the police and while we waited, I had a look at the state of the van and noticed my bike stuck under the front of it: trashed! Then it dawned on me that if I hadn't been woken and moved on by the lurcher, I'd also have been under the front of that van. I don't know if it was a ghost dog because I never touched it to find out but, ghost or not, if that hound hadn't turned up and spooked me enough to get me walking, I'd definitely be a ghost now myself!'

It is true that it is not always apparent whether such an encounter represents something 'real' or something ghostly, so the dog could have been either. But it is a strange story and one way or the other the circumstances seem to have contrived to keep Aaron alive when he could have been killed.

Name: Mister
Location: Hest Bank, Lancaster, north-west England
Date: 1990 to the present
Source: M. Walker (witness) / authors' own files

Mr Walker, who related his story of the sighting of a woman from either the Victorian or Edwardian period in the 1960s earlier in this book, also had a tale to tell of a cat that seems to be returning to its former home.

'We have been living at our present address since 1972. We have had, and still have, several cats in our time here, one in particular called Mister. He lived here at the house from about 1979 to 1990. He was a bit of a character, much loved by me and my family. Like all of our cats, Mister learned to rattle the letterbox when he wanted to come in. Up to the time of his death, whenever we heard the letterbox rattle it would be because there was a cat out there waiting to come in. But since he died in 1990 we have often heard rattlings when there is no cat there; probably about five times a year this happens. My wife and son have also heard it. We've run around to check the whereabouts of our living cats and we find they are in the house but not near the letterbox. We've checked if it's the wind and in fact we've noticed that the wind doesn't rattle the box; but we've also noticed that there is usually no wind at all when this happens. We thought it could be kids, but we've never caught anyone doing it and they would surely have given up by now – it's been 10 years. I think that for some reason it's Mister doing it.

'The reason I think that it might be Mister coming back is that out of the corner of my eye I've seen a shape in the house that I'm sure was Mister. He was very distinctive: a huge cat with clear black and white markings. Added to that, my mother, who lives just a few doors away, told me that she once thought she saw Mister walking on the road outside my house just like he had done in life; he had a distinctive walk, too, and she would know him. I only hope that he's not coming back because he's unhappy where he is now, but rather that he's coming back because he enjoyed his life here.'

Name: Mushki
Location: Hawkes Bay, New Zealand
Date: 1990
Source: *Ghost Encounters* by Cassandra Eason

This story of a returning pet was recalled with obvious affection by Janette, who lived with her family in a semi-rural area of New Zealand. Their house stood in about four acres, which Janette said was 'a paradise for Mushki and my three other cats, Horse, Tigger and Toby'. Mushki, who had come to the family nine years earlier as a black and white kitten, was a dominant, affectionate cat with a habit of sleeping with Janette.

Crossing the road one night in March 1990, Mushki was killed. Almost immediately her spirit was seen around the house. Janette's mother saw Mushki running on the lawn and her father saw Mushki standing at the door. Several times they noticed their pet dog barking and wagging her tail at an empty point in the room.

One night Janette woke up when something jumped on the bed, walked beside her, lay down and began purring. Janette was somewhat frightened by the incident but thought perhaps the duvet was slipping off the bed. When she switched on the light, the duvet was in place and she could feel a physical presence curled up against her. It was, she believed, Mushki.

Janette has two beliefs as to why Mushki might have stayed around. As she explained: 'Since she died so suddenly and unexpectedly, she was trying to reassure me that she was fine. When she was alive she would always jump up for a cuddle if any of the family was upset.' Another possibility relates to her father's nickname for Mushki, the 'clerk of the works'. In life, Mushki had always been intensely interested in everything the family did and could not bear being other than the centre of attention. Perhaps Mushki has decided to keep the job even in death.

Name: Pepper
Location: Not specified
Date: Not given
Source: *Ghost Encounters* by Cassandra Eason

Pets undoubtedly bring comfort to their human companions, so it is not surprising that there are times when they bring that comfort and companionship at the point of death. One nurse, Julie, described such a case. She was working in a hospice and had a 91-year-old patient, Mr Moore, who was near to death. Two years previously his wife had died and Mr Moore's companion since then had been his pet dog Pepper. Just a few weeks previously, however, Pepper had been taken from Mr Moore's home as he was no longer able to care for her, and the dog was living ten miles away with Mr Moore's daughter.

Julie was with Mr Moore as he died. He had been discharged from the hospice and sent home to be in his own surroundings for his last hours. He was comatose and not responding to anyone around him. In the house were Julie and Mr Moore's son-in-law. Mr Moore suddenly opened his eyes and said, 'Come on, Pepper.' Then he died. As Julie described it: 'Not two minutes later, Mr Moore's daughter telephoned to tell us Pepper had just died.'

Name: Phantom Cat
Location: Killakee House, Dublin, Republic of Ireland
Date: 1960s
Source: Various

When Margaret O'Brien bought Killakee House in the late 1960s, it had been derelict since the 1940s. When she moved in to create an arts centre, there were stories that the grounds were haunted by a large black cat, more the size of a dog. The stories went back over a 50-year span; clearly longer than the life of a real animal.

Mrs O'Brien became somewhat shaken when she caught glimpses of 'a big black animal' in the gardens, but it was a later experience of her colleagues which really brought the subject to the fore. Dublin artist Tom McAssey and two others were redecorating Killakee House in March 1968. They were working on the stone-flagged front hall opening into the ballroom. They secured the front door with a heavy bolt but it then just opened again. When they checked, the bolt was not only still secure but fastened on the inside. They looked out into the darkness and could see a black, draped figure. They called out, 'Come in. I see you.' A guttural voice replied, 'You can't see me. Leave this door open.' McAssey's two colleagues ran, while Tom himself slammed the heavy door and also ran. As the men looked back, the door swung open again and 'a monstrous black cat crouched in the hall, its red flecked amber eyes fixed on me'.

Another witness to the cat was former Irish pole vault champion Val McGann, who was living in a trailer in the grounds. He said, 'It is about the size of a biggish dog, with terrible eyes.'

In 1970 Mrs O'Brien saw the apparition of two nuns walking through the gallery of the centre. In July that year the house was exorcised and the disturbances mostly ceased.

Name: Sad Partings
Location: Israel
Date: 1997
Source: Michel Cromwell (witness)

'On 5 June 1997 I had to put to sleep my much-loved, 14-year-old cat, Ya'el. She had, a few months earlier, been diagnosed with cancer and her health deteriorated rapidly, until I was forced to face reality and let her go.

'I had found Ya'el abandoned on a sidewalk in Israel at just four to five weeks old. She was a beautiful cat, looking a little tabby-like but also a little Abyssinian, with rich, dark cocoa-brown markings and a white area around her mouth and a beautiful rust-coloured nose. She was a very verbal cat. All I had to do was look at her and she'd miaow at me. Or I'd call her name and she'd miaow and come running from wherever she was in the house. She would never let you hold her, however – at least, not unless she wanted you to. But her all-time favourite thing to do was to walk back and forth in front of me whenever I walked, which often led me to stumble and falter while I tried to avoid killing us both. I cried all the way to the vet's office when I put her to sleep, all the way home and for days afterwards. This was my first experience with the loss of a pet.

'A couple of days later, as therapy, I was cleaning the house and doing laundry. I was walking from my living room to the kitchen when I stumbled over what I thought was one of my other two cats. I quickly turned to apologise and give attention to whoever had been injured, but Isaac was asleep in my grandfather's rocking chair and my other cat, Ashawn, was in the dog's bed, fast asleep as well – and the dog was outside. I have hardwood floors, so there was nothing to trip on, but this was definitely a trip "over" something. I felt the impact on the top of my foot. Immediately, I had the impression that Ya'el was in the room and that she'd come to let me know she was all right. As if to say ha, ha, this is what you get for putting me to sleep! It was an eerie feeling but a joyful one for me as well.

'Then one Sunday night, 21 September, I felt like I was in a half-awake, half-dream state right before dawn. I looked over at my bedroom door, which is locked at night, and thought how odd it was that it appeared to be open. It was still quite dark and I was thinking how I didn't really want to be awake yet, since it obviously wasn't time to get up for work. A few seconds later I felt something jump up onto my bed and when I looked down towards the foot of the bed, there was my beloved Ya'el coming towards me. And, just like she'd always been, she couldn't hold still while I cuddled or at least attempted to cuddle, and pet her. I was so elated to see her and touch her. It was incredibly real. I could even bury my nose in her fur. "She" was very soft and very warm. I can't express the real joy that I had from being able to see her and touch her.

'But the oddest thoughts went through my mind. I was thinking, "Same old Ya'el . . . same old expression on her face." Just as if I expected her to smile at me or talk to me. I actually felt that she could talk, but that something, either my being human or still of this earth, prevented that kind of communication with her.

'I can only say that as my older cat nears his time to be put to sleep, I hope that he comes to visit me often, along with Ya'el. As far as I'm concerned, they're my kids and I do and will miss them more than anyone could possible know. I'd love to hear from others who've had experiences with the loss of their pets and being revisited by them.'

Name: The Scrawny-Looking Dog
Location: Dunnottar Castle, Scotland
Date: March 1995
Source: Peter McKenzie (custodian) / authors' own files

Dunnottar Castle is situated on the coast near Stonehaven, on a promontory jutting into the North Sea. It is virtually cut off from the mainland and dominates the skyline. The first castle was built there in the 12th century, though the present castle dates mostly from the 14th century, with major changes having been made in the early 17th century.

Peter McKenzie had heard many and various ghost stories from visitors to Dunnottar Castle, but he told us of one he himself had experienced: 'It was March 1995 when I saw a dog. It was like an old-fashioned, deer-hunting type, young and scrawny-looking. It was grey with a ginger tinge to it. I caught sight of it out of my peripheral vision and I looked up to shout at the people to keep their dog on a lead, and the thing disappeared. I hadn't realised anything was strange about it up until that moment.

'Three months after that, a German tourist came to the ticket office and reported seeing a dog of the very same description close to where I saw it, about ten yards away. The dog had disappeared, that's what upset him; it must have been a real surprise to him because in my experience it takes a lot to make Germans come forward like that. I told him it had been seen before, which made him feel better.'

Name: Tina
Location: County Clare, Republic of Ireland
Date: 1998
Source: Alan Broe (witness) / authors' own files

Alan told us of his surprise when seeing a dog that seemed to disappear just after he had seen it, and his realisation that perhaps it was the ghost of a loved pet.

'Five years ago my dog Tina was killed in a road accident. She was a small dog, not even up to my knees. She was hit by an oil truck. I had been talking to a friend on the street and somehow Tina had got out of the garden. I turned round to see her on the ground, it was obvious nothing could be done for her. It wasn't nice, but at least I could see she had died swiftly, without suffering. I buried her in my back garden.

'Then, just a few weeks ago, I was out walking when I noticed a small dog. As I walked I looked at the dog to try to figure out its type. I walked on, but I hadn't gone 20 feet when I stopped and ran back to see if I could locate the dog. I searched the area for 15 minutes but I could see no sign of the dog. I do not know how it disappeared from my view, or where it could have gone. I thought about it and came to the conclusion that the dog I saw was the ghost of Tina. I think she may have "crossed over" from the other side for some reason and then she was gone again. I haven't seen her since.'

High Strangeness

We have included this section in this volume as an addition to the content of the original edition. While there have always been remarkable, indeed strange, claims for ghosts there is a tendency for ghost reports to have evolved somewhat in recent years. One of the strengths of ghost, spirit and poltergeist reports has been their consistency over the past 2,000 years and so this recent change is perhaps not to be welcomed, but we must deal with the evidence as it is presented. We believe some of the high strangeness, such as a 'bridging' between the traditional ghost stories and the relatively modern stories of UFOs and aliens, has been brought about by the media and the popularity of such programmes and films as *The X Files*. By the same token, however, we have always argued that no understanding of the UFO phenomenon would be possible without understanding the similarities in ghost lore, so it is not surprising to find the situation reversing on itself. Who knows where this evolution will end?

Name: Black And White Hoops
Location: Jedburgh, southern Scotland
Date: Recent
Source: Various

The authors have a close connection with Jedburgh – it is near where Anne Spencer was born and where we still visit relatives regularly. Tales of haunting phenomena abound in a town which is rich in both history and tourism. One story, however, is particularly bizarre if only for its obvious lack of source either as an historical account – at least as far as we could tell – or for its attraction to tourists.

The story is that a couple driving in the Borders region, towards Jedburgh, saw the figure of a man crossing the road ahead of them. The man's dress was, even in design, strange: a three-quarter length frock coat, a top hat and a walking stick, brandished more ornamentally than as an aid to walking. But what made the whole thing far more bizarre was that the couple were sure that the entire outfit the man was wearing, including his walking stick, was covered in tiny black and white hoops. Quite what the couple thought as they approached the figure is unclear. They were certainly concerned that they might run down the man, but before they were able to assess that the figure just disappeared in front of them. The couple left the area somewhat shaken, without ever identifying the figure.

One other strange facet of the apparition was the top hat; it was a very stormy night with high winds and it would have been virtually impossible for the hat to have remained on his head.

Name: A Goblin Figure
Location: Woodcote, on borders of Oxfordshire, southern England
Date: 1943
Source: S. Nugent (witness) / authors' own files

Mr Nugent gave us this account of strange encounters his father had had: 'My father was in the RAF and stationed at Woodcote. He knew the family at a particular cottage very well, and had even rewired the house for them. He stayed in the cottage many times. On one occasion he had a friend staying there with him and they were put in the eldest daughter's old room.

'Father awoke in the night, sat up in his single bed and looked across the tiny room to his friend asleep in the other. There, in the window, he saw a little old man dressed in old-fashioned clothes, almost a goblin figure, sitting as if on an old chest. In the morning he recalled talking to the figure and thought that he might have dreamt it. Then he discovered that he had smoked several cigarettes during the night. On later nights he saw the old man several times, even to the extent of getting up, going to the toilet and finding "him" still there on his return.

'The creature had "sat" on the friend, who was never aware of it. The daughter enquired very persistently if he had slept well, and my father always pretended that he had, not telling anyone the actual occurrences till 20 years later. He thought the daughter had seen it, but I confirmed in 1992 that she did not. She admitted that she and her husband had seen ghosts in the hall of the cottage, but it appeared that they were "seen" when the parents' belongings were being sorted shortly after their deaths, and were of the parents themselves.

'It is interesting that in the last ten years, that cottage has been altered significantly from being a 100-year-old farmhouse with pigs and geese in the yard and a cesspool to become a modern, detached house, looking no older than 60 years, with a beautifully lawned, immaculate garden, quite unrecognisable. I wonder if "he" still lives there!

'My father was always totally honest. He never embellished things, in fact rarely told stories, so I feel sure that he told the truth as he saw it so long ago. Anyway, I think it was an unusual link between times, the ethereal and the solid.'

Name: Ouija Inspired?
Location: Cheadle, Greater Manchester, north-west England
Date: 1966
Source: Dennis Chambers (witness)

When Dennis Chambers was a serving police officer, he and his wife became curious about the use of ouija boards and decided to experiment with one. The result was two months of disturbance in their home. Dennis wrote the account up at the time for a magazine, but was forced to use a pseudonym as the police hierarchy were not sympathetic to officers attracting that kind of attention to themselves. As a result of the experiences, Dennis began a long-term interest in the paranormal which has led to him becoming a well-respected researcher.

In March 1966, a few days after his father's death – an event that was unexpected but one that had been foretold by a clairvoyant – Dennis used a ouija board to attempt communication with the spirit world and with his father. He and a group of sitters believed they contacted several spirits, including one called Ronald Lund who was, prior to his death, known to one of the sitters. But the group gained little at the time from it, apart from becoming convinced that something real was happening. The after-effects were more shattering.

Dennis's wife Marion described that on the night following Lund's ouija contact, 'I got into bed, having first switched out the light. The moonlight filtering through the curtains placed the room in a half-light. Suddenly, only a few feet from the bed and suspended midway between the floor and the ceiling, appeared a man's face. He seemed in his early thirties. The face was oval and rather full, his nose longish and hair light brown and wavy. From beneath bushy eyebrows shone eyes of a brilliant hue and the whole face appeared to be illuminated from within, like a colour transparency held before a bright light. The brightness of the face contrasted dramatically with the velvety blackness framing it. It remained just long enough for me to take in its features. I turned away, and as I did so Lund's Christian name came instantly to mind, as though I were meant to associate his name with the face I had seen.'

A few days later, when Dennis arrived back from his night shift at 2.30am, he found all the house lights on and his wife agitated. His wife had been trying the ouija board again and there had been some frightening incidents. A heavy board secured to the wall had suddenly crashed to the floor in their son's bedroom, though not waking the child. Unpleasant smells had filled the bedroom – an acrid, oily smell, like fish. There was also a sense of presence felt in the house.

That night in bed, Marion watched as the sleeve of her jumper, which she had discarded on a table beside her bed, shot into an upright position, folded over, and tucked itself into a lampshade. As Marion got out of bed, a gruff voice shouted her name and some abuse. A shadowy form could be seen moving along the wall. Marion believed that this paranormal display was being put on for one reason only – to terrify her. 'A purpose well and truly served,' she stated.

A clairvoyant friend called to the house and identified the centre of the problem as being the son's bedroom. Looking at a photograph of the boy, he clairvoyantly saw '. . . a monk in an old brown habit standing behind the boy. The monk's face, partly shadowed by his cowl, was yellow, wizened and seemed evil.' The clairvoyant believed the monk had decided to make his 'home' in the bedroom. Exorcism of the room gave only temporary relief. The room changed, but something strange was still present. The next night, the room was filled with 'an indescribably beautiful flower fragrance' which remained for several days.

Further types of exorcism and clearance seances were tried and Dennis and his family were advised to use both holy water and prayer in their attempts to rid their home of these problems. The atmosphere in the house eased, but something was still felt to be present. On one occasion the couple's daughter, aged nine, had heard what she believed to be her father's voice calling to her, although Dennis was in the garden at the time and had not called. 'I do not doubt she heard a voice,' Dennis said, 'but whose?'

It was 7 June when the hauntings again broke to a pitch. Dennis's wife woke up at around 2.30am and looked towards a chest of drawers in the corner of the bedroom. 'In front of it I saw a dark, human-like shape slowly rising from the floor,' she said. 'Its head was domed and faceless and there appeared to be no neck between the head and shoulders. Pieces of the body and arms were missing but the rest was sufficiently solid to obliterate my view of the chest of drawers. The end of the bed obstructed my view of its lower parts but from its slow, co-ordinated movements, this thing was obviously alive and about to stand up.

'I fought off my fear and started to get out of bed. The thing was stationary, crouched watching me. Dennis, awakened by my movement, sat up to see what was amiss. As he did so, the form sank back toward the floor and melted away.'

Dennis and his wife checked their children were okay; they were. But when the couple returned to their own bedroom, they found the spot where the entity had been was filled with the acrid, oily fish smell. A couple of nights later a further exorcism was tried, and another shortly after that. The atmosphere eased again but there was still a sense of something present.

It was suggested that the most likely 'doorway' for the entities was their experiments with the ouija board. People using this technique often report frightening events for some time afterwards: events such as Dennis and his wife found, spontaneous fires, poltergeistery or other strange events. It is a cautionary tale for those who think of ouija as a 'bit of a laugh'.

Name: The Running Man
Location: Bathgate, West Lothian, Scotland
Date: 1988
Source: Various

What makes this story fascinating is a parallel with a story that received ridicule in the United States in the 1970s. While it is unlikely there is a direct connection, could there be meaning in the two accounts?

The Scottish story, attributed to a ghost, or elemental, or earth spirit, started when David Colman and his wife and children were driving near their home in Bathgate late one night. As David rounded a bend in the road he saw to his right a tall, white, glowing figure running at high speed next to his car. The estimate of the figure's running speed was between 50 and 70 miles per hour. David got the impression that the figure was turned towards his family in the car and scowling. All the family saw the figure; the children referred to it as 'the silver man', though Colman was sure it was more white than silver. In fact, he referred to it as being 'like a negative image'. Of perhaps tangential interest is that the sighting took place in the general area of Livingston, which sported Scotland's most famous UFO encounter when a forester was 'knocked out' after he encountered a floating object and two 'outrider' objects in 1979.

It is a UFO case – but a quite different one – with which this 'high strangeness' encounter of the Running Man is here compared. In October 1973 police chief Jeff Greenhaw at Falkville, Alabama, armed with a Polaroid camera, drove to the scene of an alleged UFO sighting following a report that an object with flashing lights was landing near the town. Just outside the town he encountered a 6ft entity standing in the middle of the road dressed in a silver suit. Greenhaw got out of the car and took four photographs of the figure, then got back in and turned on the blue lights. The creature turned and ran down the road. Greenhaw chased him in the patrol car but couldn't catch him. Eventually, the car span off the road, and the figure had vanished.

It is interesting that Colman's sighting was described as looking like a negative image, as the photos taken by Greenhaw also look somewhat like a negative in that the figure was light and almost 'glowing' against a dark background.

Name: Star Child?
Location: Tullibody, Scotland
Date: 7 February 1995
Source: Strange Phenomena Investigations (SPI)/Malcolm Robinson

This case from 1995, investigated by one of the UK's leading paranormal researchers, Malcolm Robinson, is almost reaching outside the bounds of normal ghost and haunting phenomena, but it is important in any encyclopedia such as this to include examples of modern variations.

The case started normally enough when Malcolm was approached by Janet and her mother who told him that they believed that Janet's house was haunted. Janet told Malcolm that she and her son, then aged eight, had moved into the house seven years earlier and that the house was fairly new, erected some 13 or 14 years previously.

The first thing that Janet had noticed, a few months before, was that her bedroom would suddenly go cold. She had also noticed that her cat was disturbed, running into corners of the home with its fur sticking up. Perhaps more disturbing, on one occasion Janet saw a depression at the foot of her bed when she was lying in it one night. It was as if someone had sat down there, though there was no-one to be seen. Janet went on to tell Malcolm that her son had been found one night sitting in the front garden, though he could not remember how he got there. On another night, Janet saw the apparition of a tall, thin man standing at the foot of the bed. He disappeared after a few seconds. The following night she saw the apparition of two men in the bedroom; again they disappeared within seconds.

Poltergeist-like activity was also reported – things moving from their normal position, ornaments and lamps found moved. Over those few months there had been many events in the house and Janet's health suffered.

Malcolm decided to investigate the case along with his fellow researchers Billy Devlin and Kevin Rennie and a medium they took with them to assist. On 7 February 1995 the team arrived at the house and the family moved out for the night, leaving the investigation team to do their work. The psychic reported clairvoyantly seeing a man. She described: 'He had droopy eyes and had a "shimmering" effect all around him.' Still in the living room, the psychic 'saw' a head and shoulders suddenly appear, after which a heavy, oppressive atmosphere was experienced. Billy Devlin, at this point, claimed he saw something like a photographic negative above the psychic's head as she sat in a chair. This vision soon melted away. A short while later, the psychic 'saw' a small woman appear to her who had a small mouth from which she could clearly see this woman's teeth protruding. Only the head of this woman was seen; no body, arms or legs were observed. The psychic continued to receive impressions from the house, hearing singing, seeing circles of lights, receiving a message about the boy next door, and feeling that her ankles were becoming freezing cold.

The rest of the team then became somewhat affected by the surroundings. They entered the son's bedroom, at first noticing only that it was a typical boy's bedroom: 'Manchester United pictures adorned the walls, jigsaws, games and puzzles littered the floor . . .' but the SPI psychic shouted to them, 'Look at your hands, look at your hands.' From the report by Malcolm Robinson: 'Billy, Kevin and I immediately looked down at our hands and were gobsmacked at what we saw (apart, that is, from Kevin, because he never saw it!). For as I looked down at my hands, all I could see was a multitude of tiny white pinpricks of light all moving up and down and around my hands. I turned my hands over and it was the same. Simply incredible. I have no other words for it.

'I asked our psychic, "What is it?" She replied, "It's the psychic energy, pure psychic energy." I looked into Billy's hands; it was the same. I then looked into our psychic's hands; again the same. I also saw the same in Kevin's hands. I asked Kevin if he could see it, and incredibly he replied that he could not. I couldn't believe it, this was so clear, so plain that it was impossible for him not to see it, yet he said he couldn't . . . This incredible effect lasted only a few minutes or so and, as quick as it came, it had gone. For me, this was exhilarating stuff. It makes the study and research of such cases all the more fascinating.'

It was, however, at this point that the case took what could well be a unique swerve. To quote from Malcolm Robinson: 'The following piece of information that our psychic obtained was, to put it mildly, quite incredible and something that I never dreamed would happen in an investigation such as this. I know that what I am about to relate won't be accepted by certain people; indeed, I find it hard to believe myself. Nonetheless, and for what it's worth, not long after the episode with the multitude of tiny white lights, when the excitement had died down, our psychic started to receive a quite incredible message.

'Apparently, all the things that had been occurring in the house were centred around Janet's son. But the thing is, it had nothing to do with people who had passed into the spirit world and were, if you like, looking over him. No, our psychic said, it was extra-terrestrials who were ensuring that "their" boy was all right. He belonged to "them" and that "they" were looking in on him! The message went on to say that they were "leaving tomorrow because our work is done". The psychic then saw tears forming in the communicator's eyes.'

For Malcolm to sum up such a case was difficult. In his report, he comments: 'We can only surmise that when this "intelligence", "entity" or whatever came through, some form of portal or dimensional window opened up. I am convinced of the reliability of the SPI psychic medium. She has no reason to invent such a tale. Indeed, I think she was more surprised than anyone when this information came forward. But then again, one must allow for the possibility that perhaps she was being given false information from a spirit, from some lower astral entity. This is only speculation, however, and not fact.'

A few weeks after this overnight vigil, Janet reported that her home was back to normal and that she was happy to stay there. Her health improved and she was 'a changed woman'.

In one sense this case is not as unique as perhaps it seems. There have been many cases in the literature of UFOs and alien entities where ghosts and hauntings, and particularly poltergeist happenings, have intruded into the case. One of the most famous UFO and entity cases, that of Whitley Strieber, whose books about his experiences have included *Communion*, *Transformation* and *Secret School*, reported several haunting-like phenomena and at one time reported aliens and ghosts being seen in different parts of his house at the same time. A great many other close encounter experiences have produced reports of poltergeist activity. This is, however, a rarer case in that the witness, starting from the point of view of ghosts, has proceeded through an investigation using psychics, which might normally be expected to produce information from the spirit world but has, to everybody's surprise, veered off into this more modern interpretation of events, as we see in the UFO literature.

For decades there has been a recognition of a phenomenon known as 'star children'. These are people who some believe are physical human children of human parents but have been 'seeded' in some way by extraterrestrial intelligence, so that they are a form of hybrid human/alien. While not a new phenomenon, it is not one that has generally intruded into ghost research.

But what of the reality behind this? There is little reason to doubt the woman's report of her house being haunted; there is a mass of information from around the world suggesting that hauntings, whatever their origin may be, are real experiences. But the overlay of extraterrestrials? Perhaps, but what are the alternatives that ought to be considered? Could this be the effect of the massive amount of such material in modern film and television fiction? Could the psychic have picked up some fictional desire from the fantasies of those involved? There are many who claim that frequently entities in spirit seek to deceive or act mischievously. It will be interesting to see what evolution, if any, future reports of ghosts and hauntings produce.

Name: The Thing
Location: Blandford, Dorset, southern England
Date: October 1952
Source: Ken Goodson (witness) / authors' own files

Ken, now living in South Africa, told us of an astonishing encounter when he was in the military, in England, in the early 1950s. The incident happened at around 10.30 one evening in late October

1952. Ken was in a training battalion stationed at Blandford Camp in Dorset. He was with two other people from his platoon at the time.

'Myself, Charlie and Ron were all in our early twenties, raised in wartime London and trained in engineering. We were all newcomers to military life, and were laying around on our beds discussing the next day's work. The rest of the platoon was asleep and because our three bed spaces were adjacent at the far end of the "spider" hut, we could talk without disturbing anyone else. This was before the "lights out" call, but the area was quiet.

'Charlie's bed was opposite mine and Ron's, so he was able to see out of the windows above our two beds. He noticed a movement outside the window above Ron's bed and shouted out to him about it. Ron looked around, leapt up off his bed and shouted at me: "Get up, Ken, and look at this thing." In the two seconds it took me to realise he was being serious, the "thing" was looking at me through my window and I was off the bed and standing with the other two, our eyes like organ stops trying to understand what we were seeing.

'The "thing", as I call it, was of the classical ghostly appearance and greenish white in colour, although the head had a pink tinge. The head was clearly visible and so were the hands. It seemed to have a covering of some sort over the back of the head and down over the shoulders and body. It moved with a swaying, floating, bobbing movement.

'The head of the "thing" was completely devoid of any normal features: no lips, no nose, no ears, no eyebrows, no hair. Where the eyes should have been were just dark slits or holes. The mouth was opening and closing, fish-like, but making no sound. Most disturbing were the beckoning gestures of the hands, alternated with scratching on the window panes. The hands, or maybe I should say fingers, appeared to be skeletal, with no finger nails, very thin and dirty white in colour.

'The movements were deliberate and slow, and it was obvious it wanted to join us in the hut, or for us to go outside. The "thing" disappeared for several seconds, long enough for us to look at one another and say, "What the . . . hell is that?" Then it was back again, on the other side of the hut, outside of the double fire doors and pulling on the door knobs so violently that Charlie, whose bed was nearest to the doors, jammed his rifle through the bars to stop the doors opening outwards.

'By this time, probably 40 or 50 seconds into the incident, the rest of the platoon was beginning to wake up, disturbed by all the commotion, and the "thing" moved away without any of us actually seeing it go. While Ron and Charlie explained what had been going on to the other platoon members, I, now very angry, went outside the hut to check around but saw nothing and decided to report to the guard commander in the orderly room, a short distance away.

'While I was endeavouring to explain to one very cynical and irate NCO for the third or fourth time what I had seen, another soldier I did not know came running up to us and began to tell a very similar story. This soldier was the duty orderly and had fled the medical treatment room when it was entered by the same "thing" as had left our hut a few minutes earlier. I remember his words well: "There was a banging on the door. I opened it and this thing came in and started throwing all the stuff around. I didn't know what it was and ran out of the place and I'm not going back there on my own again tonight," he said.

'There was a search of the area, but nothing unusual was seen. Next morning we were questioned by platoon and company officers, who were very interested in what we had seen, but there the matter rested and no more was said about it. Not to us, anyway. I never met the orderly again but the three of us discussed the incident continually while we were together.'

The 'thing' Ken saw is still very much a mystery. We were fascinated by it because of its slight comparison in both time and description to a case that arose in America where, given the mood of the time in that country, the sighting was classified as a UFO entity sighting.

The Kentucky incident is described in *The UFO Encyclopedia* by John Spencer. Very broadly, during the evening and night of 21-22 August 1955, 11 members of two families were besieged in their farmhouse by several glowing, dwarf-like creatures. The first creature seen was slowly approaching the farmhouse with arms stretched high above its head. Later, one was seen on the roof. The family shot at the creatures, which fell but apparently floated gently down towards the backyard before making off on all four limbs. Police were summoned to the house but no creatures could be located, so they left. A creature was again seen in the early hours of the morning through a bedroom window. When shot at, it scampered off into the darkness. In almost 50 years since that time, the family have not retracted their claims, despite social pressures to do so, and no explanation has ever been forthcoming.

Ken confirmed that the 'thing' he saw was 'very definitely frightening'. He saw similarities between the two cases, at the broadest level. He commented on the Kentucky incident, of which we sent him a transcript: 'There is an aspect of "Blandford" that I never mentioned . . . During the time that the entity moved from the front of the hut to the back, one or both of the others (I never saw this) claimed that it appeared at a very small window high up at the end of the hut. This was ... too high to see through when standing on the hut floor. Whatever it was we saw could move vertically with ease ... Was it floating there? I don't know.'

Name: Thoughtography?
Location: Balmakeil, Scotland
Date: August 1980
Source: Strange Phenomena Investigations (SPI)/Malcolm Robinson

In August 1980 Mrs McEwan visited her family at Balmakeil, north-west Scotland. She took with her a new Polaroid instant camera and, spending a beautiful day at Balmakeil beach, decided to take some pictures. She took a picture of the beach and the sky, a picture designed to reflect the magnificent desolation of the area. When the picture developed she was quite shocked to see the gable end of a house and another building to the right in the photograph. She had seen no buildings in her direct line of vision while she was taking the picture, with the nearest buildings some 20 to 30 yards away.

In fact, Balmakeil beach is supposed to be haunted, according to local stories. Malcolm Robinson's own summary: 'It is my personal opinion that Mrs McEwan is relating the facts of the photograph as carefully and honestly as she can. She is still very much puzzled by what the photograph shows and would like someone to tell her exactly what she has photographed. I firmly believe that Mrs McEwan has been one of the fortunate people who have taken a photograph of what was (to the naked eye) just a normal scene and was astonished to see unseen images appear on her picture. I should also like to point out that more pictures were obtained by this camera on her holidays up at Balmakeil and some more were taken on the beach. None of those showed anything out of the ordinary.'

There are many reports in ghost literature of timeslips, i.e. of people seeing buildings which existed in the past, but it is extremely rare for such 'out of time' visions to be unseen by the naked eye and yet recorded on film. There was, however, the phenomenon of thoughtography, most identified with Ted Serios in the 1960s, where it appeared that the mental impressions of the photographer were imprinted on the film. One of these interpretations, possibly a combination of two, or maybe something quite different, seems to be at play in Mrs McEwan's photograph.

Name: The Vanishing Island
Location: Essex/Suffolk Border, eastern England
Date: Mid 20th century
Source: *Stories of Ghosts and Hauntings Along the Essex and Suffolk Border*
by Wesley H. Downes

The location of this story, verified by researcher Wesley Downes, has been withheld as it is a strictly private property and the estate managers do not want to encourage sightseers. Nevertheless, they confirmed that several people had reported to them a similar incident.

A young man was fishing from the bank of a lake in the grounds of a house when he became aware of another man fishing from a small island. He paid little attention to it other than registering that he had not been aware of the island previously, but thought perhaps he hadn't noticed it or was seeing it from a slightly different perspective. As the day wore on, the boy decided to ask the man how he had got onto the island since there was no obvious bridge and no boat tied up. The angler simply waved back, laughed and carried on fishing.

A little while later a mist appeared around the edge of the island and the boy watched as the whole island, the angler and all his equipment slowly began to sink into the lake, 'hardly causing a ripple'.

We look forward to hearing of future sightings of the island.

THE WORLD OF GHOSTS

A Comparative Study Of Beliefs

In one sense it is true that a belief in ghosts and spirits is global, with every culture having a belief in some form or another. But in another sense the 'Western' belief about ghosts is quite different from traditional beliefs elsewhere. The differences may relate to religious belief in God, or gods, and the role they play with ghosts and spirits.

There is no culture that does not have some sort of belief in something spiritual, something bigger than itself, yet intangible. A belief in God or gods and a belief that something of the human personality goes forward after death is probably a universal human concept.

The ancient Egyptians believed that the spirit left the body on death. These spirits (known as khu) were held to be responsible for illnesses and misfortune within the deceased person's family. Rituals would be held to appease them.

In Assyria there was a belief in evil spirits called utukku. Some made ghastly wailing sounds which terrorised people, not unlike the cry of the banshee in Irish folklore. Such ghosts were held to arise because of failures to perform the correct burial rituals on death. One tribe in Nigeria makes pleas to the deceased at his or her funeral not to return and haunt the tribe.

One well-known spirit of the Middle East is the jinn. Usually not thought to have been human but rather conjured by a magician, the jinn is very similar to the poltergeist; a mischievous spirit.

Several European countries have ghosts, or spirits, similar to the English 'silkie', an entity that would perform routine domestic chores for a family in return for respect. In Slavic folklore the same spirit is known as a kikimora; in Russia, a domovoy.

Western belief has many stories of protective or helpful ghosts. In our previous volume, we described the case of William Corfield whose deceased brother Jimmy, he believed, took over the controls of a plane during a dangerous flight and steered the aircraft to safety. This is foreshadowed by the beliefs of Native American Indians, who tell of the 'spook'; a spirit that temporarily possessed a person and would help them achieve some desired success.

And there is a belief that the souls of humans are recycled on death, either to return in another human guise, as in the widespread belief in reincarnation; to become a protective ghost, as is believed in the South Pacific; or sometimes to be 'trapped' as a ghost unable to 'move on', as is believed in the West.

Along with the belief in spirits is an equally widespread belief that communication between humans and the spirit world is possible. In less technological cultures, such communication might be effected by the shamans, the spiritual leaders of tribes who are the channel between mortals and the deities. In the widespread formalised religions around the world such channels are the priests, by whatever name they are known. Every culture has developed a belief that in order to communicate with the gods some individual must stand out above the others, must be special and must undergo training.

Perhaps the most shocking of variations from this universal theme is the Western move towards New Age beliefs, which effectively dismiss the priests of the formal religions as having failed to meet the people's needs, replacing them with a belief that anyone can effect contact with the spirit world. The New Age has effectively sacked the spiritual leaders.

In most cultures the realm of the dead and the realm of the gods are either the same or related places. The ancestors or deceased elders are powerful 'ghost' figures because they now dwell with the gods and therefore can influence them to produce benign decisions for the living. In the Bismarck Archipelago near New Guinea, for example, the skull of a deceased patriarch of the household is displayed over the entrance to the family dwelling, as he becomes, in death, the family's protective guardian. His skull keeps away the influences of other families, and his spirit watches over the family and can reward or punish good or wrongdoing. The former head of the family becomes a minor deity because he now dwells with the gods. The Ghost Dance tradition of the Rocky Mountains and Great Plains Indians started around 1870 after a vision of a 'Great Train' that would bring back all the ancestors from the land of the dead to see off the white settlers. Men, women and children would perform the shuffling dance accompanied by singing, and many of the participants would go into trances and communicate with the dead ancestors, asking for their return and their help.

But in the West, in the Christian traditions particularly, there is a dislocation between the realm of God and the realm of ghosts. God exists in Heaven, and the spirits of the deceased occupy a realm that seems to have nothing to do with religion per se. The world of the dead is regarded as just another dimension where a person can choose to stay, or can move on from, or even be reincarnated from. There is some reconciliation in these beliefs in that some who believe in God and Heaven would argue that ghosts occupy a world of purgatory, a 'waiting room' before Heaven or Hell.

In the West, ghosts are thought to be haunting the physical world either because the deceased do not yet understand their new state and are clinging to their old life, or because they are trapped by a sense of emotional tie or purpose, or because they seek to help. In this we see a connection to the skull of our head of household in the Bismarck Archipelago, perhaps. He is continuing to do his duty, having been translated to the world of the gods; but if a Western deceased grandfather chooses to stay around and occasionally guide the family, that is regarded as a matter of his personal choice.

It is therefore only in the West that we see the study of ghosts as parapsychology, or a study of the paranormal. It is an academic study, one of trying to understand mechanisms at play in the natural world. In any other part of the world, awareness of ghosts would be a religious observance.

But if the above is true, it is also not that clear cut. The Christian and other Western beliefs are actually quite new as beliefs go, and the influences of earlier religions and beliefs permeate our instincts. There is a suggestion that Western ghosts do occupy a world of gods; the spirits of the dead are often attributed special knowledge of the future that could come from divine interaction. Ghosts that return to earth to warn family members of impending deaths or ill-fortune are possibly bringing back information from somewhere in the realm of the gods.

And there are few cultures left that have not been influenced by others given the mass communication and ease of travel that is now a major feature of our world. For example, South America has a rich mixture of cultural overlays, creating a varied belief in ghosts and spirits. The Christian beliefs of European conquerors and immigrants – Portuguese and Spanish, mainly – have mingled with the local Indian beliefs and have been further overlaid by the traditions of the Africans who were first taken to the land as slaves. In Brazil, which rivals England as the world's most haunted country, these combinations are further enhanced by 19th-century Spiritualism which arrived there from France. A belief strong in Brazil, a result of Spiritualism, is that the dead come back to intervene in human affairs. For example, psychic surgery – channelling the talents of deceased surgeons to perform supernatural operations on the living – has been most pronounced in Brazil.

Indian ghosts are divided into four types: the *bauta*, the *paisachi*, the *virika* and the *mumiai*. Throughout the Indian countryside are small shrines where gifts can be presented to these ghosts to gain their good favour. Seeing certain ghosts is an omen of impending death. This is not unlike the various beliefs of the Celts, with the banshee serving the same purpose and phantom drummers acting in the same capacity for certain Scottish clans.

Most African cultures believe in a universal God, but they also respect or worship ancestral ghosts and spirits. They believe in good and bad spirits and it is essential that burial customs are adhered to respectfully to avoid the visitation of the latter. The Mashona tribe of Zimbabwe believe that the 'normal' spirit that leaves a person on death, called the *mudzimu*, can be called upon by their children to return and look after them. The *shave* is a wandering spirit that seeks manifestation through a medium (a *svikiro*). The *chitokwane* is something akin to a zombie of Voudun belief; a resurrected spirit under the control of a wicked medium.

In China it is believed that each person has two spirits within them: one good, known as *shin*, and one bad, known as *kuei*. The body of the deceased must be buried correctly or the *kuei* wanders the mortal world, haunting it. The Chinese offer cakes to the ghosts in the hope that they do not haunt. Perhaps this division into two types of ghost is mirrored in the ancient Roman belief in evil ghosts called *lemures*, which persecuted living relatives if the ghost was unhappy; and *lares*, which were the spirits of virtuous people and usually made themselves known by acting as poltergeists do.

The tradition of Chinese ghost marriages is as yet one that is not found in parallel in the West, though the adoption of cultural beliefs from the East such as alternative healing approaches may well bring something akin to this in the future. The Chinese ghost marriage is based on the belief that single people suffer in the afterlife, being deprived of a mate to share their existence with. This leads to several customs. One is the marrying of corpses to each other and burying them together so that they can be together in the afterlife. It is not necessary for the couple to have met in life; they will get to know each other in their new realm. Unfortunately, this has led to an illegal trade in corpses – female corpses, known as ghost brides, in particular – and illegal exhumations.

In one recent ceremony the couple had both died 25 years earlier, the 'bride' in that case being an abortion when the mother was two months pregnant. The family had been having difficulties and the mother's living son had been having trouble finding a wife, and a medium explained that it was because of the unhappy spirit of the

25-year-old who had never had the chance to live in the mortal world. She felt unwanted but would be happy if united with a spouse in the afterlife. The 'husband' was a boy who had died of pneumonia at the age of three and had communicated with his mother in a dream that he wanted to be married.

The rich variety of ghost beliefs around the world provide a fascinating insight into the various cultures. And as a virtually universal belief it must be meeting a need, whatever the level of 'objective' reality is thought to be. To study ghosts and spirits is to study something fundamental within humanity.

Ghosts And Poltergeists Under The Eye Of The Law

There have been a few attempts to 'prove' the existence of haunting phenomena in court, not for its own sake but as a means to another end.

The *Daily Mail* of Thursday 5 March 1998 carried the story of Andrew and Josie Smith, who were to go to court to defend their withholding the balance of the sale price of a house they purchased. They did so on the grounds that the property was haunted and that the vendors, Susan Podmore and Sandra Melbourne, had failed to disclose that to them. In four years of occupancy of Lowes Cottage in Hollow Lane, Mayfield, Derbyshire, the Smiths claimed to have experienced 'malevolent apparitions'. The action was brought by the vendors and a county court judge in Derby agreed that there was a case to be heard. The vendors claimed never to have experienced any such phenomena. The hearing was in January 1999. The case went against the Smiths; the court did not, in effect, accept the existence of the paranormal phenomena.

The Smiths' case was not the first time the paranormal had been tested in court. The Spanish jurist Didacus Covarrubias, in the 16th century, stated that cases had been laid before the Spanish courts in Granada relating to the question of rental payments and haunted houses. The courts had decreed that any tenant who found himself disturbed by a haunting was justified in withholding his rent.

A specific case arose in France in 1575. Monsieur Gilles Bolacre, having rented a house in Tours, found that it was infested by a 'turbulent spirit'. He applied to the courts to nullify his lease. The application was successful in the lower court but then reviewed in a higher court. The original defence against his petition was that, aside from the unbreakable nature of contract, a belief in ghosts was the superstition of 'common people'. Indeed, it was argued that the judge in the lower court should not have reached the decision he did as it would 'encourage vulgar credulity'. Bolacre, however, pointed out that ghosts, and presumably poltergeist activity as indicated by the phrase 'turbulent spirit', were a 'fact of common experience'.

Sadly for poltergeist verification, the courts avoided the issue on a technicality. The judge declared he had no power to invalidate the lease unless 'letters royaux' were obtained, and the lease would have to stand. It is held that when the 'letters royaux' were subsequently obtained, the lease was voided.

In 1850-51 the Cideville case in France brought the haunting phenomena back into court. Two boys, Gustave, aged 12, and Brunel, aged 14, were allegedly haunted by a local shepherd named Thorel. Gustave had recognised a ghostly figure as Thorel. Other incidents had included knockings and rappings, the movements of the boys' desks and their receiving slaps by invisible hands. A witness, farmer Cheval, described seeing tongs and a shovel in the fireplace move into the middle of the room and, on being replaced, moving out again. 'My eyes were fixed on them to see what moved them, but I saw nothing at all,' he stated. The parish priest of Saussay, Father Leroux, stated, 'I saw things which I have been unable to explain to myself. I saw a hammer, moved by some invisible force, leave the spot where it lay and fall in the middle of the room without making more noise than if the hand had gently laid it down.'

The children had naturally become frightened and the poltergeist had become well known in the neighbourhood. Thorel, whether he was involved at any level or not, apparently indicated that he possessed occult power. The boys' teacher, the Curé of Cideville, accused Thorel of being behind the diabolical happenings. When later meeting the priest, Thorel threatened violence, to which the priest responded by striking him. Thorel brought an action against the priest for defamation of character and for assault. Of course, the poltergeist was not itself on trial but the disturbances became the focus of the proceedings; witnesses, on oath, verified the manifestations they had seen.

The Marquis de Marville tested the poltergeist and made statements in court affirming the work he had done. Having examined the poltergeist in some detail, he was asked in court whether the Curé could have faked the poltergeistery and replied, 'I should be much surprised if anyone within these walls could seriously believe that. I cannot think it possible to produce such disturbances by natural means. The cause must be supernatural.' As in other cases, the poltergeist phenomena were somewhat sidestepped by the court. But as researcher Harry Price states in his book *Poltergeist*, 'By implication, the phenomena were accepted as genuine.'

Father Herbert Thurston in his book *Ghosts And Poltergeists* reports that there were disturbances on government property in Russia which became the subject of an official enquiry. A cavalry post in Kharkoff, commanded by Captain Jan de Chenko, became subject to poltergeistery in early January 1853. The house, which was the official residence of the captain and his wife and their staff, suffered small objects being thrown about and, somewhat alarmingly, 'an axe was thrown from the loft in the passage against the doors with remarkable velocity and noise.' The church was called in, but during a service of blessing stones were thrown in the kitchen, wood and a pail of water flew at the assembled people and a stone fell into the basin of holy water. The phenomena continued despite the church's best efforts. Spontaneous fires broke out and strange banging and groaning noises were heard. The roof of the house was eventually burnt off and an enquiry was set up by the head of the local police.

Captain de Chenko was, in the meantime, staying in another house and poltergeistery was taking place there as well. It was of much the same nature and included spontaneous fires. The result was that the captain's second house and four cottages were razed to the ground. There was a second official enquiry which reached no effective conclusion and, perhaps most tellingly, concluded only that 'there was no ground of suspicion against any of the people connected with the case.' The poltergeist was not overtly but implicitly accepted.

The poltergeist seems to have come most prominently to court in its own name in 1888-89 near Berlin, Germany. Activity had arisen in a farmhouse belonging to Karl Böttcher. Pigs had got out of their pigsty by an unknown force which had unfastened the locks, knockings had been heard on the walls of the farmhouse and stones had broken windows. Over the next few days the activity increased, some of the stones now breaking the windows of a neighbour, Herr Neumann. Several independent witnesses, including the pastor Dr Müller, also saw the activity. Dr Müller had been assailed by potatoes and a baking dish which flew horizontally from the stove and then fell at his feet. A certain hysteria was beginning to build up locally, so much so that even thefts were being put down to the 'spuk'.

Neumann became convinced that Karl Wolter, a 15-year-old farm helper, was deliberately breaking his windows and prosecuted him for causing the damage and for impersonating a 'spuk' and thereby causing disturbance in the district. Wolter's lawyer argued that what was happening was the result of invisible forces of nature. The court was not, however, impressed by the paranormal and decided to take its stand on the basis of science; it imposed a full penalty on Wolter. They did, however, allow for appeal to a higher court, where more details of the poltergeist were revealed, not least the flight path of some of the objects that had been seen moving. Potatoes, turnips and other objects had been seen flying round corners and even coming to a dead stop in mid flight. These movements certainly put the phenomenon out of Wolter's capabilities. But the paranormal lost and Wolter's sentence was confirmed.

A curious case arose in 1838 at Baldarroch in Aberdeenshire, Scotland. Sticks, stones and soil were spontaneously flung about in the farmyard, apparently impressing 'hundreds of observers'. Inside the farmhouse, several flights of spoons, knives, plates, rolling pins and other ornaments were occurring. Two servant girls were identified as the foci of the activity. The farmer made the rather questionable decision of calling in a conjuror, Willie Foreman, who it is said 'speedily put an end to the trouble', to quote Ronald Pearsall in *The Table Rappers*. Apparently the girls admitted that they were responsible and were sent to prison. We are forced to wonder how Foreman put an end to these disturbances and what the girls were charged with – or indeed what the girls meant when they admitted they were responsible. It is difficult to believe that two untrained young serving girls could fool hundreds of observers, but possibly they may have accepted that they were the foci. Imprisonment is surely not the usual penalty for breaking plates and throwing dirt around and it may be that the phenomenon was regarded as supernatural and the girls charged with witchcraft. The last execution of a witch took place less than 50 years before this and may have frightened the girls. If they were imprisoned because they could prove that the phenomenon was supernatural, then the poltergeist has been confirmed in court.

In 1964 in Marilao, Bolacan, in the Philippines, Ildefonso Santos filed a criminal action against his neighbours who he believed were causing 'malicious mischief'. Rains of stones were falling through the night, witnessed by the parish priest, other residents and a former councillor. This had started since a 14-year-old boy, Ernesto Rabanzos, had moved in. However, it turned out that Rabanzos was always asleep when the stones were thrown. The boy was moved to a convent and on that very day windows and chandeliers were pelted with stones and several people hit. Blessing the church had no effect. In the end the criminal action failed 'for lack of anybody to accuse'.

One of the most famous poltergeist cases which involved the courts arose in September 1960 at Lynwood in California. The basic manifestation was one of a stone-throwing poltergeist which was bombarding a used-car lot. This began shortly after Anthony Angelo began working there. Some 200 missiles including stones, rocks, nuts and bolts were seen flying into the area, often with abnormal trajectory. The manager, Claude Mock, asked the police to help and up to 30 officers were put on the case. Angelo was prosecuted by the police on the basis of one incident, the details of which appear to be somewhat confusing. The police believed that Angelo had been seen throwing one rock at a car and denting it. Angelo denied he had done this, though it seems highly likely that he held a rock in his hand and smashed it against the side of the car. However, even the police were quite satisfied that there was no question of Angelo being the person who was throwing the missiles into the car lot, as quite often this was happening while Angelo was in custody. When the police were put on the spot in court and asked whether they had seen any rocks thrown, they admitted that they had not. The case is a rather curious one, as Angelo was in fact charged with obstructing the police.

In court, the case seemed to be going badly for Angelo on the grounds that someone had to be throwing the rocks and he seemed to be the only one implicated. But Raymond Bayliss, a noted investigator of the paranormal, was in court and he explained the nature of rock-throwing poltergeist phenomena. The judge was quite receptive to the explanations and when Angelo took the stand, the poltergeist was the focus of the testimonies. The question of Angelo obstructing the police seemed to be buried under the question of the source of the rock-throwing poltergeist. Angelo's defence pointed out that there were no facts for conviction. The court went as far as it could to involve the paranormal, stating that 'due to the strange nature of the case, there must have been a supernatural cause, a cosmic disturbance, responsible.' Angelo was found not guilty. The paranormal scored a hit against the establishment at last.

We see then that the paranormal has found itself in the dock on several occasions. From the researcher's point of view the conclusions have never been satisfactory. Either poltergeist disturbances have been a sideline or they have been dismissed in the face of accepted science. But on several occasions it appears that acceptance of haunting phenomena has been able to swing judges in favour of defendants when they have been sympathetic to the testimony of 'the great and the good' of the locality.

Most of the cases have tended to be, from a legal point of view, minor misdemeanours rather than anything serious; breakages and malicious damage at worst. As such, therefore, poltergeists and the like have yet to really put themselves on the line in court. Should a case arise where, say, a poltergeist is suspected of something much more serious, such as actual bodily harm or even murder, then the courts will be forced to examine such a case in microscopic detail. Then the paranormal will truly have its day in court.

Solving Mysteries

Ghost and spirit research is not simply a search for proof of life after death, though the popular image of ghosts is as 'spirits of the dead'. It is a search first for the evidence to prove that the phenomena we call 'ghosts' exist at all, and then to identify what is their origin. Perhaps it will turn out to be the dead, but it certainly does not have to be that, and indeed cannot only be that. For example, a large number of apparitions turn out to be of people who are alive at the time 'their' ghost is sighted.

To determine what a ghost is, there must also be a process of proving what ghosts are not. When ghost researchers solve ghost mysteries and produce non-paranormal explanations for what people have believed are hauntings, they are succeeding in their task. While perhaps many ghost researchers would be happy to prove a positive – what ghosts are – they are also happy, along the way, to prove what they are not.

To be fair, though, there are also many others – some ghost researchers among them, as well as the general public and the media – who are unhappy to accept the mundane and for whom what should be scientific analysis becomes more a question of conviction and belief.

Take, for example, the work done by the authors as part of a larger team in Rochester Castle in the summer of 1992. Two mysteries there we solved for certain. We had been told that two of the castle windows glowed on occasions with an eerie, flickering green light. Several hours of careful observation showed that the flickering was caused by the uplights from the castle grounds, passing through the leaves and branches of trees waving in the wind, and reflected off perspex sheeting at the back of the windows in question. The second solved mystery at Rochester related to the sounds of 'galloping horses' that had been heard racing through the castle late at night. After midnight several of the team heard the sounds and agreed that it sounded exactly like horses running at speed. But a careful check of the castle revealed that the source of the sounds was in fact the wind flapping the loose rope of the flag against the pole. Several of the team on the ground floor watched the flagpole in their torch beams for several minutes to confirm the fact. At midnight the flag was lowered, leaving the rope flapping freely, and this explained why the sounds had only been heard at night.

As a team we were delighted to have made such good progress. But we didn't, to be frank, get the impression that everyone in the public and media were as happy; it seems that many like a mystery and feel let down when a mundane solution is revealed. On those occasions when we have concluded in favour of a paranormal explanation, we have noticed people seem happier with our findings. But clearly there is a difference between what we see our job to be and how it is perceived by others.

Beams of light

A quite different set of circumstances led to the same kind of accusation of being 'overly sceptical'.

Our first encounter with ghostly images on film that resembled spiralling beams of light was while investigating a woman who had manifested the stigmata (the wounds of Christ's crucifixion on her body). The claimant, Heather Woods, (the subject of our book *Spirit Within Her*) believed that she was in contact with the Holy Spirit, which had become visible as a sign of her healing ministry. She described the Holy Spirit as 'a curving beam of white light, with a spiral inside it'. She was 'given' – told in channelling – that she should invite a friend to take a photograph of her house church. As we described in *Spirit Within Her*:

The friend came, and took the photograph. Heather hoped that the Holy Spirit would be visible to the photographer and was disappointed when it was not. However, when the photo- grapher received her pictures back from the chemists, one of the images was clearly overlaid with this beam of light, exactly as Heather always described it. On the original, and some reproductions, the spiralling within the light is clear.

After we received the photograph it happened that we were having dinner with Maurice Grosse, the head of the Spontane- ous Phenomena Committee of the Society for Psychical Research (SPR). He was to show us some photographs he had been examining; we showed him the 'Holy Spirit' photograph. He smiled and handed us two photos that he had been going to show us; the exact same beam of light was on two photographs taken during a christening ceremony. In one photograph the light comes down into the font, in the other it comes down directly onto the baby's head. The family concerned replied to our enquiries, confirming that they hadn't seen any lighting effects when the ceremony was underway, and that it had been quite a surprise to them when they saw it.

Maurice told us that many such pictures had been sent to him in recent months.

At that time no explanation had yet been found for the images. It was interesting, but not unexpected, that different people were interpreting the images in different ways; to Heather it was the Holy Spirit, to other claimants the images were apparitions of ghosts. We sought out as many such pictures as we could and obtained details of how each picture had been taken as far as could be remembered by the photographers.

Two common factors were that the pictures were most often taken indoors, with flash, in dim lighting, and that they were taken with instamatic-type cameras. As luck would have it, before we had formulated enough data to move on to experimental research, our youngest daughter solved the mystery.

She was taking some pictures of our cats with one of our cameras. When developed they showed spiralling beams of light, similar to the other pictures. However, the several pictures provided enough clarity for us to identify the source of the beams. They were in fact the camera strap in front of the lens. The spiral was the grain, and the twist, of the strap. It was white because it was blasted with light from the flash; that was why most of the pictures arose in dim lighting and indoors. The cameras used were not 'through the lens' types (where the photographer would see the obstruction when looking through the viewfinder) but rather the type of all-in-one-camera with built-in flash that has become increasingly common. As the photographer does not actually see through the lens, if the strap obscures the lens it may not be visible through the viewfinder. Such cameras have the flash very close to the lens, creating the whitening of the strap.

We started further experimenting. In our first 24 shots we only got one clear beam of light, but we also got purple and pink images and a few vague shadows. We had to refine our use of the flash, and of lighting conditions, and then experiment by overdeveloping and underdeveloping the prints. We encouraged our local Boots photographic department to help us with different types of development.

Over time we got really good at it. We could produce, to order, spiral beams of various thickness and various hues from white to purple with the help of the developers.

The fact that we could predict our results, and produce them as predicted, proved beyond doubt that this was a mystery solved, and solved with the best techniques of science.

But there are plenty of anomalous photographs as yet unexplained and some may well represent proof of the paranormal – the work goes on. And there are plenty of other mysteries relating to ghosts and spirits yet to be solved. While we have always believed that they will be explainable in scientific terms one day, we take note of the most famous of statements by J. Allen Hynek, a leader in the field of UFO research until his death in the 1980s, that, 'there is a tendency in 20th-century science to forget that there will be a 21st-century science, and indeed, a 30th-century science, from which vantage points our knowledge of the universe may appear quite different.'

What Can We Learn From Animal Ghosts?

The most frequently offered explanation for ghosts is that they are the spirits or echoes of people who once lived, either coming back from the grave with intelligence, as suggested by the 'interactive' ghosts, or recordings and replays akin to a video replay where there is no intelligence noticeably present. All well and good, but why then do ghosts seem to be such a uniquely human experience? Does that tell us something about ourselves, and does it also tell us something about the phenomenon and its origin?

'Humans produce ghosts; animals do not.' That is not strictly speaking true, but the degree to which it is not true – as we shall come to later – may tell us even more about ourselves and the phenomenon.

Humans produce ghosts. Individual ghosts that slink about in buildings and on highways, or even whole troops of ghosts replaying battles of long ago. The wide variety of reports in this encyclopedia is evidence of that. Sometimes ghosts seem to exhibit a purpose. For example, in this volume there are three cases of ghosts which seem to have sought to secure justice for their own murders: the Green Briar Ghost, the Red Barn Murder and the Bell Farm Apparitions. We might learn something from the extraordinary apparitions that arose at Edgehill in Warwickshire, set out in the previous volume of this encyclopedia. Significantly, it was possible to recognise in the 'replay' of the battle people who were still alive. Therefore, while the replay was of apparitions, it clearly did not represent the return of the dead.

We can consider the wide range of ghost stories that make up the genre: phantom hitchhikers; apparitions of the famous and not-so famous; sounds and voices of people who once lived; and so on and so on. Why do they appear? It is often argued that they do not realise they are dead, or have a mission to complete, or that their emotional ties to this world are too strong to let go. Of replays it is suggested that somehow a moment – often a seemingly unimportant one, sitting on a bench perhaps – is 'embedded' somehow into the fabric of the locality to be replayed when conditions are right.

Yet no animals.

Millions of animals die all the time. Hedgehogs, rabbits and fowl die on roads every night of the year. Presumably some are cut off in their prime, perhaps some at least do not realise they are dead, some surely have 'loved ones' they feel pulled away from. Certainly we have watched animals at close range appear to be emotionally distraught at the death of a mate. In the *Mail on Sunday* of 10 October 1999 there was the story of a swan whose mate had been accidentally killed on a golf course and who was now mooching around looking for her and acting uncharacteristically. The authors live with swans in their garden; we have seen them act in a very loyal and devoted way, and they certainly seem to exhibit what humans call emotions. Yet we do not see lonely-looking phantom swans walking up the riverbanks, or apparitional animals wandering the countryside. Somehow they do not apparently either seek to leave an impression that we call a ghost or, in the case of recordings, they don't even accidentally leave one in the form of an embedded image waiting to replay.

One explanation given is that animals do not have souls. But if souls exist and humans have them, then probably so do animals; surely by now we have realised that humans are just another animal.

But we have been playing something of a game so far in this essay; in fact, a scan through the chapter of this encyclopedia entitled 'Animal Ghosts' clearly shows that ghosts of animals are in fact seen or perceived. But, and this is perhaps the important point, most of these animals were loved pets and were associated with humans to a close, personal degree. Does this signify that humans produce these ghosts to meet their own needs?

There is sufficient evidence in the literature to show that what we call 'ghosts' are genuine phenomena, but could it be that the witness creates the ghost of a loved pet rather than it being the animal that 'comes back' in some way after death? Can it be that the human wishes to know that a loved pet is safe and well after death? Can it be that some animal companions provide something so valuable that it cannot be given up by the human after the pet's death, and so the human creates an image, the presence of the pet, to continue providing that need? Or could the degree of emotion involved allow a person to see something that is genuinely there, but not normally visible? And could somewhere in this be the answer to a great many ghost sightings, whether animal or human in form?

Of course, it could be argued that we *do* see ghosts of animals, we just don't know it. If we see a deer running off across a field how do we know it is living and not apparitional? The argument has indeed been offered that we might pass a hundred human ghosts on the streets of major cities without knowing it every day, if they are there but not interacting in any way that gives away their 'true' nature. But given the millions of animals that have died, we should surely expect to see a good many that walk through trees and walls in full view of witnesses; given the millions of trees blown down in the hurricanes of the late 1980s, we should have a few reports of 'recordings-type' squirrels climbing trees that are no longer there; but we don't get these reports.

So perhaps the absence of wild animal ghosts tells us that one quality involved in the 'creation' of ghosts is a human quality. And we might extend that argument to consider that it is a human quality of living humans, not the deceased. That ghosts, though a truly paranormal experience and one yet to be understood by science, might be a construct of the living mind and fulfilling a uniquely human need.

Cross-Reference To Sections Of Common Interest

Within the broad classifcations of ghosts used in this encyclopedia there are many times when cases entered into one category overlap with another. The following is a useful guide to the major cases which have some dual aspects.

Ghosts And Visions Associated With Particular Places
see also:

Ghosts Of The Famous
see also:

Haunted Objects
see also:

Recordings And Replays
see also:

Bibliography, References And Recommended Reading

Adams, Norman	Haunted Scotland	Mainstream 1998
Ayer, Fred	Before the Colors Fade	Houghton Mifflin 1964
Blackman, W. Haden	Field Guide to North American Hauntings	Three Rivers 1998
Bord, Janet and Colin	Modern Mysteries of the World	Grafton 1989
Brooks, J.A.	Ghosts of London	Jarrold 1991
Burks, Eddie & Cribbs, Gillian	Ghosthunter	Headline 1995
Carrington, Hereward & Fodor, Nandor	The Story of the Poltergeist Down the Centuries	Rider & Co 1953
Cavendish, Richard	The World of Ghosts and the Supernatural	AA Publishing 1994
Chambers, Dennis	Haunted Pluckley	Denela Enterprises 1984
Eason, Cassandra	Ghost Encounters	Blandford 1997
Fanthorpe, Lionel & Patricia	Death – The Final Mystery	Hounslow Dundurn, Toronto 2000
Fodor, Nandor	On the Trail of the Poltergeist	Arco 1958
Forman, Joan	Haunted Royal Homes	Harrap 1987
Fox, Ian	The Haunted Places Of Hampshire	Ensign Publications 1993
Green, Andrew	Our Haunted Kingdom	Wolfe Publishing 1973
Gurney, Myers & Podmore (ed: Sidgwick)	Phantasms of the Living	Kegan Paul 1918
Guiley, Rosemary Ellen	The Guinness Encyclopedia of Ghosts and Spirits	Guinness 1992
Harris, Paul	Ghosts of Shepway	(privately published)

Hippisley Coxe, Anthony D.	Haunted Britain	Pan 1973
Holzer, Hans	True Ghost Stories	Bristol Park Books 1992
Innes, Brian	The Catalogue of Ghost Sightings	Blandford 1996
Lethbridge, T. C.	Ghost and Ghoul	Routledge and Kegan Paul 1961
Marsden, Simon	Journal of a Ghosthunter	Little, Brown & Co 1994
Myers, Frederick	Human Personality and Its Survival of Bodily Death	Longmans, Green & Co 1927
Owen, A. R. G.	Can We Explain the Poltergeist?	Helix 1964
Price, Harry & Lambert R. S.	The Haunting of Cashen's Gap	Methuen & Co 1936
Price, Harry	Poltergeist	Bracken Books 1993 (orig:1945)
Rogers, Ken	The Warminster Triangle	Coates and Parker Ltd 1994
Roll, William G.	The Poltergeist	Scarecrow Press 1976
Seafield, Lily	Scottish Ghosts	Lomond Books 1999
Spencer, John & Anne	The Encyclopedia of Ghosts and Spirits	Headline 1992
Spencer, John & Anne	The Encyclopedia of The World's Greatest Unsolved Mysteries	Headline 1995
Spencer, John & Anne	The Poltergeist Phenomenon	Headline 1997
Spencer, John & Anne	The Ghost Handbook	Boxtree 1998
Spencer, John & Wells, Tony	Ghostwatching	Virgin, 1994
Thurston S.J., Herbert (Crehan S.J., J.H. [ed.])	Ghosts and Poltergeists	Burns Oates 1953
Toynbee, Arnold	A Study of History	Oxford University Press 1935–1961
Underwood, Peter	Ghost Hunters Almanac	Eric Dobby 1993
Underwood, Peter	Ghosts and How To See Them	Brockhampton Press 1993
Warren, Melanie & Wells, Tony	Ghosts of the North	Broadcast Books 1995
Wells, Tony & Warren, Melanie	Ghost Stories of the South-west	Broadcast Books 1994

Wilson, Ian	In Search of Ghosts	Headline 1995
(Editors)	Hauntings	Time-Life 1989
(Editors)	Phantom Encounters	Time-Life 1989
(Editors)	Ghosts	Orbis 1997
Downes, Wesley H.	Essex Ghosts & Hauntings (mags) & Ghost & Hauntings (mags)	Wesley's Publications
(Editors)	ASSAP publication: Anomaly	ASSAP
(Editors)	Journals of the Society of Psychical Research	SPR

Useful Websites

In addition to websites for the organisations listed by address / phone / fax / e-mail below, the following websites are very useful, well maintained sites of interest:

Ghosts of the Prairie can be found on:
http://www.prairieghosts.com
Contact: Troy Taylor

Several items were submitted by Dale Gilbert Jarvis, a researcher and folklorist living and working in St John's, Newfoundland, Canada. He is also the host of **The St John's Haunted Hike**, a walking ghost tour of downtown St John's, which can be found online at: http://www.avint.net/hardticket
E-mail him at hike@avint.net

Ghosts of North Portland can be found on:
www.hevanet.com/heberb/ghosts/ghosts.htm
Contact: H. Michael Ball

Toronto Ghost and Hauntings Research Society (TGHRS)
Website: www.torontoghosts.org
Or try their gateway website, which is the cover-all site featuring all the research societies hosted by TGHRS at: www.ghrs.org
Contact: Matthew Didier

Obiwan's UFO-free Paranormal Pages
www.ghosts.org/stories

Contacts

We would be pleased to hear of readers' experiences. The authors can be contacted at:

The Leys, 2C Leyton Road, Harpenden, Herts, AL5 2TL, England
or by fax: 01582–461979
or by e-mail: johnandanne@paranormalworldwide.com
The authors' website can be accessed at:
www.paranormalworldwide.com

For those who would like to take a more active role in ghost research, contact:

The Association for The Scientific Study of Anomalous Phenomena (ASSAP)
Saint Aldhelm,
20 Paul Street,
Frome,
Somerset,
BA11 1DX
Contact: Hugh Pincott
E-mail: gs2@assap.org
Website: www.assap.org

The Society for Psychical Research (SPR)
49 Marloes Road,
Kensington,
London,
W8 6LA
Telephone / fax 020–7937–8984
Contact: Eleanor O'Keefe (secretary)

The Merseyside Anomalies Research Association (MARA)
52 Hawthorne Avenue,
Halewood,
Liverpool,
L26 9XD
Telephone: 0151–727–4057
Contact: Anthony Eccles
Website: www.mara.org.uk

Ghost Quest
20 McMinnis Avenue,
Parr,
St Helens,
Merseyside,
WA9 2PL
Telephone: 01744–750040
Contact: Peter Crawley

Strange Phenomena Investigations
41 Castlebar Road,
Ealing,
London,
W5 2DJ
Telephone: 020–8998–4936
E-mail spi_spi@hotmail.com
Contact: Malcolm Robinson

Reverend Lionel Fanthorpe and Patricia Fanthorpe
Rivendell,
48 Claude Road,
Roath,
Cardiff,
CF24 3QA
Telephone: 029–204–98368
Fax: 029–204–96832
E-mail: Fathorpe@aol.com
Website: www.lionel-fanthorpe.com

Index of Headings, Sub-headings and Cases

Index of Names

Index of Places